ENDORSEMENTS

This book challenges the reader with a picture of God's eternal purpose and how each man's personal destiny finds its place in this divine strategy.

—John Isaacs, president of "Pray the Bay"

The apostle Paul wrote that there are thousands of instructors in Christ but not many fathers. Barney is one of those true spiritual fathers whose wisdom, insight and love have endeared him to people around the world. His easy manner and gracious pastoral gift come through in his writings, but don't miss the profound and eternal truth that he is passionately communicating.

—Ron MacLean, senior pastor of Gateway
Christian Community, Winnipeg, Canada

Barney has skillfully managed to draw together apologetics, church history, theology, and present day missions (interwoven with his usual pastoral care), outlining the story of man's destiny. For me, the following sentences sum up the heart of this book: "Through His death, Jesus not only reduced satan to zero, He also took back the keys of death and hades that satan had acquired when Adam sinned. This was a spiritual victory of cosmic proportions, but it has a very practical and personal application to each one of us." This book is highly practical and needs to be applied personally.

—Stuart Bell, team leader of Ground Level, UK.

FINDING YOUR PURPOSE *in* GOD'S PLAN

FINDING YOUR PURPOSE *in* GOD'S PLAN

B. R. COOMBS

Cover design by Kirk DouPonce, UDG/DesignWorks
www.udgdesignworks.com

Treasure House
An Imprint of
Destiny Image₀ Publishers, Inc.
P.O. Box 310
Shippensburg, PA 17257-0310

"For where your treasure is, there will your heart be also."
Matthew 6:21

ISBN 0-7684-3019-4

For Worldwide Distribution
Printed in the U.S.A.

1 2 3 4 5 6 7 8 9 10 / 09 08 07 06 05 04 03

This book and all other Destiny Image, Revival Press, MercyPlace, Fresh Bread, Destiny Image Fiction, and Treasure House books are available at Christian bookstores and distributors worldwide.

For a U.S. bookstore nearest you, call **1-800-722-6774**.
For more information on foreign distributors, call **717-532-3040**.
Or reach us on the Internet:
www.destinyimage.com

DEDICATION

To my children, their spouses, and their children:

Stephen and his wife, Janet, and
Devon and Leighton;
Mark and his wife, Jackie, and
Jessica, Justine and Taylor;
Rachel and her husband, Jeremy, and
Estee, Samuel and Lydia

The desire of my heart is that each of you will come to understand God's eternal plan for Himself and His creation, and that in so doing, you will discover an irresistible desire to seek Him with all your heart. I pray that you will search out your life purpose—your unique place in that plan—and that when you walk in His will, you will be deeply satisfied.

CONTENTS

ACKNOWLEDGMENTS

The apostle Paul asks, "What do you have that you did not receive?" The answer, of course, is nothing. Any knowledge we have, any wisdom, any insight, any power to do the will of God—all come from our Heavenly Father, by grace and through faith. Whether directly or indirectly, everything we possess has been given to us, and I am never more conscious of that fact than when I write.

I am thankful, first of all, to the God and Father of our Lord Jesus Christ who has "blessed us with every spiritual blessing." He has poured out the Holy Spirit who leads us into all truth, and has given the ministry gifts of Christ to the church—apostles, prophets, evangelists, pastors and teachers—from whom I have learned much more than I ever could teach. This book would have been impossible without their godly input.

Once again, I am indebted to Art Enns, my dear and loyal friend. In spite of a heavy workload, he has done a superb job of editing this book. During that time, Art carried the additional pressure of his wife Margarete's fight with cancer involving radical surgery and convalescence. Margarete, thank you for encouraging Art to go ahead with the editing and for providing helpful insights. You and Art have been a constant source of joy and encouragement to Janette and me over the past 25 years. All your family and friends are delighted with your excellent recovery.

Lucy Smith, now age 85, has given the manuscript a final check for grammatical or spelling errors. It is not by mistake that I have given her the affectionate name *Hawk-eyes Smith*. Lucy is one of Canada's most senior Girl Guides and still loves camping. She is a faithful servant of the Lord Jesus, giving oversight to the prayer chain for West Coast Christian Fellowship, and actively participating in every church or house fellowship meeting—even braving snow, ice or storm to attend. Lucy, you are one of my favorite people.

I am also grateful to Fiona Peters for her helpful work in reviewing Chapters 12 to 14. Fiona discovered a number of errors in this "church history" section and made some very helpful suggestions. A special thanks as well to 14-year-old James Hamann II for his critiquing of Chapter 2.

As far as critiquing and encouragement are concerned, Don Milam of Destiny Image Publishers provided both of these vital "commodities" over the past year, resulting in many improvements. Thank you, Don, for your keen insights and helpful suggestions.

Finally, to Janette, my wife and sweetheart for the past 43 years: Your name means *God's gracious gift*, and that is who you are to me. I am deeply grateful for all your sacrificial service to the Lord on my behalf, and your indispensable participation in God's call on our lives.

Janette and I both consider that one of our greatest blessings is belonging to a spiritual family that stretches across many nations and continents. Among the members of this family are innumerable saints who have committed their time, energy and resources to the work of God's Kingdom, and others who hazard even their lives for Christ and His Church. I pray that this book will inspire you and intensify your resolve to make the Name of Jesus famous on the earth, to the end that the glory of the Lord will fill the whole earth as the waters cover the sea.

Barnabas Coombs
November 2002

INTRODUCTION

WHAT ON EARTH ARE WE HERE FOR?
Your throne was established long ago;
You are from all eternity.   —Psalm 93:2

It was the intention of our Father-God that all men
might find the answers to life's deepest enigmas.
                                        —DeVern Fromke[1]

The inspiration for this book had its beginnings about 35 years ago when I received an unexpected gift. I was attending a leaders' conference in Herne Bay, a small seaside town in southeast England, when a man approached me at the end of the conference and gave me two books—*The Ultimate Intention* and *Fullness of Stature*—both written by DeVern Fromke. The man, known to me previously only by name, was David Lillie, who explained that the books had been freight-damaged in transit from the U.S. to England and therefore were free.

Damaged or not, those two books helped open my eyes to see that God's eternal plan—His *ultimate intention*—was so much more comprehensive and purposeful than saving us from our sin. In January 1999 at a conference in Bristol, where I was sharing the ministry with George Verwer of Operation Mobilization and Terry Virgo of New Frontiers, all three of us testified to the powerful influence of DeVern Fromke's writings on our lives as young men.

Not long ago, I had the pleasure of staying briefly with DeVern. As I journeyed to his home in Indianapolis, I felt the kind of excitement and anticipation that a schoolboy might experience on his way to Disneyland. I was not disappointed. He was 78 at the time, but his mind was as sharp as a 20-year-old. I make no apology for saying that much of the key teaching in this book is repackaged *Ultimate Intention,* and that I have included some wonderful thoughts gleaned from John Piper's books, in particular *The Pleasures of God.* DeVern expressed delight that I was embarking on this endeavor.

Sad to say, we live in an age where clear, theological thinking is at an all-time low. Many who occupy the pews on Sundays are interested only in messages with good entertainment value, or sermons that support their way of thinking. The apostle Paul warned against this trend: *For the time will come when men will not put up with sound doctrine. Instead, to suit their own desires, they will gather around them a great number of teachers to say what their itching ears want to hear.*[2]

While some attend church meetings in order to be trained and equipped for service, others sit back and wait to be entertained. If the preacher fails to hold their interest, he is thought to be speaking "over people's heads" or considered to be just plain dull. I believe the issue today is not dull preachers but dull hearers. But that may not be a new problem. I recall the story of an old English fellow named Hodge, a 19th century hedger and ditcher, who was once heard to say, "I loikes Sunday, I do." "So, why do you like Sunday?" he was asked. "Well, I loikes ta go ta church an put ma feet up an think o' nothin'."

If Hodge's problem was lethargy, ours may be distraction. We are a generation infected with the sound-bite virus, our attention span reduced to a bare minimum by the short scenes and summaries that make up today's media programming. It's almost as if we've suffered brain damage through an overexposure to news, sports and Hollywood. As such, we're addicted to the remote control and the computer mouse: if we are not being entertained, we simply switch to another channel on TV, or else put on a video or DVD, or click to another site on the Internet. With that kind of 21st century "handicap," is it surprising that we prefer preachers with nice, topical, three-point sermons over those who ask us to reason along with them as they expound a chapter of Scripture?

It's tempting to think of the Early Church as being somewhat illiterate. After all, they lived 2,000 years ago. Wasn't that close to the

Iron Age? And don't we live in the Information Age? That may be true, but most Christians today have considerable difficulty following Paul's line of thinking in Galatians or Ephesians (not to mention Romans). It's easier to go along with majority opinion—or the latest speaker—and let others do the thinking for us. But that often leads to shallowness of conviction and unprincipled pragmatism, where we are swayed by every "wind of doctrine" or think that *the end justifies the means.*

A great many Christians—especially men—will buy books at conferences but never get around to reading them. (Yes, I know, life is just too busy. Maybe we'll have time to read once things get back to normal…and so on.) My hope in writing this book is to reach not only those who are trained to handle theological arguments, but also those who may struggle with concentration or conceptual thinking. To that end, I will frequently use stories to support my train of thought (as the Bible so often does in its teaching), and I will seek to be practical in my application of truth.

Finally, I would ask you, the reader, to walk with me on a journey that stretches, in terms of biblical thought, from eternity to eternity. I hope you will persevere through the parts that may be difficult to understand. And I pray that, in some small way, God will use this effort to motivate you (in the words of Paul to the Philippians) to take hold of that for which Christ Jesus took hold of you.[3]

ENDNOTES

1. DeVern F. Fromke, *The Ultimate Intention* (Indianapolis, Indiana: Sure Foundation, 1963), 21.

2. 2 Timothy 4:3.

3. Philippians 3:12.

ONE

YOU ARE NOT A MISTAKE

Your eyes saw my unformed body. All the days ordained for me were written in your book before one of them came to be.

—King David[1]

I remember lying in bed one night as a ten year old, pondering one of those questions that only philosophers and children seem to ask: *Why am I me and not my brother?* At the time, my thoughts were limited by my ignorance of the biological facts of life, but even later, the answer remained a mystery. Half a century after those childhood reflections—after discovering a few things about my own history, and learning more about our incredible universe and the God who created it all—I am amazed that I even exist, let alone that I am me and not my brother.

During the First World War, my father led a group of snipers on the battlefield. Fighting was fierce and often at close quarters. On one occasion, while looking down the sights of his gun in order to focus on a German soldier, my father discovered the same soldier focusing on *him*. His opposite pulled the trigger first—and shot with perfect accuracy. But just two feet from entering my father's brain through the left eye, the bullet struck the gun sight and, with an eerie zing, ricocheted over his head.

My father was not a committed Christian at the time, but he was so shocked at how close he had come to death that he laid down his gun and had a talk with his Creator. If that bullet had found its mark, I would not be sitting here writing this book. I would never have existed.

As a teenager, my mother attended a girls' boarding school. On the school grounds were several Laburnum trees loaded with seed-pods that, to my mother, looked very similar to runner beans. One fine autumn afternoon she persuaded a crowd of girls that these seedpods were quite edible, and began to pick them and hand them out to others.

Within the hour, ambulances were rushing the victims of my mother's "good idea" to the hospital. Included in this poisoned cav-alcade was my mother herself who, along with the others, managed to survive the ordeal. If Kathleen Good had died that day, I never would have been born; I wouldn't exist.

Despite all odds, I did come into existence—and proceeded to have some "close encounters" of my own. In 1942, at the age of five, I was taken ill with appendicitis that developed into peritonitis. My mother called the family doctor who concluded that I was suffering from a simple stomach disorder. Mother, however, was convinced that this was not the case and, sensing that my life was in great dan-ger, called another doctor.

The second doctor wasted no time. Within minutes I was rushed to Canterbury Hospital and immediately operated on. The surgeon, Dr. Beresford-Jones, later told my mother, "Another half an hour and your son would have been dead." If my mother had accepted the family doctor's diagnosis, I wouldn't be here. But there is one more timely aspect to this story. Apparently, I was one of the first civilians to receive penicillin; without it, I surely would have died.

IN SPITE OF WHO I AM...

Given the perilous events I have just described, and the fact that I was raised in a Christian home, you might assume that I grew up with an all-pervading awareness of God and my eternal destiny in Him. The truth is, unless God had taken the initiative to confront me again and again, I shudder to think what my life would look like today.

Last year while reading in the Book of Genesis, it suddenly struck me that much of my early life corresponded to that of Jacob, especially in his tendency to manipulate and deceive. Living in a very active Christian home, I soon learned how to play the role that my parents expected of me, attending church services and even teaching Sunday School when I was only ten years old.

Sunday evenings I would travel with my father as he preached in various chapels. At first, my father got me to announce a hymn and read the first verse; later he added the reading of Scripture. When I successfully handled that, I was asked to sing a solo, and then "graduated" to saying a prayer. All of this took up about 15 minutes of the 60-minute service, and the old folks loved it. What a wonderful thing it was to see a young boy in the pulpit with such a cherubic smile, pleasing manner and lovely singing voice!

At school, however, I was one of the gang—I needed to be "cool." And that, I regret to say, translated into a foul mouth and disreputable behavior like stealing cigarettes from my older brother. These I would either smoke myself or sell to one of the teachers. But that was during the week. Sunday mornings would find me pushing an elderly, wheelchair-bound Miss Shonk, accompanied by her even-more-elderly sister, Mrs. Horton, to the worship service at Hamilton Road Mission.

I would then leave the sisters and make my way to the nearby recreation ground to watch a soccer game. George McLeod, the minister, believed I went on to the church service where my parents attended, while my parents thought I stayed at the Mission with Miss Shonk. I vividly recall the many times Mr. McLeod would say, "Barney, you are doing a great work for the Lord." The strange thing was, I actually felt a certain self-righteous glow when he spoke those words.

Yet there was another side to me that no one knew but God. My first strong, personal awareness of God was at five years of age while being rushed to hospital with peritonitis. The second, at the age of seven, was a series of encounters when I was a student at Westbere Anglican Primary School. (Even there, I must confess to being caught playing hooky with Colin Long, my seven-year-old "partner in crime.") Each morning, school would commence with prayer and a hymn. There was one hymn in particular that used to touch my young heart:

> It is a thing most wonderful,
> Almost too wonderful to me,

That God's own Son should come from Heav'n and die
To save a child like me.

Later, in verse three, I would come to the line, *But 'tis more won-derful to me, my love for Him so faint and small*. For some reason, I could never sing that line without choking back the tears. I knew I was undeserving of God's love, but deep, deep down inside, I also knew that I loved this God to whom we prayed and whom my parents worshiped. I asked Him into my heart innumerable times.

As a teenager, I continued to play both sides. For a school debate in which the motion formally stated, "This house believes in the existence of Almighty God," I spoke *against* the motion. I didn't believe a word of my argument, but opposing the status quo made me "cool" in the eyes of my friends. Yet it was on days like these that I would come home from school, go to the old pedal organ in the front room, and play and sing hymns.

Again, there was one hymn that always brought me to tears: *God holds the key of all unknown, and I am glad: If other hands should hold the key, or if He trusted it to me, I might be sad*. Somewhere in the sub-terranean recesses of my soul there lurked a sense of being drawn toward the Lord, of being called to a plan and purpose that carried eternal consequence. No amount of religious performance or confor-mity would ever—nor could ever—satisfy that magnetic pull.

I was an enigma, full of contradictions. In effect, I was three dif-ferent people: one was outwardly religious, knowing how to say the right things and act the right way to impress his parents and other church members; the second was a man of the world, deceiving and bending the rules in order to feed his pride and selfish ambitions; the third was a secret, inward Christian, thirsting for the living God and who was, at times, tender, broken and deeply ashamed.

Eventually I left home and joined the London Metropolitan Police Force as a police cadet. I was looking forward to the adventure of arresting crooks but, in retrospect, I think that God was looking forward to "arresting" me! I liked the idea of being free from the influence of my parents, but I couldn't escape from God. As David once said, "I can never be lost to your Spirit! I can never get away from my God!"[2]

Just before I left home for the big city, Mrs. Horton gave me two old-fashioned, framed Bible texts and said, "Barney, I believe God is going to use you to bring many people to the Savior." Little did I realize that within four months, those two texts would be hanging from my apartment wall, and (most incredible of all) within another six months, eight police cadets would have given their lives to Christ and would be meeting in my room for prayer and Bible study.

However, I had a few tough lessons to learn before those events took place. New Year's Eve 1954, two months after my arrival in London, found me the worse for alcohol—which was a new and nauseating experience. Apart from one sip of rum while playing hooky with Colin Long at age seven, I had never before tasted alcohol. Now I felt wretchedly sick. The room seemed to be rotating around me and my head was swimming. During repeated visits to the washbasin, the contents of my stomach were being vomited down the sink; I thought I was going to die.

It reminds me of Jonah's experience in the belly of the great fish and, like him, I began to call out to God for mercy. I don't remember the exact words I used, but I can strongly identify with Jonah's prayer in that awful place:

> In my distress I called to the Lord,
> and he answered me.
> From the depths of the grave I called for help
> and you listened to my cry.[3]

A few weeks later, in a large evangelistic meeting at London's famous Royal Albert Hall, God "arrested" me and started me on a journey from which I've never looked back. One of my favorite Scriptures became this quote from the apostle Paul:

> Not that I have already obtained all this, or have already been made perfect, but I press on to take hold of [or "arrest"] that for which Christ Jesus took hold of me.[4]

I wish I could say that I have always walked perfectly in this new way, but the truth is, I have often fallen short. Because of this, I frequently pray, "Father, by whatever means You see fit, please keep me in the place where I am useful to your plans and purposes." And He has been exceedingly gracious and faithful to answer that prayer by means of His guidance, discipline, grace and kindness. He has blessed me with a loving wife, children, grandchildren, and an extended "church family" that stretches literally around the world.

A few months ago I was telling two of my grandchildren, nine-year-old Estee and six-year-old Samuel, the story of their Great Granddad Sydney Coombs and his dramatic escape in the First World War. Samuel loves dramatic adventure stories, and was highly animated as I told them of my father's escape that took place before I was born.

When I finished, I asked them, "So what would have happened if the bullet had hit Great Granddad Coombs?" Immediately Samuel replied, "You wouldn't be here." "And if I wasn't here, what would that mean?" I inquired. "Mummy wouldn't be here," Samuel responded. "You're right!" I said to him. Then posed the next question: "And what does that mean?" "I wouldn't be here," he replied confidently.

I continued, "Sam, listen to me: You are very special; you are not a mistake. God planned you before you were born; in fact, He planned you a very long time ago, and when He planned you, He had a very special reason in His mind." "What was that?" Samuel inquired. "To be honest with you, Sam, I don't know," I responded. "I only know He has a special purpose for each one of us, and that includes you and Estee. But if you keep talking to Him and reading the Bible, I promise you He will also talk to you and tell you what it is."

GOD PLANNED YOU FROM ALL ETERNITY

As we look back on our lives, we see the hand of a providential God in our encounters with death and various other crises, but what about the moment life begins? The psalmist says of God, "For you created my inmost being; you knit me together in my mother's womb. I praise you because I am fearfully and wonderfully made."[5] Think of it: the Creator of the universe gets personally involved in making us who we are!

To try to gain some perspective of this truth, let me give you a science fiction scenario that contrasts the vastness of creation with the intricate detail of our origin. (The concept is similar to those TV scenes where a camera—supposedly mounted on a space satellite—zooms in on planet Earth. The scene changes from Earth to a continent, then to a country, next a city, after this a road, and finally a house with someone sitting in the back yard reading a newspaper.)

Imagine that Earth is at the center of the universe, which happens to stretch about 14 billion light years across, and that another living being is standing on the last planet at the "edge" of the universe (if such a place exists). He wants to visit the center of the universe, so, traveling at the speed of light (186,000 miles per second), he spends about seven billion years reaching our galaxy, the Milky Way.

But after wending his way through untold billions of galaxies to arrive at the Milky Way, he still has a bit of navigating to do once he reaches our little neighborhood. *Let's see, which of these 400 billion stars is the one they call the Sun?* he says to himself.[6] As he gets closer, our cosmic visitor reaches Alpha Centauri, the nearest star to our Sun, leaving just 25,000,000,000,000 miles to go. He pauses to echo the psalmist's wonder, "How many are your works, O Lord! In wisdom you made them all."[7]

Finally, the spacecraft reaches planet Earth and lands in the front garden of 7 Sundial House, Borstal Hill, Whitstable, Kent—a small, coastal town in southeast England. The year is 1937, the month is March, the date is somewhere around the 24th. Something wondrous has just taken place. A tiny sperm has entered and fused with an egg the size of a pinhead, and a new life—a person—has just been created. Sixty-four years later, that person is seated at a computer writing this book.

Several years ago *National Geographic* published a book called *The Incredible Machine*[8] in which the journey of human life is portrayed in beautiful detail. It begins with the union of a man and woman, and the release of some 200 million to 500 million sperm that begin moving toward the woman's fallopian tube in order to interact with the egg. Within seconds, a million sperm may perish due to acids they encounter; the rest wriggle along at a rate equivalent to a swimmer's covering 12 yards a second.

Perils loom at every turn. White blood cells attack and destroy sperm by the millions, leaving only a few thousand to enter the uterus. Less than 500—sometimes as few as 10—will actually reach the part of the fallopian tube where the egg awaits.

Like a tiny space voyager meeting a huge planet, the sperm approaches the egg—which is, in fact, the largest of human cells: 85,000 times bigger than the sperm. Finally, in an heroic, supreme effort, one sperm will penetrate the egg and fertilization occurs. Seven to ten hours later, the egg nucleus containing the mother's DNA moves toward the sperm nucleus containing the father's DNA and the nuclei fuse. The miracle of new life has occurred: the two are now one.

What is even more astonishing is the wealth of genetic information packed into the two nuclei—considering that the "large" egg is the size of a pinhead and the sperm is smaller by a factor of 85,000. Genetically, they each contain three billion base pairs, or the equivalent of a thousand books of 500 pages apiece. Here the numbers get truly mind-boggling. Because of the complexity of our genetic coding, the possible number of genetic combinations in egg or sperm cells produced by any single human is, according to biologists,[9] incredibly vast: 2^{6700} or 10^{2017}. To put that into perspective, the estimated number of atoms in the whole known universe is "only" 10^{80} (that is, 10 followed by 80 zeroes).

Obviously, our brains are far too small to grasp the significance of such numbers. All we can do is acknowledge the awesomeness of our Creator—and appreciate the fact that He designed the absolute uniqueness of every individual.

Unlike the fictitious space visitor from the edge of the universe, God doesn't have to "wend His way" through time and space in order to be involved at the beginning of each new life. The psalmist says, "My frame was not hidden from you when I was made in the secret place."[10] As Creator, *He* decided which egg would be fertilized and which one of the hundreds of millions of sperm would be successful.[11] Only He knew the exact genetic code necessary to make you who you are. To put it simply, if a different "tadpole" had won the race, you wouldn't be here. That was also true for your father, mother, grandparents, great-grandparents, and every person in every generation throughout history.

Whether our parents were planning on having a baby is not the issue. It still is God who is the giver of life, the One who chooses what genetic elements to combine to make us who we are, and the

One who weaves us together in our mother's womb. As the psalmist declared, "Your eyes saw my unformed body. All the days ordained for me were written in your book before one of them came to be."[12]

Why am I me and not my brother? Because God made a deliberate decision in accordance with His pre-ordained plan for us. He chose me to be me, my brother to be my brother, and you to be you.

ENDNOTES

1. Psalm 139:16.

2. Psalm 139:7 (TLB).

3. Jonah 2:2.

4. Philippians 3:12.

5. Psalm 139:13-14.

6. Scientists currently estimate the number of stars in the Milky Way at 400 billion (plus or minus 200 billion).

7. Psalm 104:24.

8. Susan Schiefelbein, *The Incredible Machine* (Washington, DC: National Geographic Society, 1986).

9. These stupendous numbers are derived from the work of Francisco Ayala, a prominent scientist who calculated the "average heterozygosity" of humans today.

10. Psalm 139:15.

11. Some may argue that birth resulting from incest or rape cannot possibly involve God, but that view fails to consider God's sovereign role as Creator—regardless of the means of conception on the human side. The Bible contains several examples of individuals born via a "wrongful" relationship, yet who ended up in the ancestral line of Jesus! Our "wantedness" or "legitimacy" from a human standpoint has nothing to do with the fact that every human life is a person planned by God and created in His image.

12. Psalm 139:16. This wonderful truth applies even in an age of cloning and genetic engineering. Scientists may tinker with the DNA that God created, but whether an embryonic cell with a certain combination of genes actually survives and grows is still a matter of Divine determination. Even when man tries to "play God," our Creator always reserves the right to *be* God.

TWO

THIS EARTH IS NOT A MISTAKE

Astronomy leads us to a unique event, a universe which was created out of nothing, one with the very delicate balance needed to provide exactly the conditions required to permit life, and one which has an underlying (one might say "supernatural") plan.

—Arno Penzias
20th century Nobel Prize-winning physicist[1]

I am the LORD,
who has made all things,
who alone stretched out the heavens,
who spread out the earth by myself...
—The Creator of the Universe[2]

Hardly a day goes by that I don't contemplate the wonders of creation and the mysteries of eternity. Sometimes, when I'm up late on a summer night gazing at the stars and planets, I imagine someone who is spiritually unaware—perhaps a man on the other side of the world who never has seen a Bible or heard about the Creator—looking at this same, incredible, cosmic display, and I reflect on a question that he would be asking: "How did all this get here?"

While flying over the North American Rockies recently, I was struck anew by the stunning scenery below me. The landscape, as far as the eye could see, was dominated by majestic mountains—soaring, craggy peaks of white splendor, glistening in the morning sunshine. Noticing that the passenger beside me was likewise captivated by this breathtaking panorama, I offered a probing question: "Where do you think all this came from?" His reply was non-committal: "It certainly makes you think, doesn't it?"—as if to say, *I do wonder how all this came to be, but I'm not ready to consider the Creator just now.*

For a while we continued in silence and, as my senses continued to soak in the spectacular view below, my thoughts turned to the words of Psalm 19 where David speaks of God's glory in His creation:

> The heavens declare the glory of God;
> the skies proclaim the work of his hands.
> Day after day they pour forth speech;
> night after night they display knowledge.
> There is no speech or language
> where their voice is not heard.
> Their voice goes out into all the earth,
> their words to the ends of the world.[3]

King David had spent a lot of time outdoors as a young shepherd, and saw the Creator's magnificent workmanship all around him. That was about 3,000 years ago. Today, evidence for a Supernatural Designer is stronger than ever, and this generation, more than any other in history, is witness to it. As we will see later in the chapter, our 21st century scientists, peering deep into the universe through spectrographs and space telescopes, are amassing not just more "data," but more evidence of God's glory in the splendor of His creation. And it's happening literally "day after day."

This *glory* is not just a religious concept or scientific fact; it's something that touches our hearts, drawing praise, honor and renown—and sometimes a gasp of astonishment. Several years ago Janette and I were on holidays at our cabin on the west coast of Canada. One morning I rose before dawn and set off in semi-darkness for Thresher Rock, a famous fishing spot in Georgia Strait. Having arrived and set my lines, I waited with eager anticipation for that first bite. But something else was about to arrest my attention.

The sea was perfectly calm that morning, like a sheet of glass. Not another boat or ship was anywhere in sight; I was completely alone. Slowly, even as some of the brighter stars still twinkled overhead, the sky began to lighten. Suddenly, as I looked in the direction of the Coast Mountain Range near Vancouver, the sun broke into view from behind the high, snowy peaks, illuminating them in dazzling white and turning the sea to silver and gold—a spectacular sight that would forever be etched in my memory.

Instinctively, and totally unabashed, I yelled out at the top of my voice: YES! YES! YES! Then one long, drawn-out YES...followed by a hymn of praise sung with total abandon:

> O Lord my God! When I in awesome wonder
> Consider all the worlds Thy hands have made,
> I see the stars, I hear the rolling thunder,
> Thy pow'r throughout the universe displayed,
> Then sings my soul, my Savior God to Thee;
> How great Thou art! How great Thou art!
> Then sings my soul, my Savior God to Thee;
> How great Thou art! How great Thou art![4]

Gradually, tears began to stream down my face. But I continued singing. When I came to the verse, "And when I think that God, his Son not sparing, sent Him to die, I scarce can take it in; that on the cross, my burden gladly bearing, He bled and died to take away my sin," I could only whisper the words. When I finished, I found myself saying to the Lord, "Yes, that's who You are: You're the great, awesome Creator of the universe and, at the same time, my wonderful Redeemer."

What had happened? God had just been revealed to me in a tangible way through a glimpse of creation. He was glorified—and I became a humble worshiper. My hope is that, as we look at the wonders of God's handiwork in creation, we won't just respond as a student absorbing facts in a science classroom, but rather as a child overwhelmed by his Father's extravagant greatness.

One night several years ago I saw the stars as I had never seen them before. I was in Zimbabwe, off in the bush somewhere, far removed from the "light pollution" of civilization that usually affects our nighttime view. The darkness was virtually total: you couldn't see your hand in front of your face. As I looked up, it seemed like every inch of sky was packed with glittering stars. I thought I was seeing *millions* of them, but scientists tell us that even in ideal conditions, the most we can see with the naked eye is about 6,000.

When the telescope was invented in the 1600s, scientists encountered ever-increasing glory as they discovered other planets, moons and many more stars. But that was just the beginning. What astronomers didn't realize until the early 1900s was that there were galaxies beyond our own Milky Way. By the end of the century, their projections totaled *billions* of galaxies (between 120 and 200 billion, according to recent estimates), with each one containing an average of 100 *billion* stars.[5]

The Book of Job is known for its long debates by some of the great thinkers of the ancient world—and for those agonizing "why" questions from Job in his great distress. How does God respond to these questions and philosophical debates? He gives Job a nature lesson! In the space of four chapters,[6] God speaks at length—and with obvious enthusiasm—about different parts of His creation: the earth's foundations, the oceans, weather systems, constellations, and various wild animals and sea creatures.

If God were giving us a "color commentary" on creation today, He would probably highlight a few other areas. We might hear something about the biological wonders of DNA, or strange galactic objects like black holes and quasars, or perhaps elusive particles like neutrinos. He might even tell us some of the real names of the 10,000,000,000,000,000,000,000 stars that inhabit the universe (according to current estimates)—and what the exact total is. As the prophet Isaiah declares, each star is named and accounted for by God:

> Lift your eyes and look to the heavens:
> Who created all these?
> He who brings out the starry host one by one,
> and calls them each by name.
> Because of his great power and mighty strength,
> not one of them is missing.[7]

All I can say is, it's just as well that God is doing the counting. If you or I counted *one star per second* and did so continuously for *a million years*, we would have counted just 0.0000003 percent of the total. (And remember, you have to count by *name*, not just by number. I feel exhausted just thinking about it.)

Given the sheer immensity and complexity of His creation, God has ensured that no generation would have an excuse to doubt His greatness—least of all *this* one. The farther we see "out there," the more we encounter the mysterious vastness of His universe; the further we examine tiny cells and various sub-atomic particles, the more we observe His intricate craftsmanship. And in the front row seats of this cosmic theater are 21st century scientists who are now faced with overwhelming evidence of *design* in every part of creation, and who are compelled—even if reluctantly—to deal with the subject of a Designer or Creator.

"JUST RIGHT"

Eighteenth-century theologian-naturalist William Paley is best known for a famous metaphor he used in describing the universe and its Maker. His conclusion: Just as someone finding a watch lying on the ground somewhere would assume the existence of a watchmaker, we should acknowledge the fact of a "Divine Watchmaker" when we see a universe around us that is far more intricate than any watch. If Paley were alive today, he would be thrilled at the accumulation of evidence for supernatural design since he wrote that famous argument.

But someone might still wonder: *How skilled would such a Divine Watchmaker have to be? What amount of fine-tuning does it take to produce a planet where life exists? Could life on Earth be a cosmic mistake—just a happy evolutionary coincidence ("slime plus time," as someone put it)—or did the Creator specially plan it that way?*

Many people assume that there must be places like Earth all over the universe. But the more we understand the factors necessary for life, and the conditions that exist in other parts of the universe, the more we realize how unique our planet really is. Astronomer Hugh Ross has documented a variety of conditions that have to be "just right" for physical life of any kind to exist.[8] Here are just a few examples:

- *Distance from the sun:* Our planet "just happens" to be the right distance from the sun to permit an environment where water vapor, liquid water and ice are all abundant. A change in this distance of just 2 percent would upset this critical balance and render Earth lifeless.[9]

- *Type of neighboring planets:* Even our "neighbors" in the solar system are important. Planetary scientist George Wetherill discovered in 1993 that without a Jupiter-sized planet positioned just where it is, the earth would be subject to a thousand times more comet impacts. With its large mass, Jupiter draws most comets to itself or deflects them out of the solar system. Without that shield, Wetherill says, "...we wouldn't be around to study the origin of the solar system."[10]

- *Our sun:* The mass of our sun is "just right" while the mass of most other stars (99.9 percent of them) eliminates them as potential "candidates" for producing an earth-type planet.

Dr. Ross goes on to calculate the probability of finding a suitable planet *anywhere*. Taking into account a total of 128 *parameters* (or conditions) that scientists have determined to be direct or indirect requirements for life, and factoring in the maximum possible number of planets in the universe, he arrives at an astounding conclusion:

> Even if the universe contains as many as 10 billion trillion planets (10^{22}), we would not expect even one, by natural processes alone, to end up with the surface gravity, surface temperature, atmospheric composition, atmospheric pressure, crustal iron abundance, tectonics, vulcanism, rotation rate, rate of decline in rotation rate, and stable rotation axis tilt necessary for the support of life.[11]

> Thus, less than 1 chance in 10^{144} (trillion trillion trillion trillion trillion trillion trillion trillion trillion trillion trillion trillion) exists that even one such planet would occur anywhere in the universe.[12]

To me, those numbers sound like another way of saying "impossible." No wonder that British astrophysicist Paul Davies, a former agnostic, now says the "impression of design is overwhelming."[13] Robert Griffiths, who won the Heinemann prize in mathematical physics, was quoted as saying: "If we need an atheist for a debate, I go to the philosophy department. The physics department isn't much use."[14] One astronomer who obviously understood the implications of what he was seeing was George Greenstein. He wrote the following statement several years ago:

As we survey all the evidence, the thought insistently arises that some supernatural agency—or, rather, Agency—must be involved. Is it possible that suddenly, without intending to, we have stumbled upon scientific proof of the existence of a Supreme Being? Was it God who stepped in and so providentially crafted the cosmos for our benefit?[15]

Even Stephen Hawking, one of the most brilliant physicists of our time, was forced to concede:

It would be very difficult to explain why the universe should have begun in just this way, except as the act of a God who intended to create beings like us.[16]

Yet most scientists (Hawking included) still have great difficulty imagining a God who would go to all the "trouble" of fine-tuning everything in the universe just so that human beings could live on earth. With all their brilliance, they understand (more than we ever could) the sheer improbability[17] of Earth's existence, but many don't grasp the significance of a Creator who is all-powerful. They just don't "get" it. Creating a universe of 200 billion galaxies is no more difficult for God than creating a single planet or solar system.[18] Size is a non-issue, quantity just doesn't matter, complexity makes absolutely no difference, and time is completely irrelevant. All our human-based categories are totally inadequate in dealing with such a Being.

The "Unknown" God

As scientists today find themselves besieged by evidence of supernatural design, many of them are moving from an atheistic position to an agnostic one, or from agnostic to deistic (where God is acknowledged, but only as an impersonal and unknowable Supreme Being).[19] In that sense, they remind me of the first century philosophers of Athens who had built an altar with the inscription: TO AN UNKNOWN GOD. To them the apostle Paul preached the glorious truth of a Creator who is all-powerful yet *personal*:

"Now what you worship as something unknown I am going to proclaim to you. The God who made the world and everything in it is the Lord of heaven and earth..."[20]

Paul goes on to explain that God is actively at work in human history for very personal reasons:

"...so that men would seek him and perhaps reach out for him and find him, though he is not far from each one of us. 'For in him we live and move and have our being.'"[21]

And how are we to understand this "God who made the world and everything in it?" In a letter to Timothy, Paul describes Him as "the King eternal, immortal, invisible, the only God."[22] John Piper, in his book *The Pleasures of God*, declares:

What is this universe but the lavish demonstration of the incredible, incomparable, unimaginable exuberance and wisdom and power and greatness of God! What a God he must be![23]

I must say I enjoy that portrayal of One who is so awesome and extravagant in His nature, but even the best description in the best systematic theology textbook falls pitifully short in telling us what God is really like. With that "disclaimer," let us take a moment to consider some of the key dimensions of our great Creator:[24]

1. He has no beginning and no end:

God is self-existing and eternal. He created all things, including time, and He is the One, as Scripture testifies, "who alone is immortal."[25] Psalm 90 declares that "from everlasting to everlasting you are God."[26] Here is how Erich Sauer describes this amazing God in his book *From Eternity to Eternity*:

While as yet no star traversed its course, no sun threw its flood of light and energy through space, no systems of stars and suns swept through infinity in mighty curves and uniform relations, there God was; He the eternal without beginning, He who is above the whole course of time, He who in harmony beyond explanation possesses unity and life, the Father, the Son, and the Holy Spirit, the basis of eternity, the Living One, the only God.[27]

2. He knows everything:

Theologians refer to this attribute as *omniscience*, while scientists often think of God as *Supreme Intelligence*. But the Bible puts it in more personal terms. To paraphrase David's words in Psalm 139:1-6: *God knows me and everything about me. He knows when I sit down and when I stand up. He knows my thoughts from a long distance. He knows where I've been and where I'm going. In fact, He knows me not in some vague sort of way, but completely—every intimate detail. He even knows what I am about to say before I say it.* As far as David was concerned, that sort of knowledge was far beyond his ability to understand (and probably a little scary). We will examine this subject in more detail in Chapter 3.

3. He is everywhere:

The Bible speaks of God as the One who "fills everything in every way,"[28] meaning He is everywhere or *omnipresent*. That is in stark contrast to us as human beings, who can be in only one place at a time, and who fill a space of five or six cubic feet (and don't necessarily regard filling more than that as an accomplishment). Even the devil can be in only one place at one time.[29] Compare this with God's words through the prophet Jeremiah:

"Am I only a God nearby,"
  declares the Lord,
"and not a God far away?
Can anyone hide in secret places
so that I cannot see him?"
  declares the Lord.
"Do I not fill heaven and earth?"
  declares the Lord.[30]

4. He is all-powerful:

As members of the human race, we constantly are faced with our limitations. But God's power has no boundaries, He never falters, and He never sleeps: He is *omnipotent*. After receiving a direct revelation in the form of a science lesson from the Creator, Job acknowledges, "I know that you can do all things; no plan of yours can be thwarted."[31] When King Nebuchadnezzar's sanity was restored, he declared of God, "He does as he pleases with the powers of heaven and the peoples of the earth. No one can hold back his hand or say to him: 'What have you done?'"[32]

5. God in Three Persons:

There is one God (not three), yet each Person in the Trinity is fully God. In referring to His eternal nature, Jesus declared that He existed before Abraham and before the creation of the world.[33] New Testament writers identify Him as Creator,[34] the divine Word,[35] and the Almighty.[36] The Holy Spirit is also called God,[37] and is referred to as being eternal[38] and omnipresent.[39] As expressed by the ancient Athanasian Creed: "We worship one God in trinity, and trinity in unity, neither confounding the persons, nor separating the substance."

Each member of the Trinity was involved in creation, but functioned in a distinct role as we see in the opening verses of Genesis and the Gospel of John:

> In the beginning God created the heavens and the earth. Now the earth was formless and empty, darkness was over the surface of the deep, and the Spirit of God was hovering over the waters.[40]

> In the beginning was the Word, and the Word was with God, and the Word was God. He was with God in the beginning. Through him all things were made; without him nothing was made that has been made.[41]

[Some readers may be quite familiar with the truths in this section, but for others—even church members—the essential nature and attributes of God are rather vague notions. My hope is that this brief summary will not only inspire greater appreciation for our Creator, but also lay solid theological foundations where they may be lacking.]

GOD'S ULTIMATE CREATION

"The heavens declare the glory of God," says the psalmist, but the crowning touch of God's creative output was not expressed in galaxies, quasars, black holes, and planets, but in the creation of Adam and Eve. Made in the very image of God, man was given a body and brain perfectly designed to carry out the role of governor and caretaker of planet Earth, but (as we shall see in Chapter 6) he failed miserably in carrying out this mandate. For now, our focus will be on the incredible, marvelous, complex piece of "machinery" that a human being represents.

In case you thought I was using too many superlatives in that last sentence, consider the following quote from Dr. Hugh Ross:

> For the universe and the solar system, some characteristics must be fine-tuned to better than one part in 1037 for life to be possible. But, the fine-tunings necessary to build an independent, functioning organism require precision crafting beyond what people have ever imagined possible, precision to one part in a number so big that it would fill thousands of books to write out.[42]

James Watson, co-discoverer of the DNA helix, is quoted as saying, "The brain is the most complex thing we have yet discovered in the whole universe." Neurosurgeon Robert J. White commented: "I am left with no choice but to acknowledge the existence of a Superior Intellect responsible for the design and development of the incredible brain-mind relationship."[43]

But our non-brain parts are also amazing components of God's ultimate creation.[44] Take, for example, the part you are using to read this page: your eyes. No bigger than a ping-pong ball, each eye has tens of millions of electrical connections and can handle 1½ million simultaneous messages. The retina, situated at the back of the eye, is an amazing photographic screen less than an inch square, yet it contains 130 million black and white receptor cells shaped like rods, and 7 million color receptor cells shaped like cones. Everything you see is received onto the retina from where it travels to your brain through the optic nerve. (It's no wonder that the least successful part of making robots is trying to replicate a human's ability to see and interpret images.)

Then there is skin—which is actually our largest organ: it retains fluids, provides insulation, and protects against disease. Take a look at the back of your hand. Below that thin top layer (epidermis) lies the dermis containing an intricate collection of nerves, blood vessels and glands. The skin also features a special air conditioning system set at 98.6°F. To prevent dangerous changes in body temperature, our skin's surface area contains almost 2½ million sweat glands, each consisting of a tightly coiled tube less than one-quarter-inch long, but adding up to over six miles of tubing!

Now put your hand on your chest. That *boom-diddy-boom* you are feeling is your heart, which, under normal circumstances, will beat 2½ billion times in a 75-year life span. It pumps five quarts of blood continuously, delivering nutrients and oxygen to every cell in the body and removing waste at the same time. Think of it as a combined food delivery and garbage collection system. The heart with its circulatory system has been described as a river—a crimson stream that courses through every organ and twists past every cell on a journey that stretches about *100,000 miles*—long enough to circle the earth four times!

Speaking of cells, our bodies contain 20 to 30 *trillion* of these complex life structures. Despite the fact that cells are so tiny (an average 10,000 of them could fit on the head of a pin), they come in a variety of types and sizes depending on their task. Red blood cells, for example, transport life-giving oxygen to every part of the body. In the time it took you to turn this page, you lost 2 to 3 million red blood cells, yet during that moment, your bone marrow produced the same number.[45]

But it's not just those amazing "building blocks" of the body that are cause for wonder. I vividly remember the time I was present for the birth of our daughter Rachel, and how fascinated I was by her tiny, perfectly formed fingernails. Turning to the midwife, I exclaimed, "How can anyone not believe there is a God?"

Even without knowing all the incredible details of the human body that we know today, King David long ago prayed these words:

> For you created my inmost being;
> you knit me together in my mother's womb.
> I praise you because I am fearfully and wonderfully made;
> your works are wonderful,
> I know that full well.[46]

Is this earth a mistake? Could a universe that allows for life be a coincidence? Are we here by chance? The answers from science—based on the most up-to-date evidence—declare the opposite: that there is a Supreme Being, a "Divine Watchmaker," who designed it all. Over and above that testimony we have the revelation of God in Scripture, His acts in history and His Incarnation, all pointing us to a wonderfully *personal* God who made us for Himself: the great Creator who became our Savior.

The purpose of these first two chapters is not to impress you with amazing facts from science and the Bible, but rather to convince you that you are not a mistake or a child of chance. You are "fearfully and wonderfully made." The God who created the universe planned you in eternity and created you to live here at this time on this specially-constructed, purpose-built planet called Earth. The ultimate reason for our being here is that in some profound way we might play a small but unique and vital role in His grand design—a plan that was corrupted by Adam and Eve (and all of their offspring, including *us*), but redeemed by the "Last Adam," our Lord Jesus Christ.

ENDNOTES

1. Henry Margenau and Roy Abraham Varghese, eds., *Cosmos, Bios, and Theos* (La Salle, Illinois: Open Court, 1992), 83, quoted in Hugh Ross, *The Creator and the Cosmos*, 3rd ed. rev. (Colorado Springs, Colorado: Navpress, 2001), 159.

2. Isaiah 44:24.

3. Psalm 19:1-4.

4. *How Great Thou Art*, copyright 1955 by Manna Music, Inc., Hollywood, California.

5. We have become so used to hearing big numbers like *billions* that we probably don't appreciate their size. Here is an illustration that may help put it into perspective: If a man were given a billion dollars to spend at $1,000 per day, every day of the year, how many years do you suppose it would take to spend that money? (We'll exclude the factor of interest, and assume that he would pass on the remainder to one of his children when he died, and so on.) If the man started his spending at the time of Christ's birth, his descendants would still be spending that $1,000 per day now, and their descendants likewise until the year A.D. 2732.

6. Job chapters 38 to 41.

7. Isaiah 40:26.

8. Ross, op. cit., 154-157. I do not necessarily subscribe to all of Dr. Ross' theories, but his books contain a wealth of useful information.

9. Ibid., 180.

10. Ibid., 183.

11. Ibid., 185. As an example of how rapidly the evidence for design is increasing, Ross points out that between the second and third edition of his book (a period of six years), the list of parameters grew from 41 to 128!

12. Ibid., 198. Nevertheless, Dr. Ross predicts the discovery of life forms on Mars. His reasons? "Meteorites large enough to make a crater greater than 60 miles across will cause Earth rocks to escape Earth's gravity. Out of 1,000 such rocks ejected, on the average, 291 will strike Venus, 20 go to Mercury, 17 hit Mars, 14 make it to Jupiter, and one would go all the way to Saturn." He concludes: "The discovery of microbial life and creatures perhaps as large as nematodes on Mars—a discovery we can expect as technology continues to advance—will probably be touted as proof of naturalistic evolution, when in truth it proves nothing of the kind. It will prove something, however, about the amazing vitality of what God created." (Pages 209-211.)

13. Paul Davies, *The Cosmic Blueprint* (New York: Simon and Schuster, 1988), 203, quoted in Ross, op. cit., 157.

14. Tim Stafford, "Cease-fire in the Laboratory," *Christianity Today*, April 3, 1987, p. 18, quoted in Ross, op. cit., 160.

15. George Greenstein, *The Symbiotic Universe* (New York: William Morrow, 1988), 27, quoted in Ross, op. cit., 158.

16. Stephen Hawking, *A Brief History of Time* (New York: Bantam Books, 1988), 127, quoted in Ross, op. cit., 159.

17. The numbers would say *impossibility*, but the fact is, we're here!

18. Aside from God's intention to display His power and glory in the vastness of creation, there is evidence that the size of the universe itself is necessary for life to be possible (Ross, op. cit., 161).

19. This was essentially the position of Albert Einstein (Ross, op. cit., 73-74).

20. Acts 17:23-24.

21. Acts 17:27-28.

22. 1 Timothy 1:17.

23. John Piper, *The Pleasures of God* (Portland, Oregon: Multnomah Press, 1991), 94.

24. Some people see a clear separation between theology and science, but God is the Supreme Author of things both "spiritual" and "natural," everything from faith and holiness to mathematics and quantum physics. It's all His.

25. 1 Timothy 6:16.

26. Psalm 90:2.

27. Erich Sauer, *From Eternity to Eternity* (London: Paternoster Press, 1957), 13.

28. Ephesians 1:23.

29. Job 1:7, 2:2.

30. Jeremiah 23:23-24. (These are arguably the ultimate in rhetorical questions!)

31. Job 42:2.

32. Daniel 4:35.

33. John 8:58, 17:5, 24.

34. Hebrews 1:10; Colossians 1:16.

35. John 1:1-2.

36. Revelation 1:8.

37. Acts 5:3-4; 2 Corinthians 3:17-18.

38. Hebrews 9:14.

39. Psalm 139:7-10.

40. Genesis 1:1-2.

41. John 1:1-3.

42. Ross, op. cit., 201.

43. Quote from a letter to *The Daily Mail*, a national British newspaper, by Nick Welham of Verwood, Dorset, October 19, 2001.

44. For this section I am using information from sources that are factual but not overly technical, including: *Your Body and How it Works* by J. D. Ratcliff, a *Reader's Digest* publication; *The Incredible Machine* by Susan Schiefelbein, published by *National Geographic*; and various Internet sites.

45. Space does not permit a description of white blood cells, which form the core of our immune system, and the scores of other intricate biological systems in our body.

46. Psalm 139:13-14.

THREE

MADE FOR THE GLORY
AND PLEASURE OF GOD

*You made us for Yourself and our hearts find no peace
till they rest in You.* —Augustine

*Our evangelistic task is not to persuade people that the
gospel was made for their felt needs, but that they were
made for the soul-satisfying glory of God in the gospel.*
—John Piper[1]

The last words I heard from my 93-year-old mother were words
she had spoken to me many times before.

We had been on a long-distance call between Canada and England for some time, so I suggested, "Mum, it's time to hang up." "Yes
it is," she replied, "bye bye." Then she added with a commanding
tone, "Now, Barney my boy, don't you ever forget: remember, *give
God all the glory.*" Soon after, Mother was no longer able to commu-
nicate and, within two weeks, had gone to be with the Lord.

Give God all the glory. What does that really mean? I am quite
certain that when my mother said those words she was thinking of
my response to being used as a minister of the gospel. But this principle actually applies to all of life: we are here on planet Earth to live
to the praise of His glory. In fact, all of creation, both in Heaven and
earth, exists to bring glory to the Lord Jesus Christ. Here is how the
Scriptures describe the centrality of Christ in creation:

> For by him all things were created: things in heaven and
> on earth, visible and invisible, whether thrones or powers

or rulers or authorities; *all things were created by him and for him*. He is before all things, and in him all things hold together.[2]

Why do I have a body? The ultimate answer is: to bring glory to God. To the carnally-minded Corinthians Paul said, "You are not your own; you were bought at a price. Therefore honor God with your body."[3]

Why do I have a voice? To glorify God in what I say or sing. The apostle Peter refers to believers as "a people belonging to God, that you may declare the praises of him who called you out of darkness into his wonderful light."[4]

What about eating and drinking or celebrating special days? In his letters to the Romans and Corinthians, Paul gives a very clear answer:

> One man considers one day more sacred than another; another man considers every day alike. Each one should be fully convinced in his own mind. He who regards one day as special, does so to the Lord. He who eats meat, eats to the Lord, for he gives thanks to God; and he who abstains, does so to the Lord and gives thanks to God. So whether you eat or drink or whatever you do, do it all for the glory of God.[5]

Even the way we *die* is to glorify Him. John's Gospel records Jesus telling Peter that when he reaches old age someone else will dress him and lead where he does not want to go; then it adds this interpretation: "Jesus said this to indicate the kind of death by which Peter would glorify God."[6] As Paul says to the Romans: "For none of us lives to himself alone and none of us dies to himself alone. If we live, we live to the Lord; and if we die, we die to the Lord."[7]

Why do the stars and planets exist? "*The heavens declare the glory of God.*"[8] And the many thousands of species of animals, birds, fish, flowers and trees?[9] Consider this psalm of praise:

> How many are your works, O Lord!
>   In wisdom you made them all;
>   the earth is full of your creatures.
> There is the sea, vast and spacious,

> teaming with creatures beyond number—
>   living things both large and small.
> May the glory of the Lord endure forever;
>   may the Lord rejoice in his works...[10]

Why does the Church exist? In writing to the church in Ephesus, Paul says, "In him we were also chosen...in order that we, who were the first to hope in Christ, might be for the praise of his glory."[11] Chapter 3 ends with this doxology: "Now to him...be glory in the church and in Christ Jesus throughout all generations, for ever and ever! Amen."

We may agree that the Bible teaches that everything exists for God's glory, but what does that actually mean in practical terms? If God's glory is ultimately an expression of His eternal plan, how does that plan come about in our everyday lives? How do we get there?

STARTING WHERE GOD STARTS

If we truly want to discover God's plans, we must start where He starts. And that usually involves reconsidering our point of view.

DeVern Fromke tells the story of a theology professor who marked two dots on a blank sheet of white paper and then joined them with a straight line. "Explain to me what you see," he challenged the students. Many and varied were the replies, but all concentrated on the two dots and the line. Finally the professor asked, "But don't any of you see the white paper I wrote on?"

The Irish are known for their quaint sayings (which, in view of my part-Irish ancestry, may explain a few things). The story is told of a woman inquiring of a Dublin police officer as to where she might find O'Connell Street, to which he replied, "Well, madam, if I was you, I wouldn't start from here."

The lost Irish woman in our story may have had little choice where she started from, but we do have a choice in our *theological* starting point. For many Christians, that starting point is the Garden of Eden: specifically, the fall of man and God's plan of redemption. The problem with that kind of focus is that it tends to put man at the center and views God as existing in order to bless us and help us— like a glorified Santa Claus or genie of the lamp. We would never put it that way, but that is what can actually happen in our thinking.

Some like to quote Paul's statement in Ephesians chapter 1 that God has blessed us with every spiritual blessing in Christ. But that is not where the apostle starts. He begins with: "Praise be to the God and Father of our Lord Jesus Christ…"[12] The focus is not on us, it's on God. Dr. Martyn Lloyd-Jones in his exposition of Ephesians 1 writes:

> Because of our wretched subjectivity, our tendency always is to concentrate at once on the blessings; we always want something for ourselves. The apostle insists, however, that we start with God, and with worship.[13]

While Paul reminds the Ephesian believers that they have indeed been blessed with every spiritual blessing in Christ, he quickly establishes the fact that God chose us to be holy and blameless in His sight (1:4), that He predestined us in accordance with His pleasure and will (1:5), and that this is all to the praise of His glorious grace (1:6). Furthermore, he points out that God has a claim on their lives—because they were called by Him and were part of Christ's *inheritance* (1:18).

Paul states this truth even more emphatically to the Corinthian church: "…for us there is but one God, the Father, from whom all things came and *for whom we live*…"[14] God doesn't exist for *me*; that idea is ludicrous! In fact, it's pathetic. No, we exist for God. We were designed to bring *Him* glory and pleasure. We are here to live for Him as sons in His worldwide family, as members of the Body of Christ, as living stones in the temple of the Holy Spirit.

The fact that we live for *Him* (not the reverse) is foundational in our understanding of the Christian life—and should be so obvious that it need not be stated. Nevertheless, it can easily be overlooked, even in the midst of spiritual revivals. I sadly note that both the Charismatic Movement of the 1960s and the more recent renewal movements have at times over-emphasized *receiving, refreshing* and *experiences* instead of God's glory and purposes. However, I am encouraged that in many places this is now being rectified. The words of a prayer often associated with Francis of Assisi are still relevant today:

> O Master, grant that I may never seek
> so much to be consoled as to console,

to be understood as to understand,
to be loved as to love with all my soul.

Several years ago, Jim Bakker, a well-known proponent of the "prosperity gospel" during the 1980s, came face to face with the bankruptcy of his focus and his theology while serving time in prison. In his book *I Was Wrong*, Bakker writes:

> As the true impact of Jesus' words regarding money impacted my heart and mind, I became physically nauseated. I was wrong. I was wrong! Wrong in my lifestyle, certainly, but even more fundamentally, wrong in my understanding of the Bible's true message. Not only was I wrong, but I was teaching the opposite of what Jesus had said.
>
> Although I was committed to following Jesus, I wanted to do it my way rather than His; I had given my life to Him, but I was still in control of it...In prison, I came to the end of Jim Bakker.[15]

But a gospel that focuses on material blessings and "giving in order to get" is not the only way we can get sidetracked from the centrality of Christ. Those who view life from a "Christian Reconstruction" framework (and I am one who acknowledges much helpful truth from these sources) often start with the "kingdom mandate" of Genesis 1:28 where God blesses Adam and Eve and says, "Be fruitful and increase in number; fill the earth and subdue it. Rule over the fish of the sea and the birds of the air and over every living creature that moves on the ground."

"Kingdom mandate" may sound more spiritual than self-absorption in terms of material blessing but, as a theological starting point, it too fails. The problem is, we start seeing history in terms of man ruling, a viewpoint that fosters triumphalism and human effort—the idea that "we can make it happen." In other words, we focus on the kingdom but not necessarily the King. Or worse, we become our own little self-crowned monarchs running our own inconsequential kingdoms.

If we do that, we have failed to understand that the only way we can live for God is to live through Christ. While some contemporary

Reconstructionist material hardly mentions the name of Jesus or refers to the Holy Spirit, this has not always been the case—as we see in this quote from Geerhardus Vos, a highly respected writer in the Reconstruction movement:

> First of all, then, we may say that the order of things introduced by Jesus is called the kingdom of God because in it as a whole and in every part of it God is supreme. The conception is a theocentric conception which must remain unintelligible to every view of the world that magnifies man at the expense of God.[16]

Romans 14 tells us that the Kingdom of God is not a matter of eating or drinking, but of righteousness, peace and joy in the Holy Spirit. As someone once pointed out, if you took out the middle of verse 17, you would be left with the simple but profound truth that *the kingdom of God is in the Holy Spirit.* Geerhardus Vos echoes this theme:

> And Jesus ascribes all the power involved in the establishment of the kingdom to the Holy Spirit as its source…With this Spirit He has been anointed not merely to heal and set free the bodies of men, but also to preach the gospel to the poor. If, then, in its very essence the power of the kingdom is the power of the Holy Spirit, it must extend as far as the latter's operation extends and include the entire liberating, renewing, sanctifying work of grace in the hearts of men.[17]

As the Scriptures clearly show, the reason for our presence on this planet is to live for God, and the only way this is achieved is through Jesus Christ. This ensures that God's glory is safeguarded.

MAN WAS NOT CREATED IN ORDER TO BE REDEEMED

It is difficult for us *not* to see redemption as the "main event" because without it we would be forever lost.[18] But from God's perspective, redemption could be described as a Divine parenthesis. Dr. Martyn Lloyd-Jones elaborates on this in his exposition of Ephesians 1:

> Neither does he [Paul] start even with the work of the Lord Jesus Christ Himself. Many would probably put that in the first place. They would say that all this has become possible for us because of what the Lord Jesus Christ did for us

when He came into this world—in His life and death and resurrection—and what He is still doing. But the apostle does not put even that first. Indeed, we observe that he does not start with anything that first happened in time and in this world. He goes right back into eternity, before the foundation of the world; and he starts with that which has been done by God the Father.[19]

Because Adam originally lived in an innocent, sinless state, we may have assumed that this was all he was ever meant to be. But that assumption does not stand up to Scripture. First Corinthians 15:45 tells us that Adam was a living being (or soul), but that Jesus, the last Adam, is a life-giving Spirit. The next verse goes on to say, "The spiritual did not come first, but the natural, and after that the spiritual." Adam still would have had to be born spiritually in order to be able to say, in the words of Colossians 3:3, "My life is hidden with Christ in God."

The Bible also teaches that God "...has saved us and called us to a holy life—not because of anything we have done but because of his own purpose and grace."[20] What exactly is that purpose? If the purpose goes back further than the fall of man, we need to ask ourselves what would have remained the same if man had not sinned.

But before we do that, it may be helpful to consider a key attribute of God that is linked to His eternal purposes, namely His *omniscience*. This is foundational and pivotal to all that follows.

Most Christians have no difficulty believing that God knows everything about the past and the present. What some find difficult is the thought that God also knows everything that is going to happen in the future—whether good, bad or indifferent. They feel that the doctrine of God's foreknowledge somehow contradicts the fact that He gave us free will. It is not my intention to try to provide the definitive answer to a centuries-old debate, but I do believe we need to be clear on the fact that God dwells in eternity and knows all things. As the writer to the Hebrews points out:

Nothing in all creation is hidden from God's sight. Everything is uncovered and laid bare before the eyes of him to whom we must give account.[21]

Creation, of course, includes each one of us. God can see us inside out, at all times. But does that have to do only with the past and present? According to Scripture, God the Father "chose us in him [Christ] *before the creation of the world* to be holy and blameless in his sight."[22] As far as God is concerned, our true beginnings go back long before our parents ever met, or before there was any life on this planet, or before there were any planets or stars anywhere!

For God to have chosen you and me before He even started creating time and space is truly a mind-boggling concept. Actually, *foreknowledge* and *predestination* are simply words that describe things from our perspective—from the viewpoint of creatures living within time. To God who dwells in eternity, it's simply *knowledge.* Philip Yancey describes it this way:

> Unlike us, God has an all-encompassing point of view that takes in the world as we see as well as other realms hidden to us. Moreover, God sees all our history at once, as a ball of yarn compared to the short, consecutive scraps of thread we experience.[23]

While some debate whether the sacrifice of Jesus was planned in the Father's mind before Adam sinned, or whether this was a "divine afterthought," the Bible itself refers to Jesus as the Lamb "chosen before the creation of the world."[24] Clearly there would have been no need for a Sacrificial Lamb to be chosen *before* creation if God was unaware that man would sin after creation. And as has already been mentioned, Scripture teaches that we, too, were chosen *before* creation. Erich Sauer comments:

> From eternity God foresaw the irruption of sin, before all time He appointed the Son to be the Redeemer, to be the Lamb...

> Before the foundation of the world, the Father had appointed the Son to be Mediator. It therefore followed that the creating of the world itself came to pass through the Son (Colossians 1:16)...Therefore as the center of salvation of the Universe, Christ must be viewed as connected with the cross from eternity.[25]

Dr. Martyn Lloyd-Jones echoes this truth: "Let us get rid forever of the idea that salvation was an afterthought in the mind of God. It was not a thought that came to God after man had fallen into sin—it was planned *before the foundation of the world.*"[26]

Some Christians believe that God only knows what He Himself is going to do in the future, and not what evil deeds man may decide to enact. However, the Scriptures show us numerous examples of God's omniscience concerning man's sinful behavior. In Deuteronomy 31 He clearly describes Israel's future rebellion:

And the Lord said to Moses, "You are going to rest with your fathers, and these people will soon prostitute themselves to the foreign gods of the land they are entering. They will forsake me and break the covenant I made with them. On that day I will become angry with them and forsake them; I will hide my face from them, and they will be destroyed."[27]

Note also Jeremiah's prophecy about the future deeds of Herod:

This is what the Lord says:
"A voice is heard in Ramah,
mourning and great weeping,
Rachel weeping for her children
and refusing to be comforted,
Because her children are no more."[28]

Matthew's Gospel records that this prophecy was fulfilled when Herod, in his demonic rage, gave orders for the slaughter of all male children up to two years of age living in the Bethlehem area. The fact is, God sees everything: good and evil, whether past, present or future.

Recently, I was going through some old Super-8 film footage of a trip to Disney World in Florida. The first scenes of the big parade showed only the bands and floats immediately in front of me. I remember being dissatisfied with this limited view and finding a higher vantage point. Suddenly I was able to pan most of the parade at one sweep of the camera. God in His infiniteness is able to view our finite events in one sweep as if they had already happened. If you have a problem getting your mind around that, try spending a few minutes contemplating the fact of God's eternal existence: forever and ever and ever, no end, and—what is even more difficult to imagine—no beginning. Gulp!

Another reason why we struggle with this truth is because we cannot imagine an all-knowing God interacting with us in human history and doing so with true emotion. For us, emotion is linked to happenings or experiences in time. How could an eternal, almighty, omniscient God feel anger or joy over human behavior when He is not experiencing events in time the way we do?

I don't think anyone has a final answer to that question, because no human mind can begin to grasp the greatness of God. But perhaps a small example can shed light on this subject. Have you noticed how you can *know* something as a fact—for instance, a sad event such as a tragic death, or a joyous event such as reunion—but experience anew the strength of the emotion when you are telling someone else about it? If the mind of God is so great that He can hear and respond to millions of prayers simultaneously while sustaining the operation of the whole universe, then He can also enter into the emotional experience of human life at any point He chooses.

In relation to the sovereignty and omniscience of God, Dr. Martyn Lloyd-Jones makes some rather direct comments while quoting from the venerable King James Version:

> Indeed we must go further; we can say in the second place that not only does the Bible not argue with us about these doctrines, it reproves us and reprimands us when we begin to argue because we do not understand them. The Apostle states this clearly in his Epistle to the Romans (9:19): "Thou wilt say then unto me, why doth he yet find fault? For who hath resisted his will?" Take note of the Apostle's answer: "Nay but, O man, who art thou that repliest against God?" He does not try to lead a discussion and work it out and explain it, as he could have done; he simply says, "Nay but, O man, who art thou that repliest against God?"
>
> In other words, the Apostle is telling us that we must start by realizing who and what God is, that we must realize of whom we are speaking. And he goes on to remind us that our relationship to the God of whom we are speaking is really that of a lump of clay to a potter. Realize, he says, before you ask your questions and put forward your arguments based upon your failure to understand, that you are

assuming that your little mind is capable of understanding what God does. Realize that you are really suggesting that you, simple creature such as you are, small and petty as you often are in your human relationships, you who listened to the devil and brought ruin upon yourself—realize that you are claiming that your pygmy mind is able to understand the infinite and inscrutable mind of the eternal God.[29]

(It is probably safe to say that Dr. Lloyd-Jones was not an adherent of the "self-esteem" movement.)

Another way of looking at things from God's eternal perspective is to reflect on what changed and what did not change after the fall of man. In other words, what was in the heart and mind of God concerning man beyond saving us? We will consider that question in the next chapter.

ENDNOTES

1. John Piper, *God's Passion for His Glory* (Wheaton, Illinois: Crossway Books, 1998), 39.

2. Colossians 1:16-17 (emphasis added).

3. 1 Corinthians 6:20.

4. 1 Peter 2:9.

5. Romans 14:5-6 and 1 Corinthians 10:31.

6. John 21:19.

7. Romans 14:7-8.

8. Psalm 19:1.

9. Dr. Jennifer Owen counted 1,786 different birds, bugs, blooms and bees just in an average English country garden.

10. Psalm 104:24-25, 31.

11. Ephesians 1:11-12.

12. Ephesians 1:3.

13. Martyn Lloyd-Jones, *The Exposition of Ephesians, Vol.1* (Grand Rapids, Michigan: Baker Books, 1998), 57.

14. 1 Corinthians 8:6 (emphasis added).

15. Jim Bakker, *I Was Wrong* (Nashville, Tennessee: Thomas Nelson, 1996), 393, 402.

16. Geerhardus Vos, *History and Biblical Interpretation* (Phillipsburg, New Jersey: Presbyterian and Reformed Publishing Co., 1980), 311.

17. Ibid., 313.

18. DeVern Fromke describes redemption as *Divine rectification.* Whatever term we use, it is important to understand that it involves not only God redeeming man, but also God redeeming the Plan.

19. Martyn Lloyd-Jones, op. cit., 82.

20. 2 Timothy 1:9.

21. Hebrews 4:13.

22. Ephesians 1:4 (emphasis added).

23. Philip Yancey: *Reaching for the Invisible God* (Grand Rapids, Michigan: Zondervan, 2000), 114.

24. 1 Peter 1:19-20.

25. Erich Sauer, *From Eternity to Eternity* (London: Paternoster Press, 1957), 15.

26. Martyn Lloyd-Jones, op. cit., 53.

27. Deuteronomy 31:16-17.

28. Jeremiah 31:15.

29. Martyn Lloyd-Jones, op. cit., 86.

FOUR

WHAT IF...?

For the Lord Almighty has purposed, and who can thwart him? —Isaiah 14:27

Two of the most common mistakes we make are overestimating the power of the devil and underestimating the power of God. Evil can seem so strong and so pervasive in our fallen world that we think the enemy has somehow succeeded in thwarting the purposes of God. But this never can happen. Satan is still a creature and never can go beyond the boundaries set for him by Almighty God.

But what about sin? What about the fall of man? Did Adam's rebellion not result in a complete alteration of God's plans and purposes? To explore this subject, we will need to consider a "what if?" question: *What if man had not in fact made that fateful choice in the garden?* What difference would that have made in terms of God's plan?

WHAT WOULD HAVE REMAINED THE SAME IF ADAM HAD NOT SINNED?

This is more than a hypothetical or speculative question. Because of our status as sinners saved by grace, it is easy to think of our relationship to God solely in terms of "the plan of salvation." But by considering what would have remained constant regardless of the fall, we may gain a deeper understanding and appreciation of God's eternal purposes. So, what if Adam had not sinned? What would have remained the same?

1.   The Father's plan for a family that would fill the whole earth:

Apart from issues of sin and redemption, God's eternal plan included the Incarnation, our adoption as sons, and our maturing through suffering. Christ still would have been incarnated into the human family in order to show us what a true Son of God looked like: to demonstrate in attitude and behavior how to bring pleasure to the Father and glorify Him; and ultimately to bring many sons to glory.[1]

Furthermore, the Scriptures teach us that although Jesus was the sinless Son of God, He "learned obedience from what he suffered."[2] Many Christians assume that if Adam had not sinned, we would live in a world with no suffering. It is true that sin brought suffering— due to the painful consequences of wrongdoing as well as God's judgment against sin—but that is not the whole story.

Suffering is also God's method of making us mature as His sons and daughters. If that was true for Jesus the Son (as Hebrews 5:8-9 indicates), it is certainly true for us. The God who created time also chose to create beings who could grow and mature over time, a process that even applied to the eternal Son when He took on human form. The process of maturing necessarily involves suffering be- cause we have to learn self-denial, sacrificial love and servanthood— qualities that reflect the character of God Himself. In fact, Jesus is depicted in Isaiah chapters 42-53 as the suffering Servant—a portrayal not only of what was to happen historically, but also of the inherent nature of God. DeVern Fromke refers to this as the *eternal* Cross:

> We see then that the Cross is far more than an act in history. It expresses the very qualities and manner of life of the tri- une God. It is the life-giving, light-sharing and love- bestowing principle by which God has dealt with man from the beginning...(T)his *eternal Cross in God* was to become the *inwrought Cross in man*. Only when man refused this, was it necessary for an outward demonstration of the *historic Cross on Golgotha*.[3]

In the life of Christ, the *eternal* Cross was expressed ultimately in His death, but it was also evident in His attitude toward the Father and His humble, sacrificial service to man. One of the most powerful examples of such servanthood is found in John's account of what happened during the Last Supper:

> Jesus knew that the Father had put all things under his power, and that he had come from God and was returning to

God; so he got up from the meal, took off his outer clothing, and wrapped a towel around his waist. After that, he poured water into a basin and began to wash his disciples feet, drying them with the towel that was wrapped around him.[4]

Can you imagine the scene? It probably took place after the disciples had finished one of their recurring arguments, which, as Luke reports in his account of the Last Supper, was about who among them was the greatest.[5] How would you feel if you were one of the disciples at the table? Still hungry? To put it in a modern context, how would you feel if Jesus came to your house and washed your car, or cleaned the toilet in your bathroom?

The Scriptures specifically note that Jesus washed His disciples' feet in the full knowledge of who He was and where He was going. This was no emotional outburst or sudden lapse of judgment. It also accords with what He taught them earlier about the nature of their heavenly Master:

> It will be good for those servants whose master finds them watching when he comes. I tell you the truth, he will dress himself to serve, will have them recline at the table and will come and wait on them.[6]

In case they didn't quite "get it" earlier, the disciples would receive a final lesson in servanthood after the resurrection when Jesus, in His glorified body, cooked breakfast for them after they had been fishing all night.[7]

But God's eternal plan goes beyond servanthood. It was the Father's good pleasure to choose an enormous *family*—men, women and children drawn from every corner of the globe, all of whom would call Him *Father*. As Paul writes, "he predestined us to be adopted as his sons through Jesus Christ, in accordance with his pleasure and will."[8] This theme of family and fatherhood is also found in the writings of Jeremiah the prophet in these touching, paternal words: "How gladly would I treat you like sons...I thought you would call me 'Father' and not turn away from following me."[9] God planned that this family would share His life, nature, Spirit, vision, purpose and dedication. To that end, He sovereignly predestined us, and in fulfillment of that goal He regenerates us (new birth), He adopts us, He sanctifies us, and presents us complete (mature) in Christ.

Without losing the wonder of God's amazing love and purposes, let us look further at the meaning of adoption. Some commentators see adoption as being distinct from regeneration, but taking place at the same time. Others link this truth more closely with the maturing process. Perhaps the application is twofold: we are, for example, already complete in Christ *positionally*, but we are also in the process of being *made* complete in Him *experientially*.

DeVern Fromke explains that in eastern lands it was the custom for a nobleman father to submit his male child to the training and tutelage of a trusted, educated, qualified servant. It was the task of this guardian (tutor) to train the child in the ways, purposes and spirit of the father. When the child was 14 to 16 years old, it was customary to hold a formal celebration for his coming of age. This ceremony was called *adoption* and meant the son was coming into his full rights in the family. Paul expresses a similar theme in Romans 8:

> The Spirit himself testifies with our spirit that we are God's children. Now if we are children, then we are heirs—heirs of God and co-heirs with Christ, if indeed we share in his sufferings in order that we may also share in his glory.[10]

In other words, we are heirs because we are children (via regeneration, new birth) *and* because we share in Christ's sufferings. Suffering is an essential part of our growing up as mature sons and daughters and cannot be avoided if we want to share in His glory as we were intended to.

Just as the Kingdom of God has a future dimension as well as a past and present application, our adoption also incorporates a wonderful future hope. Paul writes in verse 23 that "we ourselves, who have the firstfruits of the Spirit, groan inwardly as we wait eagerly for our adoption as sons, the redemption of our bodies."

Our future inheritance as sons and daughters of Father God includes new bodies that are free from the ravages of sickness and aging. Meanwhile, in this life, no matter what trial, persecution or deprivation comes our way, we can say together with Paul in verse 28, "And we know that in all things God works for the good of those who love him, who have been called according to his purpose."

And what is that purpose? Paul answers in the next verse: "For those God foreknew he also predestined to be conformed to the likeness of his Son, that he might be the firstborn among many brothers." Notice that Jesus is the firstborn of this vast family! To the Corinthians Paul wrote, "Therefore, if anyone is in Christ, he is a new creation..."[11] As God originally created man in His own image, He is now, in the new creation, *re-creating* us in the image of Christ.

Being conformed to His likeness—or image—is a glorious outcome, but the process can be painful. The story is told of a man who visited a gold refinery many years ago. He watched as the refiner took the iron crucible and placed some nuggets of gold in the bowl. Next, he observed the bowl being held over an extremely hot burner. Soon the gold began to melt, but instead of the appearance of shiny, molten gold, there lay on the surface a film of dull dross. "Are you going to skim off the dross?" the visitor asked. "Oh no," the refiner answered, "if I did that, I would lose some of the precious gold. No, we keep the heat applied until all the dross is burned up." "So how do you know when all the dross is burned away?" pressed the visitor. Replied the refiner, "When I can see my face in it."

The more the heavenly Refiner does His work in each of us, the more His image will be reflected in our lives. The apostle Peter writes about "an inheritance that can never perish, spoil or fade," and goes on to say,

> In this you greatly rejoice, though now for a little while you may have had to suffer grief in all kinds of trials. These have come so that your faith—of greater worth than gold, which perishes even though refined by fire—may be proved genuine and may result in praise, glory and honor when Jesus Christ is revealed.[12]

Because our faith and maturity are of great value in God's sight, He will not spare us the fire. But it is also true that because He is a compassionate Father, He will not allow suffering unnecessarily. Jeremiah writes:

> For men are not cast off
> by the Lord forever.
> Though he brings grief, he will show compassion,
> so great is his unfailing love.

For he does not willingly bring affliction
or grief to the children of men."[13]

It is comforting to know that God is not indifferent or insensitive to our suffering: that He doesn't *willingly* bring affliction. It is also reassuring to know His purposes are much bigger than our personal sense of well-being, and that He will endure both our discomfort *and His own Paternal pain* in order to bring about His glory in our lives.

2.   The Church as the Body of Christ:

Another part of God's plan that would have remained the same if Adam had not sinned is the designation of God's people as the Body of Christ. Put another way, Christ would still have had a many-membered Body of which He was the Head. We noted earlier that God chose us "before the creation of the world." That applies to us both individually and corporately. In reference to Jesus and the Church, Paul writes to the Ephesians:

> And God placed all things under his feet and appointed him
> to be head over everything for the church, which is his body,
> the fullness of him who fills everything in every way.[14]

This is one of the most extravagant expressions of God's amazing grace that I have encountered in the Bible. Jesus' appointment as Head over everything is for the *Church*? The Church actually *is* His body—not just *like* it? And we—*as the Church*—are the *fullness* of Him who fills everything in every way? (At points like this I think of the prayer of the man who once said to Jesus, "I do believe; help me overcome my unbelief!"[15]) God's eternal plan was that "in the fullness of time" the Church, with Christ as her Head, would realize her destiny as the "fullness" of Christ who Himself (as the omnipresent God) fills everything.

Paul's teaching on the Church as the Body then goes into more detail:

> Just as each of us has one body with many members, and
> these members do not all have the same function, so in
> Christ we who are many form one body, and each member
> belongs to all the others.[16]

The body is a unit, though it is made up of many parts; and though all its parts are many, they form one body. So it is with Christ.[17]

Note that Paul doesn't say, "So also is Christ's Body," but simply, "So it is with Christ." Where did he get this revelation of the Church being Christ's Body? In all likelihood it started when Jesus confronted him on the road to Damascus where Paul was going to arrest more Christians. A bright light suddenly flashed around him; he fell to the ground and heard these words: "Saul, Saul, why do you persecute me?" When Paul asked the speaker to identify Himself, He said, "I am Jesus, whom you are persecuting."[18]

Our Lord was not being dramatic or careless with His words when He answered that way. He was telling Paul that when believers are persecuted, Christ is persecuted. But this truth applies not just to attacks from the "outside," from the enemies of Christ—it applies to all of us. When Christians are slandered, Christ is slandered. When we gossip against a fellow believer, we gossip against Christ. When we are impatient or inconsiderate toward other believers, we fail to discern (or recognize) the Lord's Body.

In first century Corinth, the church would gather to celebrate communion in the context of a full meal. This event, which became known as a "love feast," was attended by all members, including Christian slaves who, because of service obligations, often would arrive late. But many rich Corinthian church members refused to wait. Instead, they gorged themselves and even became intoxicated, leaving their poorer brothers and sisters hungry and humiliated.

Paul regards this as much more serious than just a breach of etiquette: he charges the Corinthians with not recognizing the Body of the Lord, and informs them that because of their despicable behavior, many of them were physically sick and some had even died.[19] Perhaps they viewed the Body of Christ merely as a theological concept or a pleasant ideal. Evidently God saw things very differently— and He still does today.

In his letter to the Romans, Paul writes that "in Christ we who are many form one body, and each member belongs to all the others."[20] If I live as though I am an island unto myself, or think that what I do doesn't affect anyone else, I don't understand or recognize the Lord's Body. Being the Body of Christ brings with it much bless-ing, but it also carries serious ramifications if we in any way abuse one another. We will return to this fundamental and vital truth in a later chapter.

3.   The Church as God's Dwelling Place:

Had Adam never sinned, God's plan would still have included our being built together into a holy temple for God's dwelling by the Holy Spirit. The theme of God dwelling with His covenant people is found throughout Scripture. An early example is found in Exodus chapters 24 and 25 where God is giving instructions to Moses on how He was to be approached:

> Then he said to Moses, "Come up to the Lord, you and Aaron, Nadab and Abihu, and seventy of the elders of Israel. You are to worship at a distance, but Moses alone is to approach the Lord; the others must not come near. And the people may not come up with him."[21]

When Moses tells the people what God had spoken, they respond with one voice: "Everything the Lord has said we will do." After this, some young men are commissioned to offer burnt offer-ings and to sacrifice young bulls as peace offerings to the Lord. Moses collects the blood from the animals, putting half of it into bowls, and sprinkling the other half over the altar. Then he takes the Book of the Covenant and reads it to the people, and again they respond, "We will do everything the Lord has said; we will obey." Moses then takes the remaining blood and sprinkles it *on the people, saying*, "This is the blood of the covenant that the Lord has made with you in accordance with all these words."

A scene that is unique in both Old and New Testament history followed these dramatic events:

> Moses and Aaron, Nadab and Abihu, and the seventy elders of Israel went up and saw the God of Israel. Under his feet was something like a pavement made of sapphire, clear as the sky itself. But God did not raise his hand against these leaders of the Israelites; they saw God, and they ate and drank.

The Lord said to Moses, "Come up to me on the mountain and stay here, and I will give you the tablets of stone, with the law and commands I have written for their instruction." Then Moses set out with Joshua his aide, and Moses went up on the mountain of God.[22]

The glory of the Lord covers the top of Sinai and settles there for six days. To Moses, the glory is like a cloud, but to the Israelites down below, it seems as if the whole mountaintop is on fire. On the seventh day the Lord calls to Moses from within the cloud, and Moses climbs up further and enters the cloud. There he stays for 40 days and nights. During this extended time in the immediate presence of Jehovah God, the Lord says to Moses, "Then have them make a sanctuary for me, and I will dwell among them."[23]

Six chapters in Exodus are devoted to the subject of building this sanctuary or tabernacle. God takes meticulous care in His instructions to Moses, laying out the design and precise measurements of each individual item. He specifies the material of each component as well as the method to be used in its production. And right from the start God emphasizes, "Make this tabernacle and all its furnishings exactly like the pattern I will show you," a command He subsequently repeats four times.

The tabernacle was a temporary, moveable structure, more tent than building. Why then the exact specifications, the attention to detail, the emphasis on constructing it exactly according to the plan given by God? Why? Because the earthly tabernacle was a copy of the heavenly one. Here is how the writer to the Hebrews puts it:

> They serve at a sanctuary that is a copy and shadow of what is in heaven. This is why Moses was warned when he was about to build the tabernacle: "See to it that you make everything according to the pattern shown you on the mountain."[24]

The word *pattern* is the same word used to describe the stamp or impression made from a die or seal: something very exact, very precise. Hebrews again refers to the heavenly tabernacle in speaking of Christ's priestly role:

> When Christ came as high priest of the good things that are
> already here, he went through the greater and more perfect
> tabernacle that is not man-made, that is to say, not a part of
> this creation.[25]

This reference, of course, is to the heavenly tabernacle, the eternal, spiritual dwelling place of God. The problem is, whenever we consider eternal things like Heaven, we are confronted with the restrictions of the human mind, not to mention our space-and-time perspective. We can visualize a physical altar, but what does a spiritual one look like? What exactly is the heavenly Holy of Holies? Some Bible scholars have attempted to interpret what the various items in the earthly tabernacle may have symbolized, but I would like to focus on two aspects—both rooted in Hebrews—that do not involve any speculation.

The first is linked to the theme of "types and shadows" as contrasted with spiritual reality—Old Testament symbols that pointed to a New Testament fulfillment in Christ. The writer to the Hebrews compares Moses and Jesus in these terms:

> Moses was faithful as a servant in all God's house, testifying to what would be said in the future. But Christ is faithful as a son over God's house. And we are his house...[26]

Much could be said about this rich analogy, but right now I simply want to point out that if the shadow (the physical tabernacle) pre-figured the Church as God's dwelling place, then the fact that God took such care in its design is very significant. It tells us that we also should anticipate an accurate design for the Church, His ultimate dwelling place. The building of the physical tabernacle, even though a type or shadow, wasn't left to Moses' discretion or to the haphazard choice of the builders. Neither was the building of the Church. God in fact has graciously laid out a practical, detailed plan for His Church that reflects *His* design, *His* pattern, *His* purposes, *His* glory.

Secondly, this mobile tabernacle was later to become a stationary temple, which in turn pointed to the construction of a living temple comprised of living stones.[27] Even some of David's psalms—written during the time of the tabernacle—hint at something more than just an earthly building:

Surely goodness and love will follow me
    all the days of my life,
and I will dwell in the house of the Lord
    forever.[28]

One thing I ask of the Lord,
    this is what I seek:
that I may dwell in the house of the Lord
    all the days of my life,
to gaze upon the beauty of the Lord
    and to seek him in his temple.
For in the day of trouble
    he will keep me safe in his dwelling;
he will hide me in the shelter of his tabernacle
    and set me high upon a rock.[29]

Exactly what David meant by "the house of the Lord" is debatable, but it probably was more than just the tabernacle of his day. As a king who was also a prophet,[30] David likely was speaking prophetically of the dwelling of God in His people—the future Church—in the Kingdom to be established by David's future "son," the Lord Jesus Christ.

However we may understand these psalms, there can be no doubt about what Jesus meant when He said, "Destroy this temple, and I will raise it again in three days."[31] The religious leaders to whom He spoke (spiritually dull, as usual) replied, "It has taken 46 years to build this temple, and you are going to raise it in three days?" John's Gospel then states: "But the temple he had spoken of was his body."[32]

At the end of Stephen's speech to the Sanhedrin, he refers to the tabernacle and the temple, but then adds a prophetic quote from Isaiah:

It [the tabernacle] remained in the land until the time of David, who enjoyed God's favor and asked that he might provide a dwelling place for the God of Jacob. But it was Solomon who built the house for him. However, the Most High does not live in houses made by men. As the prophet says:

"Heaven is my throne,
and the earth is my footstool.

What kind of house will you build for me?
    says the Lord.
Or where will my resting place be?
Has not my hand made all these things?"[33]

Paul said the same thing when he preached to the Athenians: "The God who made the world and everything in it is the Lord of heaven and earth and does not live in temples built by hands."[34]

Even the temple of Solomon—as glorious as any built at any time in history—was still a type and shadow of the true temple. So is the true temple a spiritual dwelling in Heaven or is it the Church now on earth?

The answer is: both. Our human minds tend to visualize Heaven and earth as two distinct geographical locations. But the Bible tells us that we are seated with Christ in heavenly places[35] even while we live on earth. In the spiritual realm (unlike real estate) "location" is not always an issue.

John 14 verses 2 and 3 traditionally are read at funeral services, often in the King James Version: "In my Father's house are many mansions...I go to prepare a place for you." While the idea of departed loved ones living in mansions may be a comforting thought, the Scriptural word used in the original Greek simply refers to *abodes* or houses. But *houses* in heaven can be misunderstood too— as we hear in Gospel quartet songs asking Jesus to "build me a little cabin in the corner of glory land." Do we really think Jesus is in Heaven building houses?

I would like to offer another interpretation. Every Jew knew the temple was "the house of the Lord." In John chapter 2 Jesus said to those selling doves in the temple, "Get these out of here! How dare you turn my Father's house into a market!" Keep in mind that this exchange took place in the outer court of the temple, and that the temple had a number of rooms besides the Holy Place and the Holy of Holies. We should remember also that the earthly temple was patterned after the heavenly; thus John 14:2 could be rendered (as in the NIV), "In my Father's house are many rooms..." or perhaps, "In my Father's temple there are many temple rooms..."

He then says, "I am going there to prepare a place for you." I believe this speaks of Jesus dying as a sacrificial Lamb for us and then, as our great High Priest, taking His own blood into Heaven itself and opening up for us a new and living way to the Father.[36]

In verse 3 of John 14, Jesus says, "And if I go and prepare a place for you, I will come back and take you to be with me that you also may be where I am." Yet in verse 23 He says, "If anyone loves me, he will obey my teaching. My Father will love him, and we will come to him and make our home with him." Is this a contradiction? Not if we understand that if we are in Christ and He lives in us, we are in fact seated with Him in heavenly places, and at the same time, He makes His home in us while we are still on earth.

One thing is for certain: wherever Jesus is, He is building His Church—and that is us! Paul tells the Corinthians, "Do you not know that your body is a temple of the Holy Spirit...?"[37] Here, the word *your* is singular. If I were talking to my friend John, I would say, "John, do you realize that your body is a temple of the Holy Spirit?" But in Paul's second letter to the Corinthians, he speaks of the *people of God* (i.e. the Church) as the temple of the living God:

> What agreement is there between the temple of God and idols? For we are the temple of the living God. As God has said: "I will live with them and walk among them, and I will be their God, and they will be my people."
>
> > "Therefore come out from them
> > and be separate,
> > > says the Lord.
> > Touch no unclean thing,
> > and I will receive you."
> > "I will be a Father to you,
> > and you will be my sons and daughters,
> > > says the Lord Almighty."[38]

In this passage, *temple* is used of God's people in the plural or corporate sense. You may have noticed that these verses also touch on our earlier reference to things that would have remained the same if Adam and Eve had not sinned: namely, that God would have a vast family of sons and daughters.

Here are two further Scripture passages that illustrate the "temple" metaphor, and bring me to a subject that I feel very strongly about:

Consequently, you are no longer foreigners and aliens, but fellow citizens with God's people and members of God's household, built on the foundation of the apostles and prophets, with Christ Jesus himself as the chief cornerstone. In him the whole building is joined together and rises to become a holy temple in the Lord. And in him you too are being built together to become a dwelling in which God lives by his Spirit.[39]

As you come to him, the living Stone—rejected by men but chosen by God and precious to him—you also, like living stones, are being built into a spiritual house to be a holy priesthood, offering spiritual sacrifices acceptable to God through Jesus Christ.[40]

These are wonderfully clear teachings on what (or more precisely *who*) constitutes God's house. And yet, so many believers use Old Covenant terminology when referring to church facilities. Let us take a moment to settle some misuses of the word *church*. To start with, the building I visit each Sunday to join with others in worshipping God is not *the* Church (nor *a* church, for that matter.) Similarly, the room in which we gather in that building is not *the* sanctuary. In biblical terms, we don't *go* to church; we *are* the Church.

In the Plymouth Brethren tradition of my youth, the buildings were called "Gospel Halls." These halls were multi-purpose in nature and were used for games and parties as well as Sunday services. Yet almost every Sunday I recall hearing prayers thanking God that we were found in "His house" on the Sabbath. But the use (or rather misuse) of this phrase is not limited to one denomination. Only this morning, in my devotional reading of Dr. Martyn Lloyd-Jones' exposition of Ephesians, I found the good doctor telling his congregation at Westminster what a blessing it was to be in the "house of the Lord."

I am in close fellowship with a number of leaders who pastor "Restoration" congregations on the West Coast of North America. These good friends are well versed in theology that correctly understands the Body of Christ to be the house of the Lord. Yet many of them commonly refer to the meeting hall as "the sanctuary." In Scripture, whenever *temple* is used in reference to God's people or to a believer's body, the word in the original is *naos*—which means *sanctuary*—referring to the holy of holies in the temple. When the New Testament speaks about the temple at Jerusalem, the Greek word *heiron* is always used. This word denotes the whole of the temple buildings. *Heiron* is never used for the Church (the body of believers) or for the individual believer.

Some of my friends have heard me speak on this subject before and may be tempted to dismiss it as a hobbyhorse of mine. But when you consider how important this is to God—the price He paid to bring about His habitation in us, and how carefully the Scriptures handle the temple metaphor—I think we should pay close attention. The truth that our bodies and the Church corporate are in fact the dwelling place of God by the Spirit is a revelation too precious—too profound—to be obscured in our thinking by wrong terminology. The physical buildings (even the best of them) belong to the realm of types and shadows. It's time to "get real."

> And I heard a loud voice from the throne saying, "Behold, the tabernacle of God is among men, and He shall dwell among them, and they shall be His people, and God Himself shall be among them..."[41]

To summarize three things that would have remained the same even if man had not sinned:

- God would still have had a vast *family* of sons and daughters who would fill the earth. This family, through fellowship with the Father and through suffering, would be conformed to the image of His Son, and would mature to the point where they were adopted into full sonship.

- Christ would still have had a many-membered *Body* equipped by His ministry gifts to the Church, a Body whose members had differing but complementary functions. This would result in the Body being built up through every relational joint with which it is supplied when each part is working properly[42]—a Body through which He would ultimately express His glory in all creation.

- God, by the Holy Spirit, would still have received for Himself a glorious temple made up of living stones as a place for His eternal habitation.

In all of these things, the Father has determined that His beloved Son should have the preeminence. He is "the beginning and the firstborn from among the dead, so that in everything he might have the supremacy"[43]—a supremacy expressed in His family role, in His position in the Body, and in His place in the temple:

- Christ is in charge of the family of God. As the first-born of the new creation and as our "Everlasting Father,"[44] he says prophetically, "Here am I, and the children God has given me."[45] The writer to the Hebrews also says:

Both the one who makes men holy and those who are made holy are of the same family. So Jesus is not ashamed to call them brothers.[46]

- Christ is Head of the Body (the Church)…"the Head, from whom the whole body, supported and held together by its ligaments and sinews, grows as God causes it to grow."[47]

- Christ is the chief cornerstone of the temple:

> See, I lay a stone in Zion,
> a chosen and precious cornerstone,
> and the one who trusts in him
> will never be put to shame.[48]

When I began to understand that these major biblical truths were part of God's eternal plan—and not just a "by-product" of man's salvation—it deepened my appreciation for God's amazing grace and wisdom. Meditating on these things makes me thankful that the Holy Spirit interprets the inexpressible responses of our heart to the Father. Words are often not enough.

When the apostle Paul was overcome with wonder and praise toward God, he sometimes wrote a psalm using quotes from the Old Testament. Here is a doxology that concludes chapter 11 of Romans, and that will conclude this chapter as well:

Oh, the depth of the riches of the
wisdom and knowledge of God!
How unsearchable his judgments,
and his paths beyond tracing out!
"Who has known the mind of the Lord?
Or who has been his counselor?"
"Who has ever given to God,
that God should repay him?"

For from him and through him and to him are all things.
To him be the glory forever! Amen.[49]

ENDNOTES

1. Hebrews 2:10.

2. Hebrews 5:8.

3. DeVern F. Fromke: *The Ultimate Intention* (Indianapolis, Indiana: Sure Foundation, 1963), 56 (emphasis in original).

4. John 13:3-5.

5. Luke 22:24.

6. Luke 12:37.

7. John 21:1-13.

8. Ephesians 1:5.

9. Jeremiah 3:19.

10. Romans 8:16-17.

11. 2 Corinthians 5:17.

12. 1 Peter 1:6-7.

13. Lamentations 3:31-33.

14. Ephesians 1:22-23.

15. Mark 9:24.

16. Romans 12:4-5.

17. 1 Corinthians 12:12.

18. Acts 9:4-5.

19. This is the context in which we find the warning against eating the bread or drinking the cup in an unworthy manner (1 Cor. 11:27). If our treatment of fellow believers shows that we don't really recognize them as members of Christ's body, we "eat and drink judgment" on ourselves in our communion services.

20. Romans 12:5.

21. Exodus 24:1-2.
22. Exodus 24:9-13.
23. Exodus 25:8.
24. Hebrews 8:5.
25. Hebrews 9:11.
26. Hebrews 3:5-6.
27. 1 Peter 2:5.
28. Psalm 23:6.
29. Psalm 27:4-6.
30. Acts 2:30.
31. John 2:19.
32. John 2:20-21.
33. Acts 7:45-50 (quoting Isaiah 66:1-2).
34. Acts 17:24.
35. Ephesians 2:6.
36. Hebrews 10:5-22.
37. 1 Corinthians 6:19.
38. 2 Corinthians 6:16-18.
39. Ephesians 2:19-22.
40. 1 Peter 2:4-5.
41. Revelation 21:3 (NASB).
42. Ephesians 4:16.
43. Colossians 1:18.
44. Isaiah 9:6.
45. Hebrews 2:13 (quoting Isaiah 8:18).
46. Hebrews 2:11.
47. Colossians 1:18; 2:19.
48. 1 Peter 2:6.
49. Romans 11:33-36.

FIVE

SO WHAT WENT WRONG?

*By obeying the serpent, Adam and Eve made them-
selves the friends of Satan and the enemies of God.*
                              —Edmund P. Clowney

We are members of a spoiled species.   —C. S. Lewis

When I first began writing notes for this chapter, it was December 21, 1999, just a few days before the last Christmas of the 1900s. It
was the season for *peace on earth, goodwill toward men* and the time for
tidings of comfort and joy. But as I scanned the headlines of a British
national newspaper, I found anything but tidings of comfort and joy.
Here are a few samples:

- "Letter-bomb killer and girl in car suicide"

- "Disgraced peer faces fresh questions over revelations
  of affair"

- "Sidney Cooke, the evil child killer, is condemned to
  die in jail"

- "Mugger steals victim's memory"

- "Grozny guerrillas kill 115 Russian troops"

- "School massacre boys' chilling boasts revealed in
  video: Two teenagers who carried out the Columbine High School massacre believed that their bloody
  exploits would turn them into Hollywood superstars." They were also celebrating Adolph Hitler's
  birthday with a memorial massacre of innocent children. What did they do? The newspaper continues:

"The rampage…ended in the pair committing suicide after killing 13 people with shotguns, automatic pistols and crude home-made bombs. 'I hope we kill 250 of you,' Klebold says."

Contrast these samples from one newspaper on just one day—or the events in New York and Washington on another horrendous day, September 11, 2001—with a totally different picture: Imagine a world in which people were free from death, sickness or disease; there was no sadness, anxiety, depression, not even disappointment; no gossip, lying, cheating or stealing; no violence, terrorism, war or starvation; work was pleasant, childbearing was only mildly painful, and even thorns were scarce or non-existent: in other words, *utopia*. This was the condition of the Garden of Eden on planet Earth before Adam and Eve fell into disobedience and rebellion. The actions at Columbine High School or the World Trade Center are ultimately linked to what happened in the Garden, but before we look at this further, we need to go back to the beginning.

After God made the universe, the earth and all that is in it, He came to the final—and finest—part of creation: man, whom He made in His own image. This little phrase *in His own image* is highly significant, as we shall see later. God's eternal purposes on planet Earth were inextricably tied to the creation of Adam who, according to Scripture, was created from the dust of the ground.[1]

Before Eve came on the scene, God took Adam and placed him in the Garden of Eden to cultivate it and care for it.[2] God had planted two unusual trees in the middle of the Garden—the tree of life and the tree of the knowledge of good and evil—and gave explicit instructions to Adam that under no circumstances was he to eat of the second tree. Any other tree, including the tree of life, was available to him, but if he ate from the tree of the knowledge of good and evil, he would die. (As we discover later in the Bible, God's plan from the beginning was that man would not live independently, but rather draw his life, wisdom, knowledge, strength and satisfaction from his Creator.)

God saw that His creation was good but, in the course of time, there is one thing He declares is *not good*, and that is for man to be alone. He brings to the man all of the various animals and birds He had made, and watches as Adam gives each one a name.[3] However, even with all the animals around him, Adam still feels alone because not one of them was a "suitable helper" for him. So God anesthetizes Adam, takes one of his ribs and—in an operation far superseding any cloning feats of the 21st century—makes a woman from it. When He presents her to the man, Adam waxes poetic and proceeds to name her:

> This is now bone of my bones
> and flesh of my flesh;
> she shall be called "woman,"
> for she was taken out of man.[4]

Matthew Henry wrote a comment that is often repeated at wedding ceremonies:

> That the woman was made of a rib out of the side of Adam;
> not made out of his head to rule over him, nor out of his
> feet to be trampled upon by him, but out of his side to be
> equal with him, under his arm to be protected, and near his
> heart to be beloved.[5]

Genesis chapter 2 ends with: "The man and his wife were both naked, and they felt no shame." In their original state, Adam and Eve were not self-conscious; they were utterly pure, innocent, free spirits.

In this context of covenantal relationship with their Creator, Adam and Eve were commissioned by God to be fruitful and increase in number, filling the earth with godly seed; to subdue the earth, ruling over the fish, the birds, and every living creature.[6] Thus they were created to live in continual fellowship with God and rule as His delegated authority on this planet.

What could be more beautiful, more perfect? But, as we now know, that idyllic state was shattered by Adam's rebellion and treason. Through one man's disobedience, billions would become infected with an incurable virus called sin, a virus that would wreak unbelievable havoc. By Noah's time, the whole earth had become saturated with violence. Eventually, this virus would dominate the souls of leaders like Herod, Nero, Hitler and Stalin—sadistic monsters devoted to new ways of torture and oppression—who would exterminate millions of innocent lives. It would give birth to the slave trade in which 12 million Africans would be wrenched from their families, treated like animals, and exported to the Americas. Worst of all, the whole human race would be plunged into the darkness of separation from the Creator.

We all know the key role satan played in man's downfall, how he deceived and manipulated our first parents. But how exactly wise and powerful is he? What was his status before he himself fell? And what was he trying to achieve when he tempted Eve?

OUR ENEMY THE DEVIL

As we mentioned in the last chapter, Christians often overestimate satan's power. But if we remain unaware of his schemes and allow him to outwit us,[7] we fall into the error of *underestimating* our foe. Furthermore, it is dangerous to engage in belittling or mocking him. Even though satan is horrendously evil, he is nonetheless a *celestial being*[8] whom we are not allowed to revile. Two New Testament writers warn us against this in their description of false teachers:

> Bold and arrogant, these men are not afraid to slander celestial beings; yet even angels, although they are stronger and more powerful, do not bring slanderous accusations against such beings in the presence of the Lord.[9]

> But even the archangel Michael, when he was disputing with the devil about the body of Moses, did not dare to bring a slanderous accusation against him, but said, "The Lord rebuke you!"[10]

1.   Attributes of satan:

The best way of understanding satan's attributes is by contrasting them with God's nature and power. First of all, satan is not omnipresent: he can be present in only one place at one time. Some people, after a particularly bad day, will complain that the devil was giving them a terrible time. But the likelihood of someone experiencing an actual attack from satan is very small. I am not saying that one or more of his demons couldn't harass you or me, but it's unlikely to be the devil himself. I'm too small a fish in the pond to warrant that kind of attention—and that would be true for most of us.

Secondly, satan is not omniscient: he doesn't know every-thing. In fact, compared to God's vast knowledge and wisdom, he and his demons know hardly anything. Nevertheless, evil spirits know enough to devise various schemes to trip us up. Sad to say, their efforts—aided and abetted by fallen human nature—have often proved successful.

Thirdly, he is not omnipotent: simply put, he is not all-powerful. It is true that he can change[11] into the form of a snake and can pro-duce supernatural signs. Examples include his appearance in the Garden of Eden and his duplication (through the magicians of Egypt) of some of the miracles God performed through Moses. It is also true that he consistently lives up to his "job description" to steal and kill and destroy.[12] However, we should keep in mind that prior to Adam's disobedience, satan had no authority on earth. And even since then, his power is circumscribed by what God in His wisdom allows.

Fourthly, he is not eternal: as with every other created being, he had a beginning. While the Scriptures speak very little about the devil's original state and his fall from grace, many commentators believe that Isaiah's prophecy about the king of Babylon[13] and Ezekiel's prophecy against the king of Tyre[14] refer to satan as well.[15] This would indicate that he was created and anointed to be a guardian cherub; he was originally a model of perfection, full of wisdom and perfect in beauty; and he was in the presence of God on the holy mountain.

2.   Satan's Intentions:

So what went wrong with this amazing being whom God had created? Ezekiel declares, "Your heart became proud on account of your beauty, and you corrupted your wisdom because of your splen-dor." And why did this happen? What were his motives? The pas-sage in Isaiah 14 suggests the answer in the form of five *I will* statements:

> You said in your heart,
> "I will ascend to heaven;
> I will raise my throne
> above the stars of God;
> I will sit enthroned on the mount of assembly,

on the utmost heights of the sacred mountain.
I will ascend above the tops of the clouds;
I will make myself like the Most High."[16]

The first (and key) evil intention of satan is to be equal with God. This is pride and arrogance in its ultimate manifestation—the creature aspiring to the place of the Creator. It is worth noting here that Jesus' attitude and actions were the exact opposite: "Who, being in very nature God, did not consider equality with God something to be grasped, but made himself nothing..."[17]

The contrast between Jesus and satan could not be greater. While Christ was exalted after humbling Himself, satan was utterly humiliated after seeking his own glory. After the five *I will* declarations, Isaiah records: "But you are brought down to the grave, to the depths of the pit." Ezekiel's prophecy says, "So I threw you to the earth; I made a spectacle of you before kings." But satan did not go alone. Revelation chapter 12 refers to "the great dragon...that ancient serpent called the devil, or Satan" taking "a third of the stars" (i.e. angels) to the earth with him.[18]

A second intention of the devil is to counter whatever God does. It seems that while he has his own particular plans and purposes, satan does not have the ability to be truly original. He does not create, but rather generates a type of originality through distorting, twisting and perverting what God has made. As such, he is a counterfeiter—a plagiarist—and his ultimate intention apparently is to produce a demonic replica of God's ultimate intention. In the Garden he had no new vision or new world to offer Eve, but simply a *counter*-vision and (as Adam and Eve soon found out) a twisted, distorted kind of world.

He also counters God by bringing accusations against those made in God's image. (Satan in Hebrew means *accuser*, while one of the names for Christ is our *Advocate*. That in itself should motivate us to avoid slander and gossip.) At the close of history, when satan's defeat is complete, there will be rejoicing:

For the accuser of our brothers,
who accuses them before our God day and night,
has been hurled down.[19]

Thirdly, he has an insatiable desire to rule this earth by any and all means. Because pride feeds on power, satan is strongly focused on the exercise of power (despite the fact that all *authority* has been given to the Lord Jesus). His modus operandi typically includes exercising power in its raw and ruthless forms—e.g. control, domination and fear—as well as in more subtle ways like manipulation, lies and deceit. In fact, the kingdom of darkness *needs* darkness in order to function; that is why deception, falsification and misrepresentation are the hallmarks of his rule.

Fourthly, he has a passion to be worshiped or, failing to achieve that goal, to draw worship away from Almighty God. His strategy to achieve the latter is to redirect people's focus onto themselves: in essence, self-worship, where they become "lovers of pleasure rather than lovers of God."[20] While this has proven to be an effective strategy throughout the ages, we in the 21st century—with all of our "creature comforts" available at the click of a button—are perhaps more vulnerable to this temptation than previous generations.

Our love of pleasure can focus on many things: sports, television, videos, houses, cars, other possessions, and of course money itself—which, as Paul writes, "is a root of all kinds of evil." He adds, "Some people, eager for money, have wandered from the faith and pierced themselves with many griefs."[21]

There is nothing wrong with having a desire for pleasure. It was God who created us with the capacity to enjoy the good things He made; pleasure was not the devil's idea. In fact, the best satan can do is to offer a poor substitute for the real thing—but you can be sure he will try to present that substitute as something better. A desire for pleasure is a normal part of life. The issue is: where do I go to get that desire satisfied? Thinking about that reminded me of a little chorus I used to sing in Sunday School:

I met Jesus at the crossroads where two ways meet.
Satan too was standing there and he said, "Come this way;
Lots and lots of pleasures I can give to you today."
But I said, "No! There's Jesus here: just see what He offers me—
Down here my sins forgiven, up there, a home in heaven.
Praise God, that's the way for me."

The psalmist puts it this way:

> You have made known to me the path of life;
> you will fill me with joy in your presence,
> with eternal pleasures at your right hand.[22]

The last thing satan wants is that our God-given desire for pleasure finds its fulfillment in Christ. He will try redirecting our focus in all sorts of ways: toward movie stars, sports heroes, famous singers, preachers, even worship leaders! Anything or anyone will do so long as it deflects worship away from God. Of course, his preference is that people would actually bow down and worship him. During the temptation of Christ in the desert,[23] he seemed willing to yield all of his "rights" to the kingdoms of this world for just a few moments of homage from Jesus. To be worshiped is very big with satan.

You will notice that the themes of worship and pleasure are interwoven in this last point. They are distinct subjects, and yet as issues of the heart—the things we value and focus on—they are inseparable. As Jesus stated in His Sermon on the Mount: "For where your treasure is, there your heart will be also."[24]

A fifth intention of satan is to live in people and express himself through them. The Gospel of John gives an account of an actual moment that satan entered into a man. It was at the Last Supper just after Jesus gave the bread to Judas Iscariot: "As soon as Judas took the bread, Satan entered into him."[25] But since he is not omnipresent—meaning he can be in only one person at a time—satan extends his influence through the host of demons that serve him, thus enabling him to affect millions of people simultaneously. In that sense he can "live" in people corporately.

Such corporate possession may take the form of mass hysteria—for example when Adolph Hitler, under the control of satan himself or perhaps the demonic prince of Germany, would whip crowds into a state of hate-filled frenzy. These scenes, captured on old World War II film footage, are a frightening reminder of how intelligent, modern man can be swept up in destructive and murderous behavior. This may happen even in the context of sporting events, whether the offenders are English soccer hooligans or Canadian hockey fans. (My home city of Vancouver will not soon forget the injuries and damage caused by rioters some years ago following a loss by the Canucks in the final game of the National Hockey League playoffs.)

A sixth intention of satan is to replace God's truth with false religions and ideologies. He doesn't care whether it takes the form of cults, various religions, nihilism, Nazism or Communism, as long as it deludes people and keeps them from the truth that would set them free. Many of these false religions and ideologies have supported massive systems and structures representing the devil's counterpart to the Kingdom of God and the Body of Christ. This was true in the first century A.D. when John wrote the Book of Revelation (during a time of intense persecution by an evil Roman empire) and still is true today. John, in the Spirit, saw this as a woman—a bride of satan— dressed in purple and scarlet, adorned with gold and precious stones, and holding a golden cup filled with abominable things. The way in which such a system is described should leave no doubt as to its true origin: "Mystery; Babylon the Great; The Mother of Prostitutes and of the Abominations of the Earth."[26]

A seventh intention of satan is to seduce people into a life independent of God: in other words, to duplicate his own rebellion and that of Adam and Eve. This aspect is related to the other six already mentioned, but has a particular application to certain types of "self-improvement" that have become popular even in Christian circles. I will go into some detail in the following example, partly as a warning against the specific dangers involved, and partly to illustrate how effective this enemy tactic has been.

The example is that of "Christian" LGAT (Large Group Awareness Training) groups that have sprung up over the past decade. These use what is known as the *marathon* method where a group of people will meet for four or five days in an absolutely controlled environment, complete with stirring background music and special lighting effects. There is no clock, and the trainees are normally required to give up their watches and commit themselves to everything the leader requests. Days often include 12 hours of training plus "homework," typically resulting in a 16-hour day. Some trainees report staying up all night in order to complete their assignments.

Various methods are used to break the thought patterns and emotional framework of trainees, in particular, public humiliation.

During the first three days, your name is replaced with a negative label such as *Bottom Feeder* or *Vertically Dead*, and you are treated negatively through assorted role-playing games. The scenario in one such game is that your cruise ship is sinking and there is only one serviceable lifeboat available. You and every other "passenger" are given eight stir-sticks and then required to give them to eight passengers whom you believe to be worth saving. Then you have to tell the other passengers why you think they are *not* worth saving. As one might expect, the result is emotional helter-skelter.

After the second or third game, you are instructed to pick a partner. These are mixed groups, but the partner cannot be your spouse. Yet that person will remain your partner for the remainder of your training, and you are encouraged and expected to share your deepest feelings and most intimate thoughts with this person. I would suggest this is just another form of "soul mating" and is a sure recipe for disaster.

Clinical psychologist Margaret Thaler Singer, a renowned expert on cults, has included LGAT in her bestseller *Cults in our Midst: The Hidden Menace in Our Everyday Lives.*[27] On federal court orders, Thaler Singer attended six LGAT training sessions. She writes:

> Because most of these programs are made up of highly scripted, standardized procedures, seeing one unfold gives a good picture of the processes and the attitudes of the trainers, as well as some experience of the group process that occurs when 250 to 300 people are being psychologically and emotionally aroused into becoming, on occasion, sobbing masses on the floor.[28]

Several years ago I was invited to arbitrate in a church situation where the elders had welcomed an LGAT program into their church, but where a third of the congregation were strongly opposed to it. This was an evangelical, charismatic, "Bible-believing" church, so I was shocked to discover that the elders had been encouraging trainees to use profanity in order to break free from religious inhibition, and hug one another cheek to cheek and with full-frontal bodily contact.[29] All of this was supposed to help them break out of their "paradigms."

Trainees were also discouraged from resisting any instruction on the basis of conscience, or on the grounds that it was contrary to their understanding of God or the Scriptures. The trainers would respond to those objections with, "Come on, stop hiding behind your religion," or, "Your beliefs are what stand in your way."

I tried to point out to the elders and wives the seriousness of what was taking place: that they, through this man-made *New Age* method, were in effect eating of the forbidden *tree of the knowledge of good and evil* rather than holding to God's instruction; and that one day they would have to give an account before God for their stewardship of those entrusted to their care. I noticed that some of the ladies paled significantly when I deliberately spelled out (using the trainers' terminology) what "full-frontal bodily contact" really meant. But in the end nothing really changed. The tragedy is that those in deception resist change because they cannot see that they are deceived.

THE TEMPTATION TO EAT THE FORBIDDEN FRUIT

One day when Eve was in the vicinity of the tree of the knowledge of good and evil, a snake (indwelt by satan) began to ask her about God's instructions. But this was much more than a harmless question: it suggested that God was being unduly restrictive: "Did God really say, 'You must not eat from any tree in the garden?'"[30] There was probably a note of amazement in the voice of the serpent, as though a strange rumor had been circulating through Eden. It immediately put Eve on the defensive.

Satan's challenges these days come in different words, but the tactics have not changed that much over the millennia: "Don't be so narrow-minded and old-fashioned." "Surely you don't really believe those myths in the Bible." "Only a religious bigot or right-wing fundamentalist would oppose gay rights." "Everyone smokes pot." "No one is still a virgin on their wedding day."

A clever question will also sow a seed of doubt in people's minds. When preaching on this passage I have sometimes paused to examine my watch, and then, turning to one of the leaders, ask, "What does your watch say?" I then ask the congregation whether his answer agrees with the clock on the wall. Very soon the whole church is in doubt as to what the time really is!

It is also significant that in the Genesis 3 account, satan's question and Eve's answer both exaggerated what God had said. The former (that every tree was forbidden) was a gross distortion of the truth; the latter (that if they ate *or touched* the tree of knowledge they would die) was a case of adding to God's word, and perhaps represented a small step of independence from God that made Eve more vulnerable to deception.[31]

But what began as a clever question quickly turned into a full assault against the integrity and goodness of God: "You will not surely die," says the serpent. From there he goes on to sow thoughts of discontent, suggesting that Eve was missing out on a special advantage and that God was a spoil-sport: "For God knows that when you eat of it your eyes will be opened..." He then sows the seed of pride, saying, "...and you will be like God," followed quickly by the seed of independence, "...knowing good and evil."[32]

Eve now notices that the fruit of that tree was "good for food" (appealing to the physical appetite), it was "pleasing to the eye" (appealing to the senses), and it was "desirable for gaining wisdom" (appealing to the intellect). She falls for the bait, takes the fruit and eats it, and gives some to her husband who also eats. Immediately their eyes are opened, but instead of seeing new and wonderful things as satan promised, they see only their guilt and shame. They realize they are naked, their innocence forever gone.

THE CONSEQUENCES OF ADAM AND EVE'S SIN

One of the famous songs recorded by Frank Sinatra, *My Way*, is a virtual anthem to self-will and independence. The closing words neatly sum up Adam and Eve's actions in the Garden—as well as our own sinful choices in life: *I did it my way.* The Bible speaks in terms of Eve being *deceived,*[33] while references to Adam use terms like *disobedience*[34] and *broken covenant,*[35] but they both chose to do it their own way.[36] The end result was the same: rebellion against Almighty God.[37]

Their sinful deed amounted to obeying satan, which meant that they, in effect, became slaves of satan. There is no neutral territory in the spiritual realm. Satan fooled Adam and Eve into thinking they were acting on their own—doing it *my way*—but they were actually doing it his way. Here is how the apostle Paul describes it:

Don't you know that when you offer yourselves to someone to obey him as slaves, you are slaves to the one whom you obey—whether you are slaves to sin, which leads to death, or to obedience, which leads to righteousness?[38]

Through their obedience to satan's words, our first parents came under his authority, which meant that they became subjects of the kingdom of darkness. Henceforth, all their descendants would be born in sin and born into the kingdom of darkness. That is why one day Jesus would tell Nicodemus, "You must be born again."[39]

Man now had a sinful nature from birth. Have you ever noticed that you never have to teach children how to misbehave? And you never have to train them to insist on having their own way. They do it as naturally as feeding at their mother's breast.

I have some vivid memories of encountering this element of human nature in my granddaughter Devon when she was five years old. Part of her homework one day was to read a book out loud in the presence of an adult in her family who would then sign a card confirming that she had successfully completed the task. I was the chosen adult this time. The book was called *The Green Book* and featured a different green object on each page with an identifying caption: "The color of the (object) is green."

When we came to the page showing a picture of a gooseberry and the words saying, "The color of the *gooseberry* is green," she protested that the gooseberry looked more like *kiwi fruit*. I remember agreeing with her assessment but adding, "Nonetheless, the word says gooseberry, so gooseberry it is; on you go." She promptly read, "The color of the kiwi fruit is green."

"Devon, now listen to me," I responded, "it says *gooseberry*; now don't let me have to speak to you about this again." This time it took her a while before continuing. I could tell she still had some "gas in the tank," so to speak; she was considering whether it was worth the effort. I was soon to find out. "The color of the..." (a long pause and a deep sigh) "...*kiwi fruit* is green."

"That's it, Devon. If you do this one more time you will have a spanking—and you know Granddad always keeps his word." Again there was a long pause and a deep sigh. "The color of the..." (*Please don't do it again*, I pleaded silently) "...gooseberry..." and turning her head very deliberately in my direction, she added, "*and* the kiwi fruit is green." I called it a draw and signed the card.

What I was encountering in this sweet, "butter-wouldn't-melt-in-her-mouth" granddaughter was old fashioned, straight-from-the-Garden-of-Eden rebellion! Those spiritual genes from our original parents reside in all of us, from the most obvious of rebels like a Hell's Angels biker, to a sweet little granddaughter in a Christian home.

Another consequence of the fall of man was that satan gained authority on planet Earth. (This however did not include *ownership*, because "the earth is the Lord's, and everything in it..."[40]) Adam and Eve, under the Lordship of the Creator, had been entrusted with authority over everything on earth. By obeying satan, they effectively handed over that authority to God's enemy—an act that constituted high treason—which allowed satan to become prince of this world.

Death—both spiritual and physical—now became part of man's experience. Adam's spirit, cut off from the Source of Life, was effectively shut down. No longer would he enjoy the close fellowship and spirit-to-Spirit communion he had with the Lord prior to the Fall. Physically, there were now seeds of destruction planted in his genetic code, meaning that his outer nature would eventually waste away and his body die. As the apostle Paul wrote, "...sin entered the world through one man, and death through sin..."[41] Sin's legacy included sickness, disease, demonic oppression and possession, increased pain, sorrow and tears. And satan now had the keys of death and Hades.[42]

Because of the serpent's role in Eve's deception, God curses him: henceforth he will be regarded as man's enemy: a contemptible, noxious reptile. He is consigned to crawl on his belly and, because he tempted the woman to eat forbidden fruit, he is forced to eat dust (a symbol of death).

Eve and all her female descendants would bear children with increased pain, and be ruled over by their husbands.[43] Adam would find the ground cursed with thorns and thistles, and his work marred by frustration and fatigue.

Once pure, innocent, free spirits, Adam and Eve suddenly became self-conscious and inhibited. Ashamed of their nakedness, they sewed fig leaves together to cover themselves. And for the first time, they experienced tormenting fear—something that all of their offspring would become familiar with as well. Disobedience produces guilt, guilt in turn begets shame, and shame generates fear. Thus we hear Adam explaining why he and Eve were hiding from God: "I heard you in the garden, and I was afraid because I was naked; so I hid."[44]

Adam and Eve also turned to blame-shifting—a trait that survived intact in every generation since. Adam's answer to God's question about whether he had eaten the forbidden fruit was a classic example of transferring responsibility—even though his tenure as a sinner must have been but a few hours! *The woman you put here with me*—she gave me some fruit..."[45] In other words, the fault really lay with Eve because she handed him the fruit, and even with God because He had created her and put her there. (We won't mention the fact that Eve didn't hold a gun to his head to force him to eat, nor the little issue of his choosing to listen to his wife instead of God.)

Eve was a fast learner. It wasn't her fault either: "*The serpent deceived me*, and I ate."[46] In other words, she couldn't help it; the serpent didn't tell the truth and she believed him. (Forget the fact that she chose to disbelieve God.)

I once saw a news program where 20 prisoners were being interviewed live from a prison in Scotland. To a man, each prisoner blamed someone else for his plight. Several blamed the policies of Margaret Thatcher, who was prime minister at the time. Others blamed their parents; others their schoolteachers or employers. As I listened, I thought to myself, *Nothing much has changed since Adam and Eve; it's just become more widespread.*

The tragic conclusion to this sorry saga was that they were barred access to the tree of life, driven like fugitives out of the Garden that had been entrusted to their care, and cut off from the presence of the Lord. The covenant between God and man lay shattered in pieces. Here is the epilogue to the third chapter of Genesis:

> So the Lord God banished him from the Garden of Eden to
> work the ground from which he had been taken. After he

drove the man out, he placed on the east side of the Garden of Eden cherubim and a flaming sword flashing back and forth to guard the way to the tree of life.[47]

If we were to leave the story at this low point, it would be rather depressing. But God's pronouncement over the serpent is a prophecy of hope as well as one of judgment:

> And I will put enmity
> between you and the woman,
> and between your offspring [or seed] and hers;
> he will crush your head,
> and you will strike his heel.[48]

It is important to note that ever since Eden we have been at war. And we won't escape the conflict (*enmity*) between satan's forces and God's people until the second coming of Christ. For that reason we shouldn't be surprised by opposition from the unredeemed world. But the good news contained in God's judgment of satan was that a day would come when a Descendant of Eve, although struck by the serpent on the heel, would crush the enemy's head (the head being the symbol of authority). In other words, satan's new, ill-gotten authority would not last forever. Here is how the writer to the Hebrews refers to this conquering *Son of Man*:

> Since the children have flesh and blood, he too shared in their humanity so that by his death he might destroy him who holds the power of death—that is, the devil—and free those who all their lives were held in slavery by their fear of death.[49]

There was a small but significant step taken after the judgments were pronounced in Eden: "The Lord God made garments of skin for Adam and his wife and clothed them."[50] Some might assume that was intended to improve their appearance or modesty, but I believe it had more meaning than that. It cost the life of an animal to cover their nakedness—which pointed to the animal sacrifices established under the Old Covenant, which in turn pointed to the Lamb of God who would take away the sin of the world.

This was, in effect, a promise from God that one day He would clothe repentant man with a coat of righteousness. Adam and Eve's attempts to cover themselves were totally unacceptable to a Holy God. Their "wisdom" in doing so was nothing more than man's "good idea" and evidence that the destructive virus of sin had already taken its toll. They needed God to cover them.

So, in the midst of man's darkest hour, we have two prophetic signs of God's mercy and power: a word of judgment on the enemy of our souls, and a covering for our shame. Right at the outset, God throws down the gauntlet to satan, pronouncing his ultimate doom, while at the same time, throwing out a lifeline of hope to man wherein He says, *I will provide the antidote for your sin—your disobedience, rebellion, independence and treason.*

We've looked at what went wrong after God created man, and how sin entered this world. Later, we focus our attention on the antidote to sin. But in the next chapter, we take a closer look at the underlying nature of our problem: our fatal flaw.

Endnotes

1. Matthew Henry notes that God made the world out of nothing, and man out of "next to nothing." Matthew Henry: *Commentary on the Whole Bible* (Grand Rapids, Michigan: Zondervan, 1961), 5.

2. The Hebrew word includes the sense of *guarding* it.

3. Historically, naming someone was a sign of authority over that person. This was therefore the first recorded act of ruling in accordance with the "dominion mandate" of Genesis 1:28.

4. Genesis 2:23.

5. Matthew Henry: op. cit., 7.

6. Genesis 1:28.

7. 2 Corinthians 2:11.

8. 2 Peter 2:10 (NASB: *angelic majesty*).

9. 2 Peter 2:10-11.

10. Jude 9.

11. Or, *transmogrify*, to use the technical term.

12. John 10:10.

13. Isaiah 14:12-14.

14. Ezekiel 28:12-17.

15. Many Old Testament prophecies had more than one application, e.g. those referring to the Son of David.

16. Isaiah 14:13-14.

17. Philippians 2:6-7.

18. Revelation 12:4,9.

19. Revelation 12:10.

20. Timothy 3:4.

21. 1 Timothy 6:10.

22. Psalm 16:11.

23. Matthew 4:8-9.

24. Matthew 6:21.

25. John 13:27.

26. Revelation 17:4-5.

27. Margaret Thaler Singer, *Cults in our Midst* (San Francisco: Jossey-Bass Publishers, 1995), 192.

28. Ibid.

29. The actual term they used for full-frontal bodily contact was *pee-pee* to *pee-pee*.

30. Genesis 3:1.

31. Perhaps Adam had decided it would be safer not even to touch that tree, and so instructed Eve. But whenever we construe man's rules as God's instructions, we rely on legalism instead of God to protect us, and end up becoming more vulnerable to temptation.

32. Genesis 3:4.

33. 1 Timothy 2:14, 2 Corinthians 11:3.

34. Romans 5:19.

35. Hosea 6:7.

36. Based on the specific descriptions of Adam and Eve's sin, it is possible to conclude that Adam was not deceived in the same way as Eve, and thus more deliberate and willful in his transgression.

37. Rebellion, in God's eyes, is "like the sin of divination (witchcraft)" (1 Samuel 15:23).

38. Romans 6:16.

39. John 3:16.

40. Psalm 24:1.

41. Romans 5:12.

42. These "keys" were, and are, ultimately under God's sovereign authority (cf. Matthew 10:28 and Revelation 1:18), yet Hebrews 2:14 *refers to him who holds the power of death—that is, the devil.*

43. As Jesus pointed out in Luke 22:25-26, sinful man's natural way of ruling is the opposite of servant leadership.

44. Genesis 3:10.

45. Genesis 3:12 (emphasis added).

46. Genesis 3:13 (emphasis added).

47. Genesis 3:23-24.

48. Genesis 3:15.

49. Hebrews 2:14-15.

50. Genesis 3:21.

SIX

THE FATAL FLAW

"You want it? You got it—at a price. You can marry anyone, produce an offspring made to order, have the right to decide for yourself what is right and what is wrong. With no outside authority interfering." A social critic warns that beneath such consumer bliss a 21st century dystopia[1] festers.

—Headline to a lead article
in *The Vancouver Sun,*
New Year's Day 2000

At the brink of a new millennium in world history, fears of widespread computer crashes (courtesy the infamous Y2K bug) were matched by worries about the potential fallout from current trends.[2] *The Vancouver Sun* explored this theme by quoting the views of several international commentators, including British columnist Theodore Dalrymple who writes for *The Spectator*:

Now that we have entered the new millennium we begin to see a little more clearly what the Cold War, and before it the Enlightenment, was really all about: not the extension of human freedom in its nobler aspects, but the indefinite extension of consumer choice as the highest possible good to which Man can aspire…If our spouse no longer suits, we abandon him or her for someone else; if our pregnancy is inconvenient, we terminate it; if our sex at birth feels wrong, we change it. In a world empty of higher or transcendent authority, there is only one ruling principle: our whim is law.

Dalrymple, like Malcolm Muggeridge in the century just past, offers a profound analysis of where our culture is headed. His article concludes with references to cloning and other "advances" in science:

> Science will make good the disappointment of existence, none of which is intrinsic to the human condition. It will not only pluck from the memory a rooted sorrow as easily as unwanted fetuses from the womb, but will give you everything you desire, as you desire it, from an exact copy of yourself to the gender of your dreams and the child of your desires. But life in the cosmic Wal-Mart palls even as it is lived. It is frivolous without gaiety and fast-moving without direction. When there is nothing that is not a matter of choice, life will not be free and happy, but a perpetual torment of disillusion, frustration, resentment and dissatisfaction.[3]

When God created Adam, He made him sinless and declared that His creation was "very good." It was perfectly natural for Adam to be humble, obedient, serving, responsive to the Creator's will and dependent on His wisdom and grace. But God also gave him the ability to make moral choices: he was free to choose—if he so wanted—to be proud, disobedient, selfish, stubborn and independent.

When man fell, this ability to choose was dramatically changed. Free will—in the context of a Godward orientation—now became twisted, and man became both a perpetrator and a victim of sin. In fact, free will was no longer entirely free, as there was a definite pull in the wrong direction: it became "natural" to make the wrong choice. Eventually, sinful pride, disobedience and independence became so natural that man often didn't recognize them as sin, even boasting, "I'm a bit of a rebel," or "I'm a stubborn old critter," as if these were virtues. Man was now tainted, fatally flawed.

This flaw—the sinful nature—is a major theme in Scripture and the subject of hundreds of examples in both the Old and New Testament. Why the emphasis? Why so many long, drawn-out illustrations of sinful behavior? Could it be that God wants to get our attention and help us to recognize the evil nature of sin and its destructive effect? Just a brief glance through the Bible reveals that this flaw—this malady— has tripped up even the godliest and noblest of God's servants, and is the primary hindrance to the fulfillment of His ultimate purpose.

The Bible consistently gives us the unvarnished facts; there is no anonymity for sinners. And since God never does anything by chance, we must accept that the Scripture's "unsanitized" version of history represents His deliberate choice. If they had "reality" TV shows in the Old Testament, they probably would have done a segment on Jehoram, one of the evil kings of Judah. As soon as he had secured the throne he killed all his brothers with the sword and wiped out a few Israelite princes. God responded by sending Elijah with a letter telling him that He was going to strike him and his family with a heavy blow. The outcome? An invasion from neighboring countries that took away his riches, his wives and sons. Then the following:

> After all this, the Lord afflicted Jehoram with an incurable disease of the bowels. In the course of time, at the end of the second year, his bowels came out because of the disease, and he died in great pain. His people made no fire in his honor, as they had for his fathers.[4]

The Bible is certainly not for the squeamish! Nor does it cater to sentimental souls who like all their stories to have happy endings. It records not only the exploits of the heroes of faith, but also the fiascos of the cowards of unbelief—and reveals that sometimes faith and unbelief show up in the same person! Case in point: Abraham.

FAITH, FEAR AND "GOOD IDEAS"

God promised Abraham that through his offspring (or *seed*) all the nations of the earth would be blessed, and that his descendants would be as numerous as the dust of the earth, the sand on the seashore and the stars in the heavens.[5] The Bible records that Abraham believed the Lord, and He credited it to him as righteousness.[6] In the New Testament we find many affirming comments about Abraham, such as: "If you belong to Christ, then you are Abraham's seed, and heirs according to the promise."[7] Or this example from Hebrews:

> By faith Abraham, when called to go to a place he would later receive as his inheritance, obeyed and went, even though he did not know where he was going. By faith he made his home in the promised land like a stranger in a foreign country; he lived in tents, as did Isaac and Jacob,

who were heirs with him of the same promise. For he was looking forward to the city with foundations, whose architect and builder is God.

By faith Abraham, even though he was past age—and Sarah herself was barren—was enabled to become a father because he considered him faithful who had made the promise. And so from this one man, and he as good as dead, came descendants as numerous as the stars in the sky and as countless as the sand on the seashore.[8]

But there is another side to Abraham that is not quite so flattering. It's his "man-made-good-ideas" side: his Achilles heel: his fatal flaw.[9] We find evidence of this side in an incident that happened around the mid-point of his life, long after he had come to know God and hear His promises:

Now Sarai, Abram's wife, had borne him no children. But she had an Egyptian maidservant named Hagar; so she said to Abram, "The Lord has kept me from having children. Go, sleep with my maidservant; perhaps I can build a family through her."

Abram agreed to what Sarai said. So after Abram had been living in Canaan ten years, Sarai his wife took her Egyptian maidservant Hagar and gave her to her husband to be his wife. He slept with Hagar, and she conceived. When she knew she was pregnant, she began to despise her mistress.[10]

God had made a promise to Abraham, but Sarah,[11] instead of waiting and trusting, became anxious and conjured up what she thought was an excellent plan. Why not help God out? Why not fulfill the promise through her maidservant? Abraham—apparently without consulting God—agreed.

The problem here was not the maidservant: God often uses humble people to do great things. The problem was that this "solution" was nothing more than Sarah and Abraham's "good idea." It was, in effect, eating of the tree of the knowledge of good and evil: a replay of Adam and Eve's fateful choice in the Garden of Eden, and the results again proved destructive.

Earlier in their married life, Abraham and Sarah found it necessary to travel to Egypt and live there because of a severe famine. Just before they crossed into Egyptian territory, Abraham came up with a plan to ensure his safety. Here is my paraphrase of what he told his wife:

> "Honey, we've got a little problem here. You're a very beautiful woman—any man can see that. But we're going to Egypt and you know what those Egyptians are like. One look at you and they'll consider any husband "dispensable"; my life won't be worth a shekel. Now, you wouldn't want anything to happen to me, would you, sweetheart? Here's what you need to do: just tell them you're my sister, and they'll treat me like royalty."[12]

Another "Garden-variety" good idea! My inner response to this account of Abraham is: *What a pathetic specimen of manhood! Can this be the same man who is known as the father of faith?* The Bible tells us that if we are in Christ we are Abraham's offspring, and we have the same capacity to be men and women of faith as he was. But it's also true that because we come from the same human family, we can act as cowardly as he sometimes did.[13]

I still cringe when I think back to an incident when I was 17. As a young police cadet in London, England, I was living in the *Police Section House*, which housed about 100 single officers and cadets. My friend Ian Cook, a fellow cadet, had gone home for the weekend, and I decided to borrow his bicycle (without his knowledge or permission) to ride to the local swimming pool. Without securing the bike, I parked it against the wall surrounding the pool and went on my swim.

When I returned, I found, to my absolute dismay, the bike was gone! Stolen! I spent the rest of the weekend in utter misery. How could I face Ian? What would I say? What would he think of me? I finally chose the coward's way out: I wrote him a letter explaining what had happened, and left it on his bed.

Ian returned late Sunday night. His room was four doors down the corridor from my room, but I had gone to bed early to avoid bumping in to him, and had carefully locked my door. But sleep escaped me. Eventually, I could hear his footsteps coming down the corridor. He knocked on my door as he went past, but I didn't respond. I could hear him open his door—and then, silence.

Fear had me by the throat. I felt like a wimp, a complete coward. A few minutes passed; then the sound of his footsteps. *Knock, knock, knock.* No answer. I shall never forget that moment. Then, Ian's voice through the locked door: "Come on, Coombsy, I know you're in there. Stop pretending you're asleep." I still didn't respond. The truth was, I was afraid and hid myself. Does that sound vaguely familiar?

Ian was kind enough to forgive me and, several years later, even agreed to be the best man at my wedding. Today we can laugh about it together, but at the time, it was my worst nightmare come true. I received an e-mail from him just last week asking, "What happened to my bike?"[14]

Strangely enough, when it came to sharing my faith with the police cadets, I was fearless. I even had the privilege of seeing eight of them (including Ian) make a commitment to Christ. But my fearful response when Ian's bicycle was stolen revealed a dark side—a side that went all the way back to the Garden of Eden.

Through Adam's sin, tormenting fear came into the human race—a destructive, inhibiting disease—a curse that affects all of society. Franklin Roosevelt once said, "The only thing we have to fear is fear itself," a statement that carried more truth than he may have realized.[15] Although fear is rooted in our rebellion, the enemy exploits it so that we become distracted, trapped or paralyzed by fear—which in turn leads to further rebellion.

There is a striking example of that pattern in Jeremiah's time, shortly after Jerusalem fell at the hands of Nebuchadnezzar, king of Babylon. We pick up the story where the leaders of Judah, along with the army and many women and children, are starting off toward Egypt where they think it will be safer for them:

> Then all the army officers, including Johanan son of Kareah and Jezaniah son of Hoshaiah, and all the people from the least to the greatest approached Jeremiah the prophet and said to him, "Please hear our petition and pray to the Lord your God for this entire remnant. For as you now see, though we were once many, now only a few are left. Pray

that the Lord your God will tell us where we should go and what we should do."

"I have heard you," replied Jeremiah the prophet. "I will certainly pray to the Lord your God as you have requested; I will tell you everything the Lord says and will keep nothing back from you."

Then they said to Jeremiah, "May the Lord be a true and faithful witness against us if we do not act in accordance with everything the Lord your God sends you to tell us. Whether it is favorable or unfavorable, we will obey the Lord our God, to whom we are sending you, so that it will go well with us, for we will obey the Lord our God."[16]

So far, so good. The leaders and the people seem fully committed to hearing and doing God's will. But in the space of time between this commitment and the point where Jeremiah brings back God's answer, something changes. We are not told what happened during that time (a period of ten days), but there must have been a lot of talking and speculation among the people. As they talked amongst themselves, they must have been "eating of the tree of the knowledge of good and evil" because there was a complete change of attitude: they allowed their fear to overtake faith. Here is their response after Jeremiah issued a strong prophetic warning against going to Egypt:

When Jeremiah finished telling the people all the words of the Lord their God—everything the Lord had sent him to tell them—Azariah son of Hoshaiah and Johanan son of Kareah and all the arrogant men said to Jeremiah, "You are lying! The Lord our God has not sent you to say, 'You must not go to Egypt to settle there.' But Baruch son of Neriah is inciting you against us to hand us over to the Babylonians so they may kill us or carry us into exile to Babylon."

So Johanan son of Kareah and all the army officers and all the people disobeyed the Lord's command to stay in the land of Judah. So they entered Egypt in disobedience to the Lord and went as far as Tahpanhes.[17]

It's tempting to think we would never act that way, but the truth is, we all have pockets of unfaithfulness in our hearts. Manifestations of the fatal flaw—rebellion, fear, independence, and "good ideas"— show up in even the godliest leaders. When God told Moses to speak to the rock, Moses instead shouted at the gathered assembly and dealt with the rock his *own* way:

> "Listen, you rebels, must we bring you water out of this rock?" Then Moses raised his arm and struck the rock twice with his staff. Water gushed out, and the community and their livestock drank.
>
> But the Lord said to Moses and Aaron, "Because you did not trust in me enough to honor me as holy in the sight of the Israelites, you will not bring this community into the land I give them."[18]

Notice the irony of Moses calling his countrymen *rebels* when he himself was rebelling against God's command. The judgment was severe: his rebellion cost him the opportunity of entering the Promised Land—a key part of his destiny.[19]

In 1 Chronicles 21 we find the story of David numbering the people. We are not told whether he was seeking to reassure himself of the nation's combat strength (i.e. self-reliance instead of trusting God) or whether his heart motive was pride, but either way he was wrong, and he knew it. Even his hard-headed army general Joab knew it was wrong and tried to get David to change his mind, but to no avail. The consequences were disastrous: 70,000 men died.

To close this chapter, we take a careful look at the rise and fall of one of the good kings of Judah: King Asa. Here is how he started his reign:

> Asa did what was good and right in the eyes of the Lord his God. He removed the foreign altars and the high places, smashed the sacred stones and cut down the Asherah poles. He commanded Judah to seek the Lord, the God of their fathers, and to obey his laws and commands. He removed the high places and incense altars in every town in Judah, and the kingdom was at peace under him.[20]

But this peace would soon be threatened. The biblical record shows that Asa had an army of 580,000 men: 300,000 from the tribe of Judah, equipped with large shields and spears; and 280,000 from the tribe of Benjamin, armed with small shields and bows. While this was a formidable army in its day, it was about half the size of an opposing army led by Zerah, a pagan Cushite king. Not only that, Zerah had 300 chariots, a fearsome and lethal addition to his armed forces.

As they drew up in battle formation in the Valley of Zephathah, Asa knew that, humanly speaking, he didn't have a chance. But he did have the Lord, and decided to place his hope in Him (thus, figuratively speaking, eating of the tree of life):

> Then Asa called to the Lord his God and said, "Lord, there is no one like you to help the powerless against the mighty. Help us, O Lord our God, for we rely on you, and in your name we have come against this vast army. O Lord, you are our God; do not let man prevail against you."[21]

Notice in that last sentence how Asa views the battle: it wasn't ultimately between his army and the opposing army, but between *God* and the Cushites. The result? God took the responsibility for the battle and completely routed Asa's enemies: "Such a great number of Cushites fell that they could not recover; they were crushed before the Lord and his forces. The men of Judah carried off a large amount of plunder."

After this, Asa carried on the good reforms he had begun: he removed all the idols and male shrine prostitutes from the land, and deposed his grandmother Maacah from her position as queen mother because she had made a repulsive Asherah pole. He also repaired the altar of the Lord, restored sacrifices and worship, and brought into the temple the silver and gold that he and his father had dedicated.

When people in the northern kingdom of Israel saw that God was with Asa, many relocated to Judah and Benjamin. These defections were probably one reason why Baasha, king of Israel, regarded Asa as a threat and decided to go to war against him. In any case, Baasha's strategy was to build up the fortress of Ramah in order to prevent anyone from entering or leaving Asa's territory.

This left Asa in an untenable position, but instead of taking his predicament to the Lord as he had done previously, he took the defense of Judah into his own hands. He took the silver and gold that had been dedicated to the Lord and sent it as a bribe to Ben-Hadad, king of Aram, asking him to break his covenant with Baasha, king of Israel, so that he would withdraw from Judah. Ben-Hadad agreed and began to attack Israel, whereupon Baasha withdrew from the fortress at Ramah. The strategy worked.

So, was Asa successful? Humanly speaking, yes. Some say, *you can't argue with success,* but God doesn't see it that way. "Success" achieved without God's wisdom and strength robs God of His glory. And success that is measured by visible outcomes (e.g. numbers) does not necessarily demonstrate God's blessing or approval.

Why did Asa act completely independent of God on this occasion? Had he begun to view Judah and Benjamin as belonging to himself instead of God—and therefore thought it was all up to him? Had he become prideful and self-sufficient? Perhaps he simply panicked and did the first thing that came into his mind. When man ceases to be ruled by faith, he ends up being governed by fear!

One thing is certain: despite the apparent success, Asa sinned in a big way. It wasn't long before Hanani the seer came to the king with a message:

> "Because you relied on the king of Aram and not on the Lord your God, the army of the king of Aram has escaped from your hand. Were not the Cushites and Libyans a mighty army with great numbers of chariots and horsemen? Yet when you relied on the Lord, he delivered them into your hand. For the eyes of the Lord range throughout the earth to strengthen those whose hearts are fully committed to him. You have done a foolish thing, and from now on you will be at war."[22]

Upon hearing this, Asa was so enraged that he threw the seer in prison and brutally oppressed some of the people. (Whether these were people who had disagreed with his war strategy or were simply "in the line of fire" of his fury, we are not told.) It's hard to imagine this turnaround: a distinguished, godly monarch like Asa having a temper tantrum and acting like a brute animal!

The closing event in Asa's life is also in sharp contrast with his exemplary beginning. He developed a severe medical problem in his feet, but even that was not enough to turn his heart back to God: "Though his disease was severe, even in his illness he did not seek help from the Lord, but only from the physicians."[23] What a tragic end to a great man! I think of David's lament following the death of Saul and Jonathan: "How the mighty have fallen!"[24]

Focusing on man's fatal flaw can be discouraging business—even depressing at times. But we need to face the reality of our condition. Pretending that sin isn't serious only worsens our predicament because we are so easily inclined to adopt "band aid" solutions. Furthermore, God wants us to learn from the mistakes of our forefathers, as we see in this verse referring to Israel's history: "These things happened to them as examples and were written down as warnings for us, on whom the fulfillment of the ages has come."[25]

Finally, we will not truly appreciate God's remedy if we fail to acknowledge the extent of our need. The flaw is indeed fatal—and would remain so if God did not intervene to save us and deal with our enemy. As we noted before, God promised that the seed of the woman would crush the serpent's head. But it would be another nine centuries after Asa's lifetime before God would decisively rectify what Adam and Eve had spoiled.

Someone wisely said, "God doesn't have problems; He just has timetables." The day surely would come when the Father would have His family, the Son would have His Body (the Church), and the Holy Spirit would have His temple. Nothing—none of satan's machinations nor man's fatal flaw—would be able to stop the restoration of God's original plan. To that end, God would use the seed of His flawed but beloved King David, as we see in Isaiah's ancient prophecy: "A shoot will come up from the stump of Jesse; from his roots a Branch will bear fruit."[26] Immanuel was coming.

ENDNOTES

1. *Dystopia* is an anti-utopia, a place where people lead fearful, dehumanized lives.

2. It is interesting to note that futuristic movies often portray a world that is very mechanistic, cruel and amoral—in an environment of either anarchy or despotism.

3. Theodore Dalrymple, quoted in *The Vancouver Sun* [Vancouver, Canada], January 1, 2000.

4. 2 Chronicles 21:18-19.

5. Genesis 13:16, 15:5, 22:17-18. See also Galatians 3:16 where this *Seed* is identified ultimately as Christ.

6. Genesis 15:6 (In the earlier part of Abraham's life, his name was *Abram*.)

7. Galatians 3:29.

8. Hebrews 11:8-12.

9. Some may question the term *fatal flaw* since Abraham and others apparently survived their faults. But the point is that apart from God's mercy and grace, these flaws—even in the best specimens of humanity—are quite sufficient to destroy both the offenders and their God-ordained destiny.

10. Genesis 16:1-4.

11. At this earlier point in the story, Sarah's name was still *Sarai*.

12. Genesis 12:11-13 (loosely paraphrased).

13. Genesis 12 tells of how God graciously rescued both Abraham and Sarah from what could have been a disastrous outcome in Egypt. He also rescued them in Gerer when they used the "sister" line with King Abimelech (Genesis 20).

14. An obvious attempt at "recycling" humor.

15. Even the most courageous of men deal with fear. Close friends of Winston Churchill report that he battled all his life with the irrational fear that he might throw himself in front of an express train as it thundered past the station. It was therefore his habit to stand as far as possible from the edge of the platform, preferably beside a metal roof support so that he could cling to it if necessary.

16. Jeremiah 42:1-6.

17. Jeremiah 43:1-4,7.

18. Numbers 20:10-12.

19. The severity of the judgment is tied to the level of responsibility. Jesus said, "From everyone who has been given much, much will be demanded; and from the one who has been entrusted with much, much more will be asked." (Luke 12:48)

20. 2 Chronicles 14:2-5. Asa's reforms are also recorded in 1 Kings 15:9-15.

21. 2 Chronicles 14:11.
22. 2 Chronicles 16:7-9.
23. 2 Chronicles 16:12.
24. 2 Samuel 1:19.
25. 1 Corinthians 10:11.
26. Isaiah 11:1.

SEVEN

JESUS OF NAZARETH: THE PERFECT MAN

Veiled in flesh the Godhead see:
Hail the incarnate Deity,
Pleased as man with men to dwell;
Jesus, our Immanuel! —Charles Wesley, 1739
(from "Hark the
Herald Angels Sing")

Christmas carols seem to retain their appeal year after year, even in our increasingly secular culture. Why? I believe it all has to do with the subject—the greatest event that ever took place on planet Earth—the arrival of *Immanuel*, the promised Seed, our Lord Jesus Christ. Infinity penetrating space and time, taking on the form of the finite; the Perfect One living inside the imperfect.

The tiny human egg in the womb of a teenager named Mary waits until the Holy Spirit, in some mysterious and miraculous fashion, conveys the pure life of God into that single cell, and Jesus of Nazareth is conceived. At that moment, the Son of God in human form is, physiologically, the size of a pinhead. He "emptied Himself of all but love," as Charles Wesley says in another hymn. This is the incredible truth of the incarnation. It defies comprehension, yet we (along with countless believers and unbelievers) cannot stop singing about it.

Some time after Jesus' birth, His coming is heralded to wise men in the east through the appearance of an unusual star—a star that draws the wise men westward as it moves across the heavens.

(A paradox: the Advent of the Creator of the universe is hailed by, of all things, a star!) The wise men ask, "Where is the one who has been born king of the Jews? We saw his star in the east and have come to worship him."[1]

At the time, the wise men, despite their understanding of many things, probably knew just enough to come and worship. From their present vantage point in eternity, they would, if it were possible, declare much more to those still in darkness:

- This is no shooting star that would burn up as it entered earth's atmosphere.

- This is the star that pierced the darkness: the One who John said shines in the darkness, but the darkness has not overcome it.[2]

- This is the One who has come to destroy the works of the devil.

- This is the One who has come to render powerless him who had the power over death.

- This is the One who has come to bring many sons to glory.

- This is the One who has come not only to redeem man but also to redeem the plan.

- This is the One who has come to reclaim what Adam gave away. He would recover it not in His position as Son of God, but rather as God incarnate, the Son of Man. Only a man could do it, but it would take a Man who was sinlessly perfect.

He never ceased to be God the Son, but He laid aside His divine ability to sustain Himself, and refused to use the awesome power by which He made the universe. Instead, He chose to achieve His goals by relying on the wisdom, power and knowledge supplied by the Holy Spirit through His relationship with His heavenly Father. As Peter Lewis succinctly puts it, "He had it but He didn't use it."[3]

Satan and all his cohorts were now on "red alert." That which they had dreaded through the centuries—ever since that terrible pronouncement about the serpent's head being crushed—had now arrived. No doubt they feared that Jesus would carry out the mandate originally entrusted to Adam, that He would totally fulfill the requirements of the law, and that He would be possessed with the zeal of the Lord. If so, their fears were well founded.

THE LORD IS A COVENANT-KEEPING GOD

Since the creation of the world, God's relationship to man has always been defined by specific promises and requirements in the form of covenants. God's covenants with man are similar to contracts between people in that they are legally binding, but there are some major differences. Wayne Grudem defines biblical covenant *as an unchangeable, divinely-imposed legal agreement between God and man that stipulates the conditions of their relationship.*[4] In other words, we don't get to negotiate this type of contract: we either accept or reject the terms laid down by God.

We know the Scriptures as *Old Testament* and *New Testament*, but they could just as well be called *Old Covenant* and *New Covenant* because all of God's dealings with man fall within the framework of His covenants. There were covenants established with Adam, Noah, Abraham, Moses, David and Jesus, as well as promises made to other individuals who found favor with God. One example of these smaller covenants was the unconditional promise to maintain the family of Phinehas in a lasting priesthood.[5]

But there was a problem. For thousands of years God kept His side of the covenant but man repeatedly reneged on his part: faithfulness on one side, unfaithfulness and treachery on the other. But some day there would be a Man who, for the first time, would perfectly fulfill the covenant. This is the One of whom God would say, "I will maintain my love to him forever, and my covenant with him will never fail."[6]

LIVING BY WHAT GOD SPEAKS

It was always God's intention that man would live by what God said. This is a basic rule of life taught throughout Scripture, as we find in this verse from Deuteronomy where Moses is giving the Israelites a history lesson and its application:

> He humbled you, causing you to hunger and then feeding
> you with manna, which neither you nor your fathers had

known, to teach you that *man does not live on bread alone, but on every word that comes from the mouth of the Lord.*[7]

When satan tempted Jesus, he tried to entice Him to live by His own wisdom and strength: "If you are the Son of God, tell these stones to become bread."[8] In other words, *be independent; use your own power; live by what you say. If you've got it—use it!*

Jesus resisted the temptation and replied to satan by quoting the words that Moses declared to the Israelites: "Man does not live on bread alone, but on every word that comes from the mouth of God." His response was to take a portion of the written word inspired by the Holy Spirit—Scripture that He had previously studied and treasured up in His heart—and then prayerfully speak it with faith and authority. In doing so, He didn't rely on His own power or words, but instead He repelled satan's attack by the power of the Holy Spirit and the word of God, i.e. the "sword of the Spirit."

At last! A man who truly lived by what God said. Here is how Isaiah prophesied about this One who would listen so intently to the voice of God:

> The Sovereign Lord has given me an instructed tongue,
> to know the word that sustains the weary.
> He wakens me morning by morning,
> wakens my ear to listen like one being taught.
> The Sovereign Lord has opened my ears,
> and I have not been rebellious;
> I have not drawn back.[9]

To the rebellious, arrogant, self-righteous Pharisees, Jesus could say:

> When you have lifted up the Son of Man, then you will know that I am the one I claim to be and that I do nothing on my own but speak just what the Father has taught me.[10]

LIVING FROM THE LIFE OF ANOTHER

If it were just a matter of speculation, we might be inclined to think that a perfect man would not be dependent on anyone. In fact, psychologists consider strong dependency to be a type of personality disorder. While overdependence on people is unhealthy, the Bible teaches that man was created to live in trusting dependence on God.

Jesus, the perfect Man and eternal Son of God, perfectly modeled that relationship in His attitude and way of living. Note these descriptions of Himself from the Gospel of John:

> I tell you the truth, the Son can do nothing by himself; he can do only what he sees his Father doing, because whatever the Father does the Son also does.

> By myself I can do nothing; I judge only as I hear, and my judgment is just, for I seek not to please myself but him who sent me.

> These words you hear are not my own; they belong to the Father who sent me.[11]

Let's keep in mind that, according to Hebrews chapter 1, the universe was created *through the* Son and all creation is sustained (i.e. continues to exist) by means of His powerful word.[12] In Colossians we find this truth stated very plainly: "...all things were created by him and for him. He is before all things, and in him all things hold together."[13]

In light of these facts, isn't it astounding that Jesus would say that the Son can do nothing by Himself? This is the One who created the sub-atomic particles that make up our universe, the One who flung billions of galaxies into space, the One who continues to sustain gravity, electromagnetism and all the other forces—as well as life itself.

Humanly speaking, if anyone ever had reason to be independent and self-sufficient, it was Jesus. Yet He chose to lay aside His divine prerogative and to submit Himself as a bond servant of His heavenly Father—without rights, power or possessions. He didn't even have a crib in which to be laid at birth. Throughout His life He frequently used what was borrowed from others: a coin, a boat, a donkey, and finally, a grave. He told those who wanted to follow Him that "the Son of Man has no place to lay his head"[14] (in other words, no house of his own). But the cross was His alone to bear, as was the crown of thorns.

Unless the Father gave Him words, He had no words to speak; unless the Father showed Him what He was doing, the Son had no works to do; He lived from the life of Another. "My food," said Jesus, "is to do the will of him who sent me and to finish his work."[15]

This way of life could succeed only because the Son walked in close, intimate fellowship with the Father. And that is exactly the pattern of relationship that Jesus desires with His disciples, which mirrors what God originally had in mind when He created Adam. Here is how Jesus describes it:

> Remain in me, and I will remain in you. No branch can bear fruit by itself; it must remain in the vine. Neither can you bear fruit unless you remain in me. I am the vine; you are the branches. If a man remains in me and I in him, he will bear much fruit; apart from me you can do nothing.[16]

"GOOD IDEAS" AREN'T GOOD ENOUGH

One of the slogans used by the Ford Motor Company some years ago was *Ford has a better idea.* Innovation and creativity are of course God-given gifts, but sometimes our "better idea" is simply a form of presumption—especially if we've neglected to ask God for *His* thoughts on the matter.

Bob Mumford defines presumption as *doing good things God has not asked me to do.* In other words, it's putting into action my own good ideas instead of seeking God for His will and purpose. Certain characters in the Bible were well-known for that—Saul being a prime example. When God instructed him to annihilate the Amalekites and all their livestock, Saul had a "better idea": why not save the best of the sheep and cattle and destroy just the weak ones? That way, everyone would be richer and (here was the best part!) they could offer some of those sheep and cattle as sacrifices to God. Great idea! But God called it rebellion and, as a result, rejected Saul as king over Israel.[17]

In later chapters, when we look at examples of "good ideas" from various leaders in church history, it will soon become obvious that Saul was not alone in acting presumptuously. In fact, all of us need to ask ourselves this question from time to time: *Are we doing good things that God has not asked us to do?* Some of these good things—for instance, charitable deeds or projects or even major ministries—may be highly honored among God's people. But if they are actually founded on someone's "good idea" (our own or some-one else's), we're dealing with presumption, and that—no matter what it looks like—is still sin.

The prophecies concerning Jesus present a completely different picture. In stark contrast to the presumptuous attitudes and actions of sinful man, Jesus would make His decisions based on what He saw and heard in the Spirit:

> A shoot will come up from the stump of Jesse;
> from his roots a Branch will bear fruit.
> The Spirit of the Lord will rest on him—
> the Spirit of wisdom and of understanding,
> the Spirit of counsel and of power,
> the Spirit of knowledge and of the fear of the Lord—
> and he will delight in the fear of the Lord.
> He will not judge by what he sees with his eyes,
> or decide by what he hears with his ears...[28]

Jesus as a man was tempted (as we are) to evaluate things based on what He saw and heard, and then to determine a course of action: the *good idea* approach to life. There must have been countless times as a young man, before the start of His ministry at age 30, that He had thoughts about helping, healing and teaching others—doing good things. But the Father had not yet given the go-ahead. He resisted those temptations and relied on the Holy Spirit to direct Him as to the *what*, *where*, *when* and *how* of His ministry. And that was because He had settled the *why* issue: namely, to please His Father. A verse from the Gospel of John captures this theme so well that we will read it from three translations:

> By myself I can do nothing; I judge only as I hear, and my judgment is just, for I seek not to please myself but him who sent me.[19]

> I can do nothing on My own initiative. As I hear, I judge; and My judgment is just, because I do not seek My own will, but the will of Him who sent Me.[20]

> But I pass no judgment without consulting the Father. I judge as I am told. And my judgment is absolutely fair and

just, for it is according to the will of God who sent me and is not merely my own.[21]

In other words, Jesus didn't have "good ideas," just good hearing! May that increasingly be true of His followers.

OBEDIENCE BRINGS PLEASURE TO THE FATHER

I once heard a preacher say that Jesus didn't come to be crucified; He came to do the will of His Father—which included going to Calvary. Jesus' awareness of the Father's will clearly began at an early age. As a 12-year-old He told His earthly parents, "Didn't you know I had to be in my Father's house?"[22] David prophetically spoke of Jesus' heart commitment to obeying His Father:

> Then I said, "Here I am, I have come—
> it is written about me in the scroll.
> I desire to do your will, O my God;
> your law is within my heart."[23]

Jesus could honestly say to the people of his day, "The one who sent me is with me; he has not left me alone, for I always do what pleases him."[24] Imagine having a child who always did as he was told, always finished whatever task you entrusted to him, always gave you his full attention when being spoken to, always went to bed when he was asked to and always got up as soon as he was called. Then imagine the Father's pleasure in His Son—a Son who could say, "I *always* do what pleases him."

No wonder that when Jesus was baptized, the Father sent the Holy Spirit to descend on Him in bodily form like a dove, and spoke these words in the hearing of all who were gathered: "You are my Son, whom I love; with you I am well pleased."[25] How could the Father not be pleased with a Son whose heart's desire was to serve His Father in joyful obedience, and whose actions perfectly expressed that desire?

Jesus not only set out to do His Father's will, He also *finished* the work He was assigned. In His prayer shortly before the crucifixion, He was able to say to the Father, "I have brought you glory on earth by completing the work you gave me to do."[26] This too is an amazing statement in light of a public ministry that lasted about 3½ years. If one were to view it from a purely human perspective, it doesn't look very complete: not many followers who remained faithful; few who actually understood what the Kingdom was about; His top disciples still exhibiting major character flaws; many thousands still unhealed or oppressed by demons; and an evil Roman empire as strongly entrenched as ever. Yet He had finished *His* work because He completely carried out His God-given mandate.

Finally, with His lifeblood draining away on the Cross, He shouts, "It is finished!"[27] He didn't say, "I am finished," in a weak cry of resignation, but rather, "It is finished!" because He had accomplished the purpose for which He came. The Greek word used in John's Gospel is *Tetelestai*, which carries the meaning of total realization: *It is complete; you cannot add anything to it and you cannot subtract anything from it. It is perfectly perfect!*

After this, Jesus "bowed his head and gave up his spirit."[28] Matthew records that it was at this very moment when the curtain in the temple—the barrier that kept man outside the Holy of Holies—was torn in two from top to bottom. This symbolized the new and living way that was opened up between God and man, allowing man to be reconciled to a holy God.[29] Here is how Adam Clark describes it in his commentary:

> *It is finished*, as if he had said: "I have executed the great designs of the Almighty; I have satisfied the demands of his justice; I have accomplished all that was written in the prophets, and suffered the utmost malice of my enemies; and now the way to the holy of holies is made manifest through my blood." An awful, yet glorious finish. Through this tragical death God is reconciled to man, and the kingdom of heaven opened to every believing soul.[30]

What is encompassed in those last words of Jesus on the Cross is so monumental that I want to quote the inspiring remarks of one more eminent commentator, Matthew Henry:

> *It is finished*, that is, the malice and enmity of his persecutors had now done their worst.

> *It is finished*, that is, the counsel and commandment of his Father concerning his sufferings were now fulfilled. He

had said, when he entered upon his sufferings, *Father, thy will be done*; and now he saith with pleasure, *It is done.*

It is finished, that is, all the types and prophecies of the Old Testament, which pointed at the sufferings of the Messiah, were accomplished and answered. The substance is now come, and all the shadows are done away.

It is finished, that is, sin is finished, and an end made of transgression. *The Lamb of God was sacrificed to take away the sin of the world*, and it is done.

It is finished, that is, his sufferings were now finished. The storm is over, the worst is past, and he is just entering upon *the joy set before him*. Let all that *suffer for Christ*, and with Christ, comfort themselves with this, *that yet a little while* and they also shall say, *It is finished.*

It is finished, that is, his life was now finished, he was just ready to breathe his last. This we must all come to shortly.

It is finished, that is, the work of man's redemption and salvation is now completed, a fatal blow given to the power of Satan, a fountain of grace opened that shall ever flow. *He that has begun a good work will perform it*; the mystery of God shall be finished.[31]

Through His death and resurrection, Jesus legally recovered all that Adam lost. At the same time, He dealt thoroughly and decisively with all the consequences of our sin—and the awful ramifications of the sinful nature we inherited from Adam. The apostle Paul writes:

When you were dead in your sins and in the uncircumcision of your sinful nature, God made you alive with Christ. He forgave us all our sins, having canceled the written code, with its regulations, that was against us and that stood opposed to us; he took it away, nailing it to the cross.[32]

Notice what this verse is saying: God has made us alive with Christ; He has forgiven *all* our sins; He has cancelled the written code (i.e. the judgment we were subject to under the law) that was against us and stood opposed to us; He not only took that code away, He also made certain that it stayed away by nailing it to the Cross! If that little list doesn't evoke a *hallelujah* from us, I don't know what will!

One of the most enduring songs of the past century has been *Amazing Grace*. The grace of God truly becomes more amazing the more we understand what He has done for us. Another expressive term for this grace is *outrageous*, which, though often used in a negative sense, also means *exceeding the limits of what is usual: fantastic*. It is in this sense that a Christian musician recently wrote *Outrageous Grace*, a song that speaks of what has changed since Jesus finished His work:

> There's a lot of pain, but a lot more healing;
> There's a lot of trouble, but a lot more peace;
> There's a lot of hate, but a lot more loving;
> There's a lot of sin, but a lot more grace.
>
> > O outrageous grace! O outrageous grace!
> > Love unfurled by heaven's hand—
> > O outrageous grace! O outrageous grace!
> > Through my Jesus I can stand.
>
> There's a lot of fear, but a lot more freedom;
> There's a lot of darkness, but a lot more light;
> There's a lot of cloud, but a lot more vision;
> There's a lot of perishing, but a lot more life.
>
> > O outrageous grace...
>
> There's an enemy that seeks to kill what it can't control;
> It twists and turns, making mountains out of molehills.
> But I will call on the Lord who is worthy to be praised;
> I run to Him, and I am saved.
>
> > O outrageous grace...[33]

A few years ago, a very dear friend of mine came to me and bared his soul. He was being tormented by accusations from the enemy concerning his past life and unsure of his current standing before God. Added to that misery, he was suffering from a serious, debilitating illness.

We arranged to visit a close, mutual friend whose property happened to back onto a sizeable lake. When we got there, my friend wrote out a long list of sins, accusations and issues on several sheets of paper, and then the three of us entered the lake. He laid the papers on the lake bottom and placed a large stone on top of them. Then we baptized him in the Name of the Father and of the Son and of the Holy Spirit, and into the finished work of Christ at Calvary. I do not advocate this as a biblical norm (he had been baptized years before), but it certainly helped reinforce for him the awesome deliverance that Christ secured for us on the Cross.

The Bible also teaches that Jesus shared in our humanity "so that by his death he might destroy him who holds the power of death, that is, the devil, and free those who all their lives were held in slavery by their fear of death."[34] When it refers to Jesus *destroying* the devil, the original Greek word means *bring to naught* or *reduce to zero*.

I've told this story before, but it bears repeating. When my daughter Rachel was about six years old, she came home from school one day and, looking very serious, asked me, "Daddy, what does five naughts and three naughts add up to?" (Naughts are British terminology for zeros.) Naturally I replied, "Nothing." "But Daddy," she remonstrated, "there's five of them and three of them; they must make something." "Sweetheart," I responded, "if there were five million of them and three million of them added together, there would still be nothing: just one big zero." She walked off, plainly unconvinced.

In the same way, some people (perhaps even some reading this page) still find it difficult to accept the fact that satan no longer has the power of death, and thus they keep on living in fear and torment. The devil will try to impress us with all of his "zeros" if he can, but the truth is: Jesus reduced him to *nothing*—and 8,000,000 zeros are still *nothing*. The truth sets us free, but only if we believe God's truth and reject satan's lies.

The apostle John reaffirms this truth in Revelation where he records a stunning encounter with Jesus. After one look at the risen and glorified Lord, John collapses to the ground like a dead man. Then Jesus places His right hand on him and speaks words of personal reassurance and ultimate triumph:

Do not be afraid. I am the First and the Last. I am the Living One; I was dead, and behold I am alive for ever and ever! And I hold the keys of death and Hades.[35]

Through His death, Jesus not only reduced satan to zero, He also took back the keys of death and Hades that satan had acquired when Adam sinned. This was a spiritual victory of cosmic proportions, but it has a very practical and personal application to each one of us. We are no longer at the mercy of the devil throughout life and, with Jesus holding those keys, we are absolutely secure in regard to the circumstances surrounding death. Chance, statistics, the actions of others, the efforts of the enemy—all are of no account. *He alone* holds the keys.

LIFE IN THE SPIRIT

From conception to resurrection, Jesus' life on earth was lived in the enabling, guiding and empowering hands of the Holy Spirit. The scope of the Spirit's involvement is found throughout the Gospels:

- Jesus was conceived by the Holy Spirit (Matthew 1:20).
- The Spirit descended on Him like a dove at His baptism (Matthew 3:16).
- Jesus was led by the Spirit (Matthew 4:1).
- He ministered in the power of the Spirit (Luke 4:14).
- He drove out demons by the Spirit (Matthew 12:28).
- He was full of joy through the Holy Spirit (Luke 10:21).
- God gave Him the Spirit without limit (John 3:34).
- Jesus was anointed by the Holy Spirit to preach good news to the poor, to proclaim freedom for the prisoners, recovery of sight for the blind, release for the oppressed, and to proclaim the year of the Lord's favor (Luke 4:18-19).

Even at Calvary, it was through the *Eternal Spirit* that Jesus offered Himself to God as an unblemished sacrifice.[36] It was also through the Holy Spirit that Jesus was raised from the dead.[37]

Someone has described this all-encompassing involvement of the Holy Spirit in these terms: *All that Jesus ever did, He never did!*

This way of life is precisely what Jesus has in mind for us. He wants us to live by what God says; to bring Him pleasure by our obedience; to reject the good ideas of our own invention; and to live through Him by the Spirit.

Before Jesus left this earth, He appeared to His disciples and said to them, "Peace be with you! As the Father has sent me, I am sending you." After that He breathed on them and said, "Receive the Holy Spirit."[38] Whether it's the disciples in the first century or those of us living in the 21st, Jesus wants His followers to be filled with the Spirit, to walk in the Spirit, to be led by the Spirit, to produce the fruit of the Spirit, and to edify the Church through the gifts of the Spirit.

THE NEW CREATION

Jesus of Nazareth not only lived a perfect life Himself, He also inaugurated a new humanity on earth! This was fundamental to reversing the curse of Eden. Here is how the apostle Paul describes it to the Corinthians:

So it is written: "The first man Adam became a living being"; the last Adam, a life-giving spirit. The first man was of the dust of the earth, the second man from heaven. As was the earthly man, so are those who are of the earth; and as is the man from heaven, so also are those who are of heaven. And just as we have borne the likeness of the earthly man, so shall we bear the likeness of the man from heaven.[39]

Jesus, the "last Adam," is also referred to as the *firstborn* from among the dead and the *firstborn* among many brothers.[40] In some amazing yet real way, we who are in Christ were joined with Him in His death and resurrection:[41]

We were therefore buried with him through baptism into death...If we have been united with him like this in his death, we will certainly also be united with him in his resurrection. For we know that our old self was crucified with him...[42]

In one form or another, death is unavoidable: "in Adam, all die."[43] That means every unrepentant sinner is in the same predicament as the convicted murderer on death row. Both are awaiting execution—the day of their death; both are "dead men walking." But the same Scripture just quoted goes on to say that in Christ we are made alive. And in Paul's second letter to the Corinthians, we find this wonderful promise: "Therefore, if anyone is in Christ, he is a new creation; the old has gone, the new has come!"[44]

Paul is careful to hold up the centrality of the Cross in regard to the new creation:

> May I never boast except in the cross of our Lord Jesus Christ, through which the world has been crucified to me, and I to the world. Neither circumcision nor uncircumcision means anything; what counts is a new creation.[45]

The perfect Man, Jesus of Nazareth, indeed inaugurated a new humanity on the earth and (praise God) we're included. I want to close this chapter by summarizing a few of these key truths in the form of declarations:

- We are the new creation who have been reborn, who derive our life and sustenance from Jesus (the real Tree of Life), and whose desire is to refrain at all times and in every situation from eating of the tree of self-knowledge.

- We are the family of God who have the Spirit of adoption, by whom we cry Abba, Father.

- We are the Body of Christ through whom He loves the world, through whom He shines, and through whom He expresses His manifold wisdom.

- We are the holy dwelling place of God by the Spirit.

- We are the people who, according to His eternal purposes, are destined to live to the praise of His glory!

ENDNOTES

1. Matthew 2:2.
2. John 1:5.

3. Peter Lewis, *The Glory of Christ* (London: Hodder, Stoughton, 1992), 232.

4. Wayne Grudem, *Systematic Theology* (Leicester, England: Inter-Varsity Press, 1994), 515.

5. Numbers 25:10-13.

6. Psalm 89:28.

7. Deuteronomy 8:3 (emphasis added).

8. Matthew 4:3.

9. Isaiah 50:4-5.

10. John 8:28.

11. John 5:19,30; 14:24.

12. Hebrews 1:2-3.

13. Colossians 1:16-17.

14. Matthew 8:20.

15. John 4:34.

16. John 15:4-5.

17. 1 Samuel 15.

18. Isaiah 11:1-3.

19. John 5:30 (New International Version).

20. John 5:30 (New American Standard Bible).

21. John 5:30 (The Living Bible).

22. Luke 2:49.

23. Psalm 40:7-8.

24. John 8:29.

25. Luke 3:22.

26. John 17:4.

27. Both Matthew and Mark report that He cried out with a loud voice before He gave up His spirit, while John's Gospel records the words of His shout.

28. John 19:30.

29. Hebrews 10:20.

30. Adam Clark, *Commentary* (London: Thomas Tegg & Son, 1836), 676.

31. Matthew Henry, *Commentary on the Whole Bible* (Grand Rapids, Michigan: Zondervan, 1961), 1621-1622 (emphasis in original).

32. Colossians 2:13-14.

33. "Outrageous Grace" written by Godfrey Birtill, available on One Voice from Grapevine 2000 Worship Celebration in Lincolnshire, England; *Kingsway* label.

34. Hebrews 2:14-15.

35. Revelation 1:17-18.

36. Hebrews 9:14.

37. Romans 8:11.

38. John 20:21-22.

39. 1 Corinthians 15:45, 47-49.

40. Colossians 1:18, Romans 8:29.

41. This isn't a type of time travel; it's the miraculous act of a sovereign God who transcends time and space.

42. Romans 6:4-6.

43. 1 Corinthians 15:22.

44. 2 Corinthians 5:17.

45. Galatians 6:14-15.

EIGHT

The Son of Man Ascends to the Ancient of Days

He hath left with us the earnest of the Spirit, and taken from us the earnest of our flesh, which he hath carried into heaven as a pledge that the whole shall follow after.
            —Tertullian

Many years ago I had the privilege of getting to know Sir John Hamilton who formerly served as Commander in Chief of British Naval Forces in the Mediterranean, as well as Commander in Chief of NATO Naval Forces in the Mediterranean. He had been born again while stationed in Malta, and would testify unashamedly of his personal faith in Christ.

Sir John told me of an amusing incident involving an exchange of letters between the *C in C* (Commander in Chief) of NATO Naval Forces and the *C in C* of British Naval Forces—who were, at that time, one and the same person: himself. In his role within NATO he wrote a very terse letter to himself as *C in C* of British Naval Forces, complaining of Britain's small contribution. He also asked that his letter requesting a greater financial commitment from Britain should be passed on to the British Minister of Defense. The strange thing is, it worked!

While we are familiar with the concept of "wearing two different hats," the incident involving Sir John Hamilton is somewhat unusual. What is far more unusual and difficult to grasp is the dual nature of Christ, who is both Son of God and Son of Man. People have struggled to understand this truth for centuries. The difficulty is, we have no real point of reference or comparison when it comes to a Person who is both human and divine; it defies human logic.

CHRIST'S PERMANENT HUMANITY

One of the key premises of this book is the full and permanent humanity of Jesus Christ. We need to remember that it was the human body of Jesus that was resurrected on the third day (His Spirit of course being eternal and not subject to death). After His resurrection, Jesus made a point of showing the disciples that His body was real, even though in His transformed state He could walk through walls. He ate some fish in their presence and invited Thomas to feel His wounds.[1] And it was in His resurrected body that Jesus ascended into Heaven.

When Jesus came to earth to put on humanity, it was not just a 33-year "project." His humanity was to be a permanent state. Think of it! Jesus chose to be "one of us" forever: humanity linked inseparably with Deity. In speaking of the incarnation, the writer to the Hebrews quotes a prophetic psalm of David:

> Therefore, when Christ came into the world, he said:
> "Sacrifice and offering you did not desire,
> but a body you prepared for me…"[2]

The truth about Christ's nature came under attack soon after the birth of the New Testament Church, which led church leaders to deal with the subject in the form of apostolic letters[3] and official statements of faith. In A.D. 451 the *Council of Chalcedon* declared Christ "to be acknowledged in two natures, inconfusedly, unchangeably, indivisibly, inseparably; the distinction of the natures being in no wise taken away by the union, but rather the property of each nature being preserved and concurring in one Person…"

The *Westminster Confession of Faith*, completed in 1646, used different words but carried the same message:

So that two whole, perfect and distinct natures, the Godhead and the manhood were inseparably joined together in one Person, without conversion, composition or confusion. Which Person is very God and very man, yet one Christ the only Mediator between God and man.

While these Councils stated the faith of the church regarding the Person of Christ, they did not attempt to explain the mystery involved. (They wisely recognized that some things in God are beyond human understanding.) But one distinction has always been clear: the eternal Son of God took upon Himself our humanity; it was *not* the case of a man acquiring divinity.[4]

When God became man, the two natures became *inseparably* joined—an aspect of the incarnation that is perhaps the least understood. We can picture Jesus while He lived on earth because He looked like an ordinary man.[5] But how do we picture Him in heaven? And how can we really grasp that He is there—right now—as both God and man? Hymn writer Christopher Wordsworth touched on this theme many years ago when he wrote:

> He has raised our human nature
> In the clouds to God's right hand;
> There we sit in heavenly places,
> There with Him in glory stand:
> Jesus reigns, adored by angels;
> Man with God is on the throne;
> Mighty Lord in thine ascension,
> We by faith behold our own.

THE VICTORY OF THE CROSS

To most onlookers in the first century, a crucifixion represented ultimate defeat. It was a form of torture reserved for the worst and the lowest: a man was beaten, stripped bare and nailed to a wooden frame, there to hang in humiliation and agony until he died of blood loss, shock and exhaustion. Why then does the Scripture speak of the *victory* of the Cross? What does the apostle Paul mean when he speaks of Jesus conquering and humiliating evil spirits *by the Cross*?

> And having disarmed the powers and authorities, he made a public spectacle of them, triumphing over them by the Cross.[6]

We can read about the observable events that accompanied His death—the darkening of the sun, the earthquake, the temple curtain tearing in two—as well as the awestruck response of the Roman centurion who witnessed it all. But what was going on in the spiritual realm? What happened after Jesus took His last breath on the Cross?

Some people suppose that Jesus' Spirit somehow remained with His deceased body on the Cross and in the tomb until the resurrection on the third day. But that cannot be true because He said to one of the thieves on the Cross next to Him, "I tell you the truth, today you will be with me in paradise."[7]

What did He mean by paradise?

In Jesus' parable of the rich man and Lazarus,[8] the rich man is buried and finds himself in hell (or *hades*, to use the Greek term) where he is in torment. Lazarus, on the other hand, is carried by the angels to Abraham's side. We learn from the story that Lazarus, though "far away," was visible to the rich man, and that between them existed a great divide—a divide that Abraham declares could not be bridged by either side: no one could cross over. (It is interesting that the term Jesus uses is not *ascend* or *descend* but *cross over*, which suggests a type of horizontal parity.)

The late Geoffrey King, former Baptist minister at East London Tabernacle, offered some helpful insights on this subject. He taught that the word *hell* or *hades* simply means "the underworld" or "covered-over place." The word *hell* was used in medieval England to mean "covered over," and men who thatched roofs with straw were known as *hellyers*.[9] In Jesus' parable, *hell* simply referred to the temporary abode of the dead: one part was a place of torment; the other was Abraham's bosom where the righteous (like Lazarus) were "comforted." The former was a precursor to *Gehenna*, "the eternal fire prepared for the devil and his angels";[10] the latter, a place of rest and comfort—a *paradise* that would one day be relocated to a place of ultimate glory, "the paradise of God."[11]

It is my conviction that the moment Jesus' body expired and He released His Spirit to the Father, the effects of His victorious death burst upon the unseen world like exploding fireworks: darkness was overwhelmed by a shower of dazzling light. His death was agonizingly slow, but His victory swift. The events (at least from our perspective) unfolded in consecutive order, but they all happened so fast it would have appeared that the steps of conquest were simultaneous.[12]

We read earlier in Hebrews 2:14 that satan held the power of death—metaphorically, the *keys of death and hades*. (That may explain why the witch of Endor, at King Saul's request, was able to bring up Samuel from the dead.[13]) Of course, satan's authority over death, like everything else, was still subject to God's ultimate sovereignty.

Continuing with the *keys* metaphor, we now see Jesus approaching satan, the "jailer of hades," who is, at this point, whimpering and cowering from Christ's presence. Jesus, the Son of Man and the Son of God, binds satan (that is, binds his authority to exercise legal control over mankind)[14] and repossesses the keys of death and hades.[15] The head of the serpent surely is being crushed!

Jesus then visits hades and proclaims that He is the new prison governor.[16] To those in paradise—Abraham and all the others who had died in faith—He brings the good news that they are free.[17] This news is literally earthshaking: the rocks split, tombs break open and the bodies of many Old Covenant saints are raised to life.[18] The Cross, once symbolic of utter defeat and dishonor, suddenly represents ultimate victory and glory.

Everything is now ready and waiting for the legal transfer of paradise from hades to Heaven (or, as someone aptly described it, paradise transferred to better quarters). All that remains is for Jesus to make an open display of His victory. This meant rising from the dead and rolling back the stone, then releasing the saints who had been raised from their graves—and allowing them one last tour of Jerusalem before taking them along on His return to Heaven. Matthew records that these risen saints "went into the holy city and appeared to many people."[19]

The display of satan's defeat was evident not only to the spiritual world, but also to the eyes of many who lived in and around Jerusalem: Roman guards at the tomb, Mary Magdalene, the Twelve, over 500 disciples at once,[20] and all those to whom the risen Old Covenant saints appeared. During the 40 days between His resurrection and ascension, Jesus also gave many last minute instructions to His apostles on matters concerning the Kingdom of God.[21]

THE SCENE IN HEAVEN

Whenever Heaven is described in the Bible, the writers use vivid imagery, metaphors and poetry. It plainly would be futile to depict Heaven using straightforward, didactic prose (as we might find, for example, in a book on systematic theology) because we wouldn't understand it: our earthbound minds would have no point of reference. So, in the description that follows, I trust you will allow me some "poetic license" as I draw on experience and imagination to help portray the celebration in Heaven triggered by these events on earth.

I remember one Christmas Eve when my four-year-old grandson was so ecstatic with anticipation that he couldn't refrain from hopping about the room. His mother finally said, "Sam, for goodness sake, stop jumping up and down." He replied, "I can't help it, Mom, I'm too excited to stay still!" That's how it must have been for the entire heavenly host when Jesus accomplished His great victory and prepared to return to Heaven: they were beside themselves with excitement and anticipation. (If there is rejoicing in Heaven over one sinner who repents,[22] can you imagine the elation over Christ's ascension?)

The headlines in the Heavenly Herald (if there were such a publication) would have read: *ALL AUTHORITY IN HEAVEN AND EARTH GIVEN TO CHRIST.* And in letters no less bold: *HE'S COMING BACK!* As news of the victory and the terrestrial "transfer of authority" spreads through Heaven, the thoughts of every living creature focus on one thing: the King of glory is returning!

Heaven is abuzz with excitement as final preparations are carefully reviewed for the homecoming of its conquering hero. The combined angelic choir has been practicing a special anthem that will be sung antiphonally. To start with, the choir will divide into two groups, with one meeting Jesus upon His arrival. These singers will escort Him along the celestial highway—renamed *The King's Highway*—and accompany Him right up to the gates through which He is to enter heavenly Jerusalem. The other group will wait in the city, but just *inside* the closed gates. But even before that, the moment Jesus breaks through the clouds, thousands of trumpeters will be on hand to herald their King.

As a former police officer in London, I have often witnessed the preparations that precede major events such as royal weddings or the trooping of the color. Military bands practice diligently for weeks, followed by a full dress rehearsal. Finally, the big day arrives, and the scene is truly magnificent: streets on the parade route festooned with flags, military uniforms neatly pressed, boots polished to a high gloss, every soldier immaculately turned out in ceremonial attire, and we as police officers outfitted in our special, formal uniforms.

We scan the crowds that have been gathering since 5 o'clock in the morning and those who camped out all night. Finally the procession begins. Every head is turned in the direction of the palace; necks are craned, multitudes are standing on tiptoe. Some faint, unable to contain themselves. Such drama, such anticipative joy: people gasp, others cheer; cries of "Isn't she lovely" are repeated throughout the crowd; some cannot keep back the tears.

Standing there holding back the crowds, I've seen it all before, yet I still feel my skin tingle and a shiver running down my spine. Royal horse-drawn carriages, tiara and diamond-adorned majesty, military precision and pageantry—all pass before your eyes, the dazzling sights and sounds engulf the emotions, extracting awe and wonder.

But all of this is a mere shadow compared to what happened on Ascension Day. On earth, the day seems to start like any other. Most of the world's inhabitants are oblivious to the events about to unfold and continue with their everyday business. The disciples know, but remain somewhat anxious as they cluster around Jesus on the Mount of Olives. (Some are still getting over the shock of the crucifixion and resurrection; others are grappling with lingering doubts.[23])

In Heaven, meanwhile, all preparations are complete. Celestial beings of every description are now in "standby" mode, awaiting the ascension and homecoming of their Lord. They know that Jesus will conclude His time on earth by instructing His disciples to go in the power of the Holy Spirit and make disciples of all nations. At last, Jesus begins His final words: "But you will receive power when the Holy Spirit comes on you; and you will be my witnesses in Jerusalem, and in all Judea and Samaria, and to the ends of the earth."[24]

"This is it! He's on His way!" echoes throughout Heaven. Back on the Mount of Olives, Jesus finishes speaking and is lifted up before their very eyes, a cloud hiding Him from their sight.[25] "He's gone," the disciples say to each other sadly, still staring at the cloud, hoping for one last glance. "Here He comes!" shout the sentinels in Heaven. The heralds wet their lips, take a deep breath and get ready to blow, while the angel choir members lift their heads, breathe in, and turn to face Christ's anticipated re-entry.

Unseen from earth (possibly hidden by the cloud), all those who had been in "Abraham's side"—the inhabitants of paradise—fall in behind Jesus, fulfilling a prophetic word from the Psalms that the apostle Paul applies to Christ's ascension: "When he ascended on high, he led captives in his train and gave gifts to men."[26]

There must have been millions of men, women and children. Abraham was among the throng, of course, as were other notables such as Isaac, Jacob, Joseph, Joshua, Rahab, Elisha, Samuel, David, Daniel and Ruth. But a special place of honor was reserved for certain other saints—most of them unrecognized—who had suffered for their faith. Here is how the writer to the Hebrews describes them:

> Some faced jeers and flogging, while still others were chained and put in prison. They were stoned; they were sawed in two; they were put to death by the sword. They went about in sheepskins and goatskins, destitute, persecuted and mistreated—the world was not worthy of them. They wandered in deserts and mountains, and in caves and holes in the ground.[27]

Missing from this great cavalcade were Moses and Elijah. Why? Because they never entered hades, but instead went straight to Heaven.[28] By no coincidence, it was Moses and Elijah who earlier had appeared with Jesus on the Mount of Transfiguration.[29]

But now, all attention is focused on the One leading the throng. Jesus of Nazareth, "very God and very man," pierces the cloud and ten thousand heralds blast forth their royal greeting. Accompanied by a multitude of musicians, the entire heavenly host breaks out in song: a *Hallelujah Chorus* that surpasses anything ever heard on earth. Jesus marches at the front of the assembly, singing with great joy and magnificent abandon.[30] What a sight to behold!

In no time at all, they arrive at the gates of the city of God, heavenly Jerusalem. Tens of thousands of voices sing out in perfect harmony, their exquisite sounds filling the whole of heaven. The entire escort choir, resplendent in white, addresses the gatekeepers:

> Lift up your heads, O you gates;
> be lifted up, you ancient doors,
> that the King of glory may come in.[31]

The choir in the city responds, "Who is this King of glory?"—a question to which all living beings in Heaven already know the answer, but it's an answer they just love to hear. In fact, they wouldn't find it the least bit boring or repetitive to hear the answer for the next thousand years. The first choir replies, their voices rising to a crescendo:

> The Lord strong and mighty,
> the Lord mighty in battle.
> Lift up your heads, O you gates;
> lift them up, you ancient doors,
> that the King of glory may come in.

The second choir asks again:

> Who is he, this King of glory?

Back comes the exultant answer:

> The Lord Almighty—
> he is the King of glory.[32]

At this point, the gates swing wide open and the King of glory enters. The angelic host is now caught up in pure, undiluted euphoria— happy spirits overcome with unspeakable delight at the sight of their King's return. And echoing over the city walls, then re-echoing through the sunlit mountains stretching out in every direction from the city, the sounds of celebration: songs, music, and the joyful shouts of multitudes.

Perhaps it was similar to what hymn writer Thomas Kelly saw and heard when he wrote:

> Look, ye saints, the sight is glorious:
> See the Man of Sorrows now;
> From the fight return victorious,
> Every knee to Him shall bow;
> Crown Him! Crown Him!
> Crowns become the Victor's brow.

> Hark, those bursts of acclamation!
> Hark, those loud triumphant chords!
> Jesus takes the highest station;
> O what joy the sight affords:
> Crown Him! Crown Him!
> "King of kings, and Lord of lords."

THE THRONE OF GOD

Jesus proceeds inexorably toward the heart of the city: the Most Holy Place, the Throne Room and the presence of His Father. As He once set His face toward Jerusalem and judgment, He now sets His face toward the throne, coming as the Lamb of God who takes away the sin of the world, and as the conquering Lion of Judah ready to receive His coronation as King.

Words fail completely in painting a picture of the true likeness of God. Augustine posed the question *What is God like?* and answered thus: "Surely it is he who, when he is spoken of, cannot be spoken of; who, when he is considered of, cannot be considered of; who, when he is compared to anything, cannot be compared; and when he is defined, groweth greater and greater by defining of him."[33] Indeed, how can finite creatures describe infinite Deity? It would be like a cave man trying to describe a nuclear power station, only much more daunting a challenge.

The scene that awaits Jesus is absolutely awe-inspiring.[34] In fact, when Ezekiel saw it in a vision, he fell facedown and, for a week afterwards, simply sat overwhelmed.[35] The apostle John, during his revelation on the island of Patmos, also fell down, completely immobilized—as though dead.[36]

In the Most Holy Place, the seraphim and cherubim are stationed above and beneath the throne of God. The sapphire-like throne is flaming with fire, set on wheels that are also ablaze and can move in any direction.[37]

Seated on the throne is Almighty God, the Ancient of Days. His hair is white like wool and His clothing white as snow. From what appears to be His waist up, He looks like glowing metal; from there down He looks like fire. His eyes are like blazing fire and He is surrounded by brilliant light.[38] The train of His robe fills the temple, and a river of fire is seen flowing, coming out from before the throne.

Thousands upon thousands attend Him, and ten thousand times ten thousand stand before Him. The radiance around Him is like a rainbow shining in the clouds on a rainy day. Above the throne are the seraphs, each with six wings: with two they cover their faces, with two they cover their feet, and with two they fly.[39] They continually call to one another, "Holy, holy, holy is the Lord Almighty; the whole earth is full of his glory."

Beneath the throne move the cherubim, also referred to as the four living creatures. They appear like burning coals or lighted torches. Dazzling fire flashes back and forth among them, and they move with lightning speed.

Jesus, appearing as the Son of Man, enters the Throne Room and is led into the presence of His Father, the Ancient of Days. "You are my Son," declares the Ancient of Days, "today I have become your Father.[40] Ask of me, and I will make the nations your inheritance, the ends of the earth your possession. You will rule them with an iron scepter..."[41] Then the Father adds:

> "Sit at my right hand
> until I make your enemies
> a footstool for your feet."

> The Lord will extend your mighty scepter from Zion;
> you will rule in the midst of your enemies.

> Your troops will be willing
> on your day of battle.
> Arrayed in holy majesty,
> from the womb of the dawn
> you will receive the dew of your youth.[42]

Then, with great joy and pleasure—and to the loud acclamation of the entire host of Heaven—the Father formally gives all authority to His Son. Here is how the scene is described in Daniel's prophetic vision:

> In my vision at night I looked, and there before me was one like a son of man, coming with the clouds of heaven. He approached the Ancient of Days and was led into his presence. He was given authority, glory and sovereign power; all peoples, nations and men of every language worshiped

him. His dominion is an everlasting dominion that will not pass away, and his kingdom is one that will never be destroyed.[43]

It's not too difficult to imagine the response in Heaven to the announcement of Christ's exaltation: unrestrained jubilation that seemed to go on and on. But if Heaven's inhabitants thought the celebrations ended there, they were in for a surprise. There is a further dimension to Daniel's revelation: the Son intends to *share* His Kingdom with the "royal family"—His redeemed brothers and sisters:

But the saints of the Most High will receive the kingdom and will possess it forever—yes, for ever and ever.[44]

The subject of that amazing revelation (and how it is worked out practically) will be explored in the next chapter. But before we conclude this section, let us review eight glorious outcomes of the ascension of Jesus Christ:

- First, God the Father declares Jesus to be His Son.

- Second, the Father offers Him the nations of the earth.

- Third, He invites Jesus to take His place on the throne at His right hand.

- Fourth, He promises to make Christ's enemies a footstool for His feet.

- Fifth, He promises that Christ's mighty scepter will be extended out from Zion.

- Sixth, He declares that the soldiers of Jesus will be willing on the day of the Lord's battle.

- Seventh, He announces that we, His saints, will participate in government with Jesus.

- Eighth, He proclaims that His Kingdom is an everlasting kingdom that will never be destroyed.

This promise of sharing with Christ in His rule and reign is exciting for us to consider. But it is essential that we appreciate the glory and majesty of our Lord Jesus Christ—and all that He accomplished on the Cross, in hades, and in Heaven—before we focus on His power at work in us. We exist for *Him*, not the other way around.

And ultimately He will receive *all* the glory and honor because He alone is worthy; He is our Source, our victory, our joy. We close this chapter with a stanza from one of Charles Wesley's hymns that summarizes Christ's victory and (in the third line) hints at the key for us as believers:

> Power is all to Jesus given,
> Power o'er hell and earth and heaven!
> Power He now to us imparts;
> Praise Him with believing hearts.

ENDNOTES

1. Luke 24:41-43, John 20:26-27.

2. Hebrews 10:5.

3. For example, the letters of 1st and 2nd John address the Gnostic heresies concerning Christ.

4. The bias of cults and *New Age* ideas, on the contrary, tends to the reverse: man becoming a god.

5. According to the prophetic description in Isaiah 53:2, there was "nothing in his appearance that we should desire him."

6. Colossians 2:15.

7. Luke 23:43.

8. Luke 16:19-31.

9. This term exists today as the surname *Hellyer*.

10. Matthew 25:41.

11. Revelation 2:7.

12. If man's supercomputers can now perform trillions of calculations per second, we could expect God's spiritual "program change" to be virtually instantaneous.

13. 1 Samuel 28:8-19. There are differing views on this passage, but I take the Scripture at face value when it says Samuel appeared and spoke a message of God's judgment to Saul.

14. Jesus previously taught this lesson in spiritual warfare: *how can anyone enter a strong man's house and carry off his possessions unless he first ties up the strong man?* (Matthew 12:29).

15. Revelation 1:18.

16. 1 Peter 3:19.

17. 1 Peter 4:6.

18. Matthew 27:51-52.

19. Matthew 27:53.

20. 1 Corinthians 15:5-6.

21. Acts 1:3.

22. Luke 15:10.

23. Matthew 28:17.

24. Acts 1:8.

25. Acts 1:9.

26. Ephesians 4:8; Psalm 68:18.

27. Hebrews 11:36-38.

28. Scripture tells us that God Himself buried Moses and that no one knows where his grave is (Deuteronomy 34:6); also that satan and the archangel Michael disputed over Moses' body (Jude 9). Elijah went directly to heaven in a whirlwind (2 Kings 2:11). The only other person under the Old Covenant apparently privileged to bypass hades was Enoch (Genesis 5:24).

29. Matthew 17:1-8.

30. Hebrews 2:12.

31. Psalm 24:7.

32. Psalm 24:8-10.

33. Augustine, quoted in *The Works of Thomas Brooks, Vol. 1* (Edinburgh: Banner of Truth, 1980), 419.

34. These descriptions of the Throne Room of God are taken from Isaiah 6, Ezekiel 1, Daniel 7 and Revelation 1.

35. Ezekiel 1:28, 3:15.

36. Revelation 1:17.

37. Symbolic of the omnipresence of God.

38. With reference to *light* and *fire* and *white*, note 1 John 1:5: "God is light; in him there is no darkness at all."

39. It appears that seraphs were not permitted to look directly at God.

40. A messianic prophecy from Psalm 2:7 quoted in Hebrews 1:5 and 5:5. Even as the eternal Son of God, Jesus entered a new dimension of sonship through the incarnation. Thus He "was declared with power to be the Son of God by his resurrection from the dead" (Romans 1:4).

41. Psalm 2:7-9.

42. Psalm 110:1-3.
43. Daniel 7:13-14.
44. Daniel 7:18. See also verse 27.

NINE

THE POWER OF A SHARED LIFE

I can honestly say that I had never once heard from the lips of men the message that came to me then...But God that night simply focused upon me the Bible message of Christ Who is our life...The Lord seemed to make plain to me that night, through my tears of bitterness: "You see, for seven years, with utmost sincerity, you have been trying to live for Me, on My behalf, the life that I have been waiting for seven years to live through you."
—Major W. Ian Thomas[1]

With the end of Jesus' physical life on earth came a series of events that would revolutionize the created order for all time and eternity. Nothing would ever be the same. By His sacrificial death, Jesus not only paid for man's sin but also conquered satan. Through His resurrection, He displayed the enemy's defeat and opened Heaven to both Old and New Covenant saints; and when He ascended to the throne of His Father, He received all authority in Heaven and on earth.

These "seismic" events came as a shockwave to the spiritual world—as well as to the disciples on earth who gradually learned what was going on. But something equally unexpected was to follow: Christ chose to share the Kingdom of God, including its power and authority, with His followers. They were to be His fellow workers, His representatives on earth: "As the Father has sent me," says Jesus, "I am sending you."[2]

If we had been eyewitnesses at this commissioning, we probably would have held out little hope for its success. The majority of the disciples were fishermen who were lacking in education, wealth and social standing. And none had a great track record: all had abandoned Jesus when He was arrested; the leader among them, Peter, denied Him with oaths and curses; and they repeatedly argued about who among them was the greatest. They were, at times, naïve, dull, carnal, arrogant, and even used by satan; they also faltered in times of crisis, unable to stay awake one hour when Jesus asked for their prayer support in Gethsemane.[3]

Apart from the dubious qualifications of the Twelve to represent God's Kingdom, the failings of Old Testament patriarchs like Abraham would have also raised concerns about entrusting anything important to man (that is, if normal human judgment were applied). If Father Abraham failed, what chance did anyone have? Yet the disciples, despite their spotty track record and major character flaws—and in the face of fierce opposition from both Jewish and Roman authorities—somehow managed to start a spiritual revolution that would change history! As testimony to that, the world's main calendar eventually was changed to reflect the birth of Christ—a fact we were reminded of repeatedly in the months leading up to the year 2000.[4]

What was the key to their improbable success? The Gospel of John records that after commissioning the disciples, Jesus breathed on them and said, "Receive the Holy Spirit."[5] He had spoken earlier to them about the Spirit, saying, "But you know him, for he lives *with* you and will be in you."[6] A critically important shift was about to take place in the very core of their being.

As we noted previously, "everything Jesus did, He never did." In other words, He did not act on His own initiative or do things in His own strength. He was sent to do the will of the Father *by* the Spirit and *in* the Spirit. And now He says to the disciples, "As the Father has sent me, I am sending you."

The Father didn't send Jesus to this earth to try to figure things out on His own and then do His best. Neither does Jesus commission His disciples that way. The Kingdom of God has nothing to do with people implementing their own good ideas, but everything to do with the will of God being done "on earth as it is in heaven."[7] The *way* of doing God's will was modeled perfectly by our Lord Jesus

Christ, who knew the secret and the power of the shared life: life in the Spirit. This is to be our way of living, our modus operandi for every area of life.

THE "BURDEN" OF PRAYER

Let's take the matter of prayer. No one can deny that Christians are commanded to pray, but for many, the mandate to pray has become a heavy burden of guilt. We tend to think that we pray too little, too late, and probably about the wrong things. (All of which may be correct, but it's not the whole picture.)

Adding to this burden may be messages from books, articles and the pulpit admonishing us to "pray without ceasing," to "watch and pray," and to "stand in the gap" as intercessors. The last phrase is taken from the book of Ezekiel where God says:

> I looked for a man among them who would build up the
> wall and stand before me in the gap on behalf of the land
> so I would not have to destroy it, but I found none.[8]

I must confess that the thought of the Almighty searching for one person to stand in the gap has made *me* feel miserable, because I for one have not prayed consistently. Then, in my attempt to turn from this "dereliction of duty," I redouble my efforts to be more faithful and disciplined, but in so doing, discover I am picking up a responsibility that is not from God: an "illegal" burden, one that is labeled *it all depends on me*.

If failure to pray consistently leads to guilt, you would expect diligence in this area to bring grace and freedom. The problem is: if I pray out of a sense of duty and actually succeed in achieving my goals, my effort can easily lead to pride. And pride is more than an attitude problem. Scripture says, "God opposes the proud, but gives grace to the humble."[9] I could be highly disciplined and fervent in prayer—yet totally ineffective because God was opposing me due to pride. Thankfully, our guilt-driven, human efforts at prayer are usually unsustainable.

How then do we move beyond a call-to-duty motivation in prayer, to one where we talk to our God with a delightful sense of privilege and shared responsibility? And how do we grow in our prayer life to where we "pray in the Spirit on all occasions with all kinds of prayers and requests"?[10]

WHO STANDS IN THE GAP?

There are many outstanding examples of prayer warriors in the Bible. One is Abraham who, out of concern for his nephew Lot, interceded on behalf of Sodom and Gomorrah, "standing in the gap" between God's righteousness and man's evil, between the Lord's wrath and humanity's deserved judgment. Abraham's role was prophetic and priestly, yet, as we have seen in Scripture, he failed many times as a man.

Today we live in the New Covenant, and the gap is filled, not by imperfect men like Abraham, Moses, David, the Twelve or even us, but by One who will never fail. This is the *only* One who could stand in the gap: the "one mediator between God and men, the man Christ Jesus,"[11] the high priest who "always lives to intercede" for us.[12] The good news is: God has found His man, and it is none other than His own beloved Son!

When we look at another kind of gap, the difference between what we believe and what we actually do, we are confronted with the inadequacy of our performance in every area of life. The Scriptures tell us "there is but one God, the Father, from whom all things came and for whom we live,"[13] and our heart responds with an *Amen,* but our memory reminds us that we *don't* in fact always live for Him. The Scripture just quoted is, without question, theologically correct, but how can it be true in daily life? It seems impossible. But if we finish the verse, we will see that what is impossible with man is gloriously possible with God. Here is how it continues (with emphasis on the last phrase): "...and there is but one Lord, Jesus Christ, through whom all things came and *through whom we live.*"

Think of it: When we live through Him, we are more than conquerors through Him, we resist the devil through Him, and we can face poverty or weakness because we can do all things through Christ who strengthens us. *Everything* is in the Triune God: the love of Christ, the joy of the Lord, the peace of God, the gifts of the Spirit, the armor of God, the sword of the Spirit and the fruit of the Spirit.

A NEW BURDEN

Christ actually invites us to share His life so that we can participate in what He is doing. He refers to us as *fellow workers*,[14] that is, those who work *with* the Lord rather than just *for* the Lord. As we do so, the burden we carry is His burden, and the yoke we bear is His yoke. (The *yoke* metaphor is of a team of oxen working together.) Here is how Jesus issues His invitation to us:

> "Come to me, all you who are weary and burdened, and I will give you rest. Take my yoke upon you and learn from me, for I am gentle and humble in heart, and you will find rest for your souls. For my yoke is easy and my burden is light."[15]

Perhaps we have the idea that *other* burdens—the kind we pray about—can be shared with the Lord, but that praying itself is *our* part. But Jesus does not distinguish between types of burdens. The fact is, laboring in prayer for others is both our mandate and our burden, and He invites us to share it with Him. Here is how James Torrence writes about the burden of prayer:

> The God to whom we pray and with whom we commune knows we want to pray, try to pray, but cannot pray. So God comes to us as man in Christ Jesus to stand in for us, pray for us, teaches us to pray and lead our prayers. God in grace gives us what He seeks from us—a life of prayer—in giving us Jesus Christ and the Spirit. So Christ is very God, the God to whom we pray. And He is very man, the man who prays for us and with us.[16]

A NEW PROVISION

As my divine Advocate, Christ takes even the weakest efforts and coldest thoughts we offer Him and transforms them into strong intercessions and inspired submissions. The same kind of transaction takes place when we share His praise life. Note the words of the writer to the Hebrews: *"Through Jesus, therefore*, let us continually offer to God a sacrifice of praise—the fruit of lips that confess his name."*[17] What a difference there is when we (all of us, including worship leaders) stop striving to produce the "perfect sound" or the "right feeling" on a Sunday morning, and simply draw near to our heavenly Leader of praise, the One who says:

> I will declare your name to my brothers;
> in the presence of the congregation I will sing your praises.[18]

Is there any place for passion? Yes—when it is *His* passion that motivates us. Is there any room for effort? Of course—so long as *He* is the One inspiring it. Otherwise our approach is no different (in principle) from the attempts of the prophets of Baal to call down fire. The account in 1 Kings presents a graphic picture of dedication and zeal that was completely misguided and futile:

> Then they called on the name of Baal from morning until noon...At noon Elijah began to taunt them. "Shout louder!" he said. "Surely he is a god! Perhaps he is deep in thought, or busy, or traveling. Maybe he is sleeping and must be awakened."
>
> So they shouted louder and slashed themselves with swords and spears, as was their custom, until their blood flowed. Midday passed, and they continued their frantic prophesying until the time for the evening sacrifice. But there was no response, no one answered, no one paid attention.[29]

Compare this frenzied behavior with that of Elijah, who simply repairs the altar of the Lord, cuts up the oxen, lays the pieces on the altar, drenches everything with water, and waits. Then he prays, noting that he had done all these things at God's command (i.e. not on his own initiative): "Answer me, O Lord, answer me, so these people will know that you, O Lord, are God, and that you are turning their hearts back again."[20] Then the fire of the Lord fell.

People these days may not cut themselves and shout for hours to try to gain the attention of their god, but in terms of our heart's attitude in prayer, do we more closely resemble Elijah or the prophets of Baal? Do we engage in spiritual disciplines—devotional schedules, fasting, good deeds—with the thought of earning "brownie points" with God in order that He will hear our prayers? We are indeed called to intercession (including fasting, as God leads), but it is to join Jesus in *His* intercessory ministry, and to do so in the power of the Holy Spirit:

> In the same way, the Spirit helps us in our weakness. We do not know what we ought to pray for, but the Spirit himself intercedes for us with groans that words cannot express.[21]

Isn't it reassuring to know that God not only understands our weakness, but also has made provision for it? In one of the accounts of King David's reign, we find a beautiful picture of such grace. David invites Mephibosheth, who was lame in both feet, to eat at the king's table—not just once, but every day: "So Mephibosheth ate at David's table like one of the king's sons."[22] We, though spiritually infirm, are likewise given a royal invitation: to be seated in heavenly places at the King's table, clothed in the robe of His righteousness, and encouraged to live and pray "in the Spirit." What a privilege! What a provision!

ALL THE TREASURES OF WISDOM AND KNOWLEDGE

In an observation as true today as the day it was written in the 18th century, William Law states, "Man needs to be saved from his own wisdom as much as he needs to be saved from his own righteousness, for they produce the same corruption." One of the more corrupt periods of Israel's history is recorded in the Book of Judges, where we find in the closing chapters a sordid tale of idolatry, rape, murder and injustice. The book closes with this telling phrase: *everyone did as he saw fit*, or more literally: *everyone did what was right in his own eyes.*[23]

The Book of Proverbs is well known for its wisdom as well as for its warnings against fools. One such warning states: "He who trusts in himself is a fool…"[24] Chapter 26 begins with ten proverbs about fools—how destructive they are, and how repetitive and repulsive their folly (e.g. "as a dog returns to its vomit"). But then the writer proceeds to make this astonishing declaration:

> Do you see a man wise in his own eyes?
> There is more hope for a fool than for him.[25]

When you take into account the various Scriptures about fools, and then consider that you're better off being a fool than being impressed by your own wisdom, it really makes you wonder! Why would the fool be better off in this comparison? Could it be that the pride and arrogance of being "wise in your own eyes" has more self-deception in it (and therefore is more resistant to change) than the destructiveness of folly?

That certainly seemed to be the case for those Jesus encountered during His earthly ministry. The tax collectors and sinners, who were regarded as fools by that society, came into the kingdom ahead of those who considered themselves wise. As Jesus said to the Pharisees, "If you were blind, you would not be guilty of sin; but now that you claim you can see, your guilt remains."[26]

But even when we are generally committed to "walk humbly with our God" and not "lean on our own understanding,"[27] we can still fall prey to the trap of drawing from our limited, human resources of wisdom. The example I will give is from my own experience, a story I have related before,[28] but one that is worth repeating. (It certainly made a lasting impression on me.)

A Christian medical doctor had become engaged to a man who was also a doctor—but he was a Hindu. Prior to her wedding day, she had talked him into becoming a Christian, but in her heart she knew his "conversion" was a farce. Soon after their marriage, she fell into a deep depression, and was brought to me for help.

I gave her all the verses imaginable to encourage her, especially those where God promised to forgive our sins when we confess them (e.g. 1 John 1:9). But she had already confessed her sins to God repeatedly, and nothing seemed to change.

A few months later, I saw her walk into our Sunday evening service, her countenance dark with depression, her eyes lifeless. Following the service I noticed she was being led by the arm in my direction. My heart sank. But I knew I couldn't turn her away, and ushered both her and her friend into my office. The friend explained that the next day, the doctor was scheduled to be admitted to our local psychiatric hospital for electric shock therapy. (This was the same hospital where her husband was a consultant psychiatrist.) Could I pray for her further to see if God might intervene?

Once again I resorted to the same Bible verses I had shared with her previously, but to no avail. Suddenly it dawned on me that I was relying on my own assessment of the problem and coming up with *my* choice of remedies. I immediately asked that we have a time of silent prayer—which gave me the opportunity to send an urgent "SOS" to the Lord. I was desperate. "Lord," I prayed, "forgive me for behaving independently. I've been leaning on my own understanding. For the sake of this poor lady, have mercy on her and on me."

Immediately the phrase *James 5* came to mind. But then I thought, *How can it be James 5? That has to do with being healed from sickness.* Again came the phrase *James 5,* but I continued to reason why it couldn't be healing when the real issue was *guilt.* (Of course, if I had taken the trouble to look up the Scripture, I would have noticed this prayer-of-faith *healing* passage ends with the sentence, "If he has sinned, he will be forgiven."[29])

Once more the words *James 5* came to mind. This time, faith entered my heart. I turned to the doctor and asked, "Do you believe that Jesus heals the sick?" Her answer, without speaking a word, was to get off her chair and kneel on the floor. The presence of God filled that little office; it was awesome.

Filled with faith, I laid hands on her head and prayed for healing. All I can say is that "I knew that I knew" God was healing her that very moment. She rose from the floor, her face radiant, her eyes no longer glazed and listless but sparkling with joy. It all happened in less than two minutes! My good ideas had failed miserably, only serving to prolong her suffering. But two minutes of "eating from the Tree of Life" and the result was a miracle.

The story doesn't end there. Upon arriving home, she was met at the door by her husband (the psychiatrist) who was absolutely astounded at the dramatic change in his wife's countenance. A few days later, he genuinely gave his life to Jesus, receiving Him as the only true and living Lord.

What a testimony to the treasures of wisdom and knowledge available to us in Christ! We have God's Word, which is "a lamp to my feet and a light for my path."[30] The promises in the Word of God are all "Yes" in Christ, and in Him we respond "Amen."[31] And we have Christ living in us in the Person of the Holy Spirit, the One whom Jesus promised would guide us into all truth.[32]

I can say without qualification that every time I have turned from my own good ideas or solutions and called on His Name, He has given me wisdom and knowledge. It may even be for an issue outside of my awareness. Once during a pre-service prayer time, it came to my mind to pray for another church in our city. The following Sunday the same thought again came to mind; both times I obeyed the prompts. Shortly thereafter, a man who was present in those meetings was relating to his Christian boss the fact that I had prayed for his church. The man seemed quite taken aback, and replied, "You tell your pastor to keep on praying; we're in the middle of a major church split, and we need all the prayers we can get."

We can declare with the apostle Paul, "...Christ lives in me. The life I live in the body, I live by faith in the Son of God..."[33] "...namely, Christ, in whom are hidden *all the treasures of wisdom and knowledge.*"[34]

ALL AUTHORITY IN HEAVEN AND EARTH

I vividly recall my first real experience of authority as a police officer. It was customary at that time in England for police officers to be asked by children, the elderly and the physically disabled for assistance in crossing busy streets. That day I was walking the beat at Holloway Road, a bustling access route for large transport trucks en route to the London markets, when a child came up to me and requested my help in seeing her across the road.

Here was my big moment. I found a suitable gap in the traffic, took one step onto the road, pointed to a fearsome-sized truck and held up my hand, signaling it to stop. To my great relief, the driver applied the brakes and the truck shuddered to a halt. I cannot describe the rush of adrenaline that coursed through my nervous system.

A few weeks earlier, I had taken the oath of allegiance to Her Majesty the Queen as an officer invested with her authority to serve her subjects within the London Metropolitan Police District. Now, for the first time, I was putting that authority to good use. When I raised my hand to stop the truck, I wasn't just representing myself. Behind that hand stood the entire Metropolitan Police Force, and ultimately the British Army, Navy and Air Force, the Prime Minister and his cabinet, the whole of Parliament, and Her Majesty the Queen, sitting on her throne with the crown on her head and the scepter in her hand.[35]

But there is a truth much more wonderful and awesome than that. Living inside me is One who has *all* authority in every place, be it London, the UK, the whole of Europe, North America, every continent on this earth, every planet, every galaxy, the entire universe. He has complete authority in every spiritual realm as well. There is nothing anywhere, in any shape or form, seen or unseen, that is not included in His realm of authority.

The fact that His authority is often unrecognized doesn't change the fact of its reality. Much of God's Kingdom is hidden from earthly view (probably in part to keep our free will from being overwhelmed), but the biblical record clearly demonstrates God's sovereignty over things large and small. Jesus declared that not one sparrow falls to the ground apart from the will of the Father, and that the very hairs of our head are all numbered.[36] At the other end of the scale, Isaiah says that from God's perspective, the nations are like a drop in a bucket and regarded as less than nothing.[37]

Man tends to be impressed with the trappings of earthly power, but the kingdoms of man all come and go: the Roman Empire, the Third Reich, the British Empire,[38] the former USSR—to name but a few. During their ascendancy, kingdoms and superpowers seem invincible, but eventually they fall when God decides it's time for judgment.[39]

As the Son of Man, Jesus knew His destiny. From childhood He had read Scriptures like Psalm 2, where the Father says to the Son, "Ask of me, and I will make the nations your inheritance..." Thus He could say to those who challenged His authority:

> "...the Son gives life to whom he is pleased to give it. Moreover, the Father judges no one, but has entrusted all judgment to the Son, that all may honor the Son just as they honor the Father."[40]

The nations may not know it, but their Supreme Judge and true Head of State is none other than the Lord Jesus Christ, who holds all authority in Heaven and on earth. He is the One who ultimately determines what will be permitted, how things will happen, who is judged and when such judgment will take place.[41] And our lives are bound together with His. Paul writes to the Ephesians that "God raised us up with Christ and seated us with him in the heavenly realms in Christ Jesus..."[42] We're with Him and He is in us.

This revelation of the shared life so obsessed the mind of the apostle Paul that he could say without exaggeration, "For to me, to live is Christ and to die is gain."[43] The power of this spiritual bond is such that no person or circumstance can ever come between the Lord and us. We are truly inseparable—as we see in this concluding Scripture passage:

> Who shall separate us from the love of Christ? Shall trouble or hardship or persecution or famine or nakedness or danger or sword? As it is written, "For your sake we face death all day long; we are considered as sheep to be slaughtered."
>
> No, in all these things we are more than conquerors through him who loved us. For I am convinced that neither death nor life, neither angels nor demons, neither the present nor the future, nor any powers, neither height nor depth, nor anything else in all creation, will be able to separate us from the love of God that is in Christ Jesus our Lord.[44]

ENDNOTES

1. Major W. Ian Thomas, *The Saving Life of Christ* (Grand Rapids, Michigan: Zondervan, 1961), 8.

2. John 20:21.

3. Earlier, when the Twelve were sent out to preach the gospel of the Kingdom, Jesus had said, "He who receives you receives me..." (Matthew 10:40). That raises a searching question: would *we* have received those messengers despite their obvious flaws? (The Twelve included Judas Iscariot at that time.) Character is important, but so is our willingness to receive the messages and the messengers God sends.

4. Worldwide fears of the "Y2K bug" led to many reminders of the origin of our dating system, which begins with the estimated birth-year of Christ.

5. John 20:22.

6. John 14:17 (emphasis added).

7. Matthew 6:10.

8. Ezekiel 22:30.

9. James 4:6.

10. Ephesians 6:18.

11. 1 Timothy 2:5.

12. Hebrews 7:25.

13. 1 Corinthians 8:6.

14. 1 Corinthians 3:9.

15. Matthew 11:28-29.

16. James Torrence, *Worship, Community and the Triune God of Grace* (Downers Grove, Illinois: InterVarsity Press, 1996), 64.

17. Hebrews 13:15 (emphasis added).

18. Hebrews 2:12.

19. 1 Kings 18:26-29.

20. 1 Kings 18:37.

21. Romans 8:26.

22. 2 Samuel 9:11.

23. Judges 21:25 NIV and NASB respectively.

24. Proverbs 28:26.

25. Proverbs 26:12.

26. John 9:41.

27. Micah 6:8; Proverbs 3:5.

28. Previously recounted in my book *A Guide to Practical Pastoring* (Eastbourne: Kingsway Publications, 1993), 170.

29. James 5:15.

30. Psalm 119:105.

31. 2 Corinthians 1:20.

32. John 16:13.

33. Galatians 2:20.

34. Colossians 2:2-3 (emphasis added).

35. Paul in Romans 13 takes it one step further by noting that these authorities are instituted by God.

36. Matthew 10:29-30.

37. Isaiah 40:15,17.

38. The British Commonwealth still exists, of course, but not the Empire on which the sun would never set.

39. The timing of such judgment is hidden in God's divine understanding, but we see a reference to the Lord's multi-generational

timetable in a phrase He spoke while establishing His covenant with Abraham: "In the fourth generation your descendants will come back here, for the sin of the Amorites has not yet reached its full measure" (Genesis 15:16). We have no way of knowing what constitutes a "full measure of sin" in a given situation; we simply are told that God makes those determinations.

40. John 5:21-23.

41. In biblical history, God often used ungodly men and unrighteous nations to execute His judgment. That doesn't mean what they did was right; it simply means God used their actions for His purposes.

42. Ephesians 2:6.

43. Philippians 1:21.

44. Romans 8:35-39.

TEN

PARTICIPATING IN
THE DIVINE NATURE

His divine power has given us everything we need for life and godliness through our knowledge of him who called us by his own glory and goodness. Through these he has given us his very great and precious promises, so that through them you may participate in the divine nature and escape the corruption in the world caused by evil desires. —2 Peter 1:3-4

I never tire of the extravagant truths of God's Word: "given us everything we need for life and godliness, *given us his very great and precious promises*." This is one of those "goldmines" in Scripture—filled with the riches of God's glory and grace. Here the apostle Peter speaks not only of His divine power in our lives, but also about our participation in His nature.

What does it mean to *participate in the divine nature?* Before answering that question, I want to point out two things that it doesn't mean. First, unlike most New Age philosophy, biblical doctrine never confuses the creature with the Creator. In the incarnation, God the Son permanently took on humanity but remained "very God." In regeneration, man becomes a temple of the Spirit of God, but never becomes divine. Secondly, participating in the divine nature does not come through "trying harder to be like Christ." It comes through Christ living His life in me.

I have been crucified with Christ and I no longer live, but Christ lives in me. The life I live in the body, I live by faith in the Son of God, who loved me and gave himself for me.[1]

And how does Christ live in me? Some might reply that it's through "reading the Bible," or "praying," or "going to church services." Those activities are all vitally important in our Christian life, but none of them describes the actual way Christ lives in me. The Bible, prayer and fellowship are certainly means of God's grace to me and avenues of communicating with Him, but the specific way He lives in me is by the Person of the Holy Spirit. Here is what He told His disciples:

> "I will ask the Father, and he will give you another Counselor to be with you forever—the Spirit of truth. The world cannot accept him, because it neither sees him nor knows him. But you know him, for he lives with you and will be in you."[2]

The apostle John[3] wrote these words to the early Church:

> And this is his command: to believe in the name of his Son, Jesus Christ, and to love one another as he commanded us. Those who obey his commands live in him, and he in them. *And this is how we know that he lives in us: We know it by the Spirit he gave us.*[4]

"Christ lives in me." None of the Old Testament patriarchs could make that claim, nor could pre-fall Adam, nor even John the Baptist, who "prepared the way of the Lord" and baptized Jesus. In fact, Jesus once said to the crowds, "Among those born of women there has not risen anyone greater than John the Baptist; yet he who is least in the kingdom of heaven is greater than he."[5] Matthew Henry helps to explain this paradox:

> John came to the dawning of the gospel-day, but he was taken off before the noon of that day, before the rending of the veil, before Christ's death and resurrection, and the pouring out of the Spirit; so that the least of the apostles and evangelists, having greater discoveries made to them, and being employed in a greater embassy, is *greater than John*...What reason we have to be thankful that our lot is

cast in the days of the *kingdom of heaven*, under such advantages of light and love![6]

Because of the limitations of our earth-bound understanding, we cannot fully grasp the magnitude of what took place at Pentecost. When Peter refers to "the sufferings of Christ and the glories that would follow" and "the Holy Spirit sent from heaven," he adds: "Even angels long to look into these things."[7] This is no side issue or minor point of doctrine.

If there were such a thing as a "top 10 list of blessings," the truth of Christ *living in me* surely would rank among the very highest. It means not only that I have access to divine power and wisdom, but also that I have the Spirit of Christ at work in me to change my character, alter my attitude, and transform my motivation. In other words, all that Jesus *has* and all that He is, resides in the Person of the Holy Spirit, and the Holy Spirit lives in me!

Jesus Loves Righteousness and Hates Wickedness

In my adopted homeland of Canada—and to some extent throughout the Western world—*tolerance* is regarded as one of the greatest of virtues. But it is often a very subjective, "politically-correct" kind of tolerance that permits or even encourages hatred of certain groups like polluters, "right wing extremists" and pro-life advocates. On the other hand, those who oppose certain behaviors that the Bible calls sinful—for example, homosexual sin—may be charged with hate crimes and brought before human rights tribunals.[8] Our culture seemingly will tolerate anything but intolerance of sin.

But this type of tolerance is in direct opposition to the divine nature, as we see in this prophetic word about the Son of God recorded in Psalms and quoted in Hebrews:

"Your throne, O God, will last for ever and ever,
and righteousness will be the scepter of your kingdom.
You have loved righteousness and hated wickedness;
therefore God, your God, has set you above your companions
by anointing you with the oil of joy."[9]

Some Christians are comfortable with the "loving righteousness" part of Christ's attitude, but would rather steer clear of "hating wickedness." It avoids troublesome conflict and awkwardness, and doesn't "make waves." But that approach is not a valid option for us. We are *predestined to be conformed to the likeness of his Son*,[10] and part of His likeness (that is, His character or nature) is to love what is right *and* to hate what is wrong.

This truth was impressed upon me in a powerful way during a Christian protest march I had organized many years ago in Basingstoke, a town in southern England. It was part of the 1970 "Festival of Light," which was a national movement led by Peter and Janet Hill along with personalities like Colonel Dobbie, Mary Whitehouse and Malcolm Muggeridge. One of the movement's slogans was *Moral Pollution Needs a Solution*—the aim being to call our nation back from the morass of sexual permissiveness.

Two years before this event, our local police had laid charges against a news agent for selling a special children's edition of *Oz*, a monthly pornographic magazine. Sad to say, the prosecution was unsuccessful, leaving many Christians dismayed by the court decision and discouraged about future trends.

It so happened that our procession took us right past this news agent's shop. We were heartily singing "Light Up the Fire," a song written especially for the *Festival*, and I recall my mood being somewhat cavalier and triumphalist. But as we came to the front of the news agent's shop, a still, small voice whispered in my spirit, *Do you really love righteousness and do you really hate iniquity?* It was like an arrow that pierced my soul; I simply dissolved in tears. I remember crying out to God, "To be quite honest, Lord, I don't. But I really, really want to."

A week later, I visited the owner of the shop and complained about how easy it was for youngsters to view these filthy magazines. He was unexpectedly compliant and promised that when they moved to a nearby location they would confine this material to a special section out of children's view. I thought this concession was better than nothing.

However, about six months later when I stopped by the new premises to buy a newspaper, I discovered that not only was the offensive material still out in the open, it was located right next to the comics and within reach of the smallest child! I was stunned. Then, somewhere inside of me, there rose up a deep-seated anger against satan and his demonic minions, and a hatred—a God-induced hatred—of the evil perpetrated by these pornographers and distributors who were corrupting the vulnerable minds of the young.

I immediately left the news agent, headed straight for the police headquarters and asked for the senior officer.[11] That would have been the Police Superintendent, but he wasn't on duty just then. Next in line was the Chief Inspector who *was* available, and who also happened to be the officer in charge of the failed *Oz* prosecution. The Chief Inspector welcomed me like a long lost brother and then introduced me to another Inspector for the purpose of taking down a written complaint. When the Chief Inspector had left, the other Inspector turned to me and said, "Barney, you and I have two things in common: we have both been police officers, but even better than that, we both love the Lord Jesus." I thought, *fantastic*.

As it turned out, he and the Chief Inspector decided that, rather than prosecute the news agent, it would be better to seize the pornography and issue a summons whereby the onus lay on the defendant to show cause why the offending material should not be destroyed. Unbeknownst to me, the Basingstoke police, in cooperation with several other police forces, decided to simultaneously raid over a dozen warehouses in six different counties, seizing hundreds of tons of pornography.

I learned the outcome of these efforts the following year in a most unlikely place. Janette and I were in Kathmandu, Nepal, on a tour of the various countries to which our church had sent missionaries. We arrived there the same day that two editions of the *Daily Telegraph*, a British daily newspaper, happened to show up. Imagine my amazement and delight when I took the papers up to my room and discovered reports in the *Telegraph*, for two days running, on the Court's decision to destroy by fire all the magazines that had been seized. Millions of dollars' worth of smut had gone up in smoke! It was deeply gratifying to experience Christ's love of righteousness and hatred of wickedness flowing through me—and to discover anew that when I am cooperating with Christ in what *He* is doing, *His yoke is easy and His burden light*.

Let me turn to a more recent example that followed my reading of a *Focus on the Family* magazine article entitled, "Why I Don't Do *Titanic*." The writer tells of hearing about the movie from various people, including a high school student who told her, "You won't be happy with this movie. Everyone else will love it, but you'd better not see it." After hearing more about the film, the writer thought to herself, *I knew she was right. I could not justify sitting through nearly three and a half hours of a movie that glamorized hedonism and dishonesty. Nor could I support a film that romanticized pre-marital sex in a way that has captured the hearts of millions of young, impressionable girls.*[12]

The following Sunday I was preaching in our home church on the subject *Christ lives in me*, and highlighted His love of righteousness and hatred of wickedness. I then took the opportunity to read from the article, hoping it would illustrate how we as believers sometimes compromise our Christian witness.

Suddenly, without premeditation, I found myself presenting to the congregation an imaginary scenario where I go to a theater showing *Titanic*, accompanied by Jesus. As we come to the scene in the film depicting an unmarried couple committing fornication in the back seat of a car, I turn to the Lord and ask, "Jesus, are you enjoying this?" After a long pause I discern a note of pain in His voice as He slowly replies, "Actually, no, I am not. This is the reason I shed My blood on Golgotha: I died in order to cleanse people from the sin that you are treating as entertainment."

You could have heard a pin drop in the service. Some faces looked stunned and turned pale; it wasn't difficult to discern those who had already seen the movie. Was I laying a guilt trip on people, or did this imaginary exchange represent how God sees these things?

I realize there are many factors that apply to our decision-making concerning television and movies: elements such as profanity, graphic violence, occult and sexual content; age of the viewers (especially if they are children); our motivation in seeing a particular film; and its effect on our minds, attitudes and actions.[13]

Apart from weighing these factors, I believe we need to ask ourselves whether we have become gradually desensitized through increased exposure to evil, and whether we have deluded ourselves into thinking something is acceptable just because our culture says it is. But most important of all is how *God* sees these issues, and whether we are pleasing *Him* by what we are watching and hearing. Jesus really does live in me, and He really does want to love righteousness and hate iniquity *through* me.

As it happened, no one argued with what I said that Sunday morning. On the contrary, I have seldom had a more appreciative response in 35 years of ministry. I am thankful for that, because my intention was not to bring condemnation or to promote legalism, but to help us relate honestly to a holy God who loves righteousness and hates wickedness.

Jesus Is Full of Grace

Full of grace and truth is how John describes the glory of the Father's Son.[14] It was a grace that expressed itself in word and deed throughout Jesus' life on earth. Grace to show love to the unlovely. Grace to sit and eat with sinners. Grace to be regarded as unclean because He touched lepers. Grace to allow His feet to be anointed with oil and kissed by a prostitute.

Grace to pray for those who had shamefully mocked Him, spit in His face, and unmercifully crucified Him, saying, "Father, forgive them, for they do not know what they are doing."[15] Grace to cover all my sins—past, present and future. Jesus is full of wonderful, amazing, astonishing, awesome, breathtaking, beautiful grace. What we *deserved* was judgment; what we *earned* was death; but what we are *given* is Jesus, who is full of grace.

No evil act perpetrated against me, no unkind or untruthful words spoken about me, no act of rejection or betrayal that I experience—none of these need to remain unforgiven. In an instant, through the grace of our Lord Jesus Christ, I have the ability to approach His great well of salvation and draw on His living water, allowing me to bless those who curse me and pray for those who mistreat me. I am neither a victim of circumstance nor a prisoner of resentment, but one who is set free by the One who is full of grace—and who lives in me!

Jesus Is Full of Truth

"I am the way and the *truth* and the life,"[16] said Jesus: Truth that reveals the Father. Truth that is reality. Truth that is uncompromising.

Truth that reveals our sinful condition. Truth that promises eternal life to those who put their trust wholly in Him. Truth that is pure, undefiled and untarnished by hidden motives or selfish intent. He is full of integrity. And He lives in me!

I don't have to exaggerate, cheat, lie or manipulate. I don't have to live with the guilt that sours my soul when I tell an untruth or speak an ungracious, biased word against another. Because He lives in me, I can walk in the light as He is in the light.

But the truth is, I have not always made that choice. One Saturday morning many years ago, I was awakened by the ringing of the telephone. I glanced at the time: 7:30 A.M. "I hope I didn't wake you up," the voice greeted me. It was Gerald, one of the church members. "No," I answered confidently. "You sure?" he further enquired. "Sure I'm sure."

My heart sank. First I had lied unintentionally (my initial response), but now I had lied deliberately. However, I soon shrugged off my dampened feelings and got on with my day, preparing for a meeting at which I was to preach in a town some 35 miles away.

Later that morning I met Gerald at a church event in aid of charity. Gerald enjoyed soccer, and his friend Danny, who had recently received Christ, was a fan of Southampton United Soccer Club. It so happened that Southampton had a game that afternoon, and where I was going to be preaching that evening was only a few miles from the stadium. "How about you and Danny coming with me to the match?" I asked. "We could grab a quick bite to eat after the game and still be in plenty of time to go the meeting." They jumped at the idea.

The game and the meal went well and we arrived for the meeting early, so I excused myself and went off to pray in the pastor's office. But it wasn't working. Whatever I sent up seemed to bounce right back down, as if the ceiling were three-foot-thick reinforced concrete. I felt utterly miserable. Darkness separated me from sweet fellowship with the One in whom there is no darkness at all. Finally, I prayed, "Lord, I was wrong: I lied. Please forgive me and cleanse me from my sin. I promise that as soon as the meeting is over, I'll confess my sin to Gerald and ask for his forgiveness." Immediately the heaviness lifted and the presence of God filled the room.

Before the service began, I quickly told Gerald that as soon as we got back on the road later, there was something I wanted to talk to him about. It wasn't the best of meetings, but I was free in my spirit and enjoyed ministering.

After the usual goodbyes, the three of us jumped into the car and set off for home. It occurred to me that it might not be a wise thing to confess my sin in front of a new believer, so I reminded Gerald of our intended talk but suggested that we could leave it until we got home. "No, you don't have to wait; I don't mind," responded Gerald. "Well, I'm sure you don't," I replied, "but I still think it would be best if we waited."

"No, honestly, I really don't mind," Gerald continued, "Danny and I don't have any secrets, do we Danny?" I can recall thinking, *Lord, you do make humility difficult sometimes.* "Alright," I said, "Gerald, when you asked me this morning whether you had woken me up, I said no. And when you further questioned me as to whether I was sure, I again said no. I'm sorry; that was not the truth." "Oh," he replied matter-of-factly, "I knew that." I could have punched him (or, as we say in England, I felt like bopping him one).

The prophet Jeremiah writes: "The heart is deceitful above all things and beyond cure. Who can understand it?"[17] Yet he also prays, "O Lord, do not your eyes look for truth?"[18] And David declares, "Surely you desire truth in the inner parts..."[19] So how do we bridge the gap between an incurably deceitful heart and a God of truth? It's through our Lord Jesus, the One who is full of truth, who cleanses us from sin, who changes our hearts, who now lives in us!

Jesus Is Gentle in Heart

Gentleness is often viewed as somewhat unmanly or even effeminate. It's a characteristic you would expect to find in nursing mothers, but not necessarily in men, and perhaps not in women who find themselves in the workforce (where "assertiveness" is more often espoused than gentleness). Yet, gentleness is listed as a fruit of the Spirit,[20] and the apostle Paul reminded the church at Thessalonica that he, along with fellow apostles Silas and Timothy, had been *gentle* among them, "like a mother caring for her little children."[21]

There was nothing effeminate about Jesus. He was utterly fearless when confronting the Pharisees or other ungodly authorities of

His time. But for Him, courage and gentleness were not at odds with each other. Note an example from Luke 13 where some Pharisees came to Him with warnings that Herod planned to kill Him. His reply?

> "Go tell that fox, 'I will drive out demons and heal people today and tomorrow, and on the third day I will reach my goal.' In any case, I must keep going today and tomorrow and the next day—for surely no prophet can die outside Jerusalem!"[22]

In the very next verse, Jesus turns His attention to Jerusalem, and from out of the depths of His innermost being spring forth tender longings in the form of a lament:

> "O Jerusalem, Jerusalem, you who kill the prophets and stone those sent to you, how often I have longed to gather your children together, as a hen gathers her chicks under her wings, but you were not willing!"

Godly leadership displays strength of purpose, but the gentleness of the Spirit is never far from view. The antithesis of being gentle is to be abrasive, biting, harsh, strident, imperative or insensitive. Any of those traits may be symptomatic of more deep-seated problems such as pride, anxiety, and "illegal ownership."

I recall an example from several years ago while traveling in a ministry team with Ron MacLean of Winnipeg, Canada and Bryn Franklin of Basingstoke, England. One evening as we sat with the elders of a related church, we got into a strong theological discussion. The discussion was not heated (in terms of anger), but it definitely crossed the line of courteous, brotherly love.

I went to bed that night feeling quite downcast. I was not pleased with my conduct and attitude, and came to the conviction that I had acted out of my own wisdom and strength rather than resting in Christ's grace. As we say in Canada, I was not a happy camper! The next day when Ron and Bryn asked to see me privately, I was ready to listen, and it didn't take them long to convince me that I was carrying a burden that was not given me by the Lord.

It can be so tempting to behave like an owner instead of the Lord's steward. The work is *His*, not mine; the future is also His, not mine. In the words of an old hymn:

> God holds the key of all unknown
> And I am glad:
> If other hands should hold the key,
> Or if He trusted it to me,
> I might be sad.
> What if tomorrow's cares were here
> Without its rest?
> I'd rather He unlocked the day.
> And, as the hours swing open, say,
> "My will is best."[23]

Our family of churches numbers several hundred congregations in 29 different nations. The responsibility for all this has at times weighed heavily on my shoulders but, in recent years, I have been releasing more and more of my leadership duties to the next generation. In doing so, I had determined that I would not release authority with one hand while holding on to it with the other—because that would be a sure recipe for disaster.

However, that process was not always easy for me, nor did it take place without experiencing a certain amount of anxiety. Along with that, I watched a third generation of leaders emerge who, from my perspective, did not always place the same value on some of the building principles that have been so precious to me. (Examples would be in the areas of worship and the ministry of God's Word.)

Coupled with this was a concern for the condition of the larger evangelical church, which, I believed, had gradually moved away from its evangelical orthodoxy, increasingly embraced process theology, and replaced the authority and efficacy of Scripture with an inordinate reliance on psychology. I found myself frequently waking up in the morning feeling discouraged and irritable.

Then one night I had a vivid dream. I was holding a small, cultivated Christmas tree by the trunk. But as I was looking at the tree (which was about three feet high), my attention was drawn to some small feathers and tufts of straw that were sticking out from the tight foliage. Clumsily, I stuck my hand into the tree and pulled out a small bird's nest—the type of nest that is entered from a hole in the side.

I discarded the tree and focused on the nest. Rather carelessly, I pulled the top off, wondering if there was anything inside. To my dismay, there was a mother wren sitting on her nest, who appeared highly distraught and soon flew away. From the angle I was viewing I couldn't see any eggs, but when I drew the nest closer I was surprised to discover a tiny baby bird with furry down sticking out between its feathers. It seemed obvious to me that it was nearly ready to fly.

But my actions had created a problem. *Now what are you going to do, you clumsy thing?* I reproached myself. It was no use trying to cut up worms to feed the baby wren (it wouldn't be able to swallow them) and it was impossible to catch insects. What was I to do?

At that very moment, out of the corner of my eye I noticed a rock about 1 foot thick, 8 feet long and 4 feet wide. There was a small niche at the far end of the rock, so, without further thought, I walked over and placed the nest into the hole. I was immediately impressed by how snugly it fit, as if the hole was made for the nest. Then, as I walked away, I noticed the mother bird had returned with insects sticking out of her beak. She was perched on the end of the rock nearest me, but then, to my delight, hopped over to the nest and began feeding her fledgling chick. My relief was indescribable.

For several weeks I tried to understand what the dream was all about. I even shared it with other mature Christian leaders in the hope that they could shed some light on its meaning.

Finally it hit me like a sledgehammer: the nest represented the family of churches God had entrusted to my fatherly oversight. The baby bird signified the new generation of young leaders who were nearly ready to fly, and the rock as well as the mother wren represented different aspects of Christ's ownership and ongoing provision for His Church. If I were not careful, my paternal instincts and protectionism would end up producing the very opposite of what I passionately desired.

Furthermore, if Jesus was able to entrust the whole future of the fledgling Church into the hands of a small group of imperfect men with whom He had spent about three years, what basis did I have for hanging on to the controls of something that I claimed was owned by Him anyway?

Recently I visited a business owned and operated by a godly group of Christians where each senior staff member makes a New Year's commitment to the rest of the 240 workers. These commitments are printed out and posted on the wall for everyone to see. My attention was drawn to one that said, "I commit myself to not interfere with those whom I have empowered, for the sake of long term success, even at potential short term expense." I discovered that this was the commitment of the company boss.

Last year at our *Salt and Light* European Leaders Conference in Bristol, England, 450 leaders from various countries were gathered under the leadership of Steve Thomas who also leads our European Apostolic Team. I couldn't help but be impressed as I observed how graciously and competently Steve handled the whole conference.

Eighteen months earlier, at our *Days of Destiny* summer camp with over 2,500 people present, I had taken off my jacket and draped it over Steve's shoulders as a prophetic gesture that he should take my place as leader of the European Team. I had passed on the mantle! As I drove away from the Bristol conference, I found my mind was at peace: *Everything is going to be just fine.*

A short time later, in obedience to the leading of the Lord, I relinquished the pastoral leadership of West Coast Christian Fellowship in Vancouver, Canada to 31-year-old David Bornman. David and his godly wife Tina, with their three young children, came to us from the U.S. Midwest. He is a gifted, personable leader who had walked with me in a discipleship relationship for two years. I had grown to love and trust him, and so did the whole church.

I had only one concern: I wasn't sure how well David could handle expository teaching from Scripture. The following Sunday he taught from Philippians 2, and the message was superb. Again, I left with the reassuring thought, *Everything is going to be all right.* The gentleness of Christ was at work, helping me to release younger leaders to God's purposes, for the building up of the church and the ultimate glory of God.

JESUS IS HUMBLE IN HEART

Pride is a dreadful malady—and I am ashamed to say I can speak from first-hand experience. As the Scriptures tell us, God opposes the proud but gives grace to the humble.[24] I well remember experiencing God's opposition during a certain period of ministry until He spoke to me through an unlikely word from Proverbs: "The poor use entreaties, but the rich answer roughly."[25] I recognized that I had been acting like a rich man, not one who was poor in spirit, and I repented both privately and publicly.

One of the most dangerous characteristics of pride is its deceptive, hidden presence. It's like bad breath: the person who has it is often totally unaware of the problem—unlike others who happen to be nearby! And just when you think pride has been dealt a death-blow, it resurfaces in some new form. (The classic example, of course, is the man who was awarded a medal for humility, but then had it promptly taken away because he wore it.)

Pride comes in many shapes and sizes. One of its telltale manifestations is taking credit for what rightfully belongs to God or to another person. We see it in politics, in business, in school and even in preaching. It wouldn't be too difficult to relate negative examples, but I want to offer a positive one: A while ago I attended the Sunday morning service of The King's Community Church in Langley, B.C., Canada, which is pastored by my good friend Brian Watts. When Brian stood up to preach, he introduced his sermon by saying, "Most of what I'm about to say comes from a book written by James Packer entitled *Laid Back Christianity*." That's humility as well as honesty.

As we have already noted earlier, the credit for everything Jesus said or did was given to His Father. Jesus was absolutely secure in His Father's love. He did not humble Himself because He was unaware of His identity or unsure of His worth. Instead, as the Gospel of John tells us, "Jesus knew that the Father had put all things under his power, and that he had come from God and was returning to God; so he got up...and began to wash his disciples' feet..."[26] Is there a more striking picture of divinity embracing humility?

Jesus' identity and security were all wrapped up in His relationship with His Father. There is no need for pride when you are satisfied with your Father's commendation that says, "You are my

Son, whom I love; with you I am well pleased."[27] In turn, our security and identity must be wrapped up in Jesus, who "lives in me."

I don't have to try to prove anything, to promote myself, to draw attention to my accomplishments or claim the credit—even if I was the one who said it or did it. Why? Because if it has any eternal value, I could not have been the source of it in the first place. As Paul writes to the Corinthians:

> For who makes you different from anyone else? What do you have that you did not receive? And if you did receive it, why do you boast as though you did not?[28]

If, on the other hand, the accomplishment does not have eternal value, there's even less reason for pride. So if we live in the reality of who we are and who Jesus is, pride has no ground in which to take root. It can, in fact, survive only in the soil of deception.

Jesus, the "image of the invisible God"[29] and "the exact representation of his being"[30] says to us, "Take my yoke upon you and learn from me, *for I am gentle and humble in heart*, and you will find rest for your souls."[31] I cannot get over the fact that the Almighty God is *humble in heart*, but that is what the Scriptures teach us, and that is what Jesus demonstrated throughout His life.

In light of that, is there any reason—even the tiniest shred of an excuse—to harbor pride? Is there any basis for boastfulness when we have a humble *King* living inside of us? Not for a moment. Nor do we have to succumb to that age-old temptation. Praise God for the awesome privilege and the incredible honor of participating in the divine nature!

ENDNOTES

1. Galatians 2:20.
2. John 14:16-17.
3. John, who was known as "the disciple whom Jesus loved," seemed to have a special understanding of relationship with the Lord Jesus—the Master he followed on earth and the Son of God he knew by the Spirit after the ascension.
4. 1 John 3:23-24 (emphasis added).
5. Matthew 11:11.

6. Matthew Henry, *Commentary on the Whole Bible* (Grand Rapids, Michigan: Zondervan, 1961), 1259 (emphasis in original).

7. 1 Peter 1:11-12.

8. In some Canadian cities, the human rights tribunal has fined the mayor for refusing to issue proclamations promoting "Gay Pride Week."

9. Hebrews 1:8-9.

10. Romans 8:29.

11. A word of advice: If you want action at a police station, always ask for the senior officer; don't just file your complaint with the desk sergeant.

12. Susan Perrin Rooke, "Why I Don't Do Titanic." *Focus on the Family Magazine*, February 1999.

13. *Focus on the Family* sponsors a helpful, Christian-based movie review service called *Plugged In*. It can be accessed online at www.family.org/pplace/pi/

14. John 1:14.

15. Luke 23:34.

16. John 14:6 (emphasis added).

17. Jeremiah 17:9.

18. Jeremiah 5:3.

19. Psalm 51:6.

20. Galatians 5:23.

21. 1 Thessalonians 2:7.

22. Luke 13:32-33.

23. J. Parker, "God Holds the Key," *Redemption Hymnal*.

24. James 4:6.

25. Proverbs 18:23 (RSV)

26. John 13:3-5.

27. Luke 3:22.

28. 1 Corinthians 4:7.

29. Colossians 1:15.

30. Hebrews 1:3.

31. Matthew 11:29 (emphasis added).

ELEVEN

FROM SHADOW TO SUBSTANCE

The law is only a shadow of the good things that are coming—not the realities themselves.

—Hebrews 10:1

I am often away from home, speaking at churches or conferences in various parts of North America, Europe, Africa, Asia, Australia and New Zealand. During those times, I am always delighted when Janette is able to travel with me, but that is not always possible. And so I have often experienced the keen anticipation of homecoming after days or weeks of ministry.

Willie Burton used to say, "Home is not a place; home is a person," and he was right. While I am away, my interest is not centered on our house, but on my wife. I find that the night before returning, my thoughts increasingly turn to what is happening at home. If I am in India—which is 13½ hours ahead of Vancouver—I picture Janette waking up as I am going to sleep. And I think to myself, *Tomorrow I will see my sweetheart and hold her in my arms.*

I am always excited when I finally board the plane. We leave on time, and there is even a tailwind to increase our speed, but the journey still seems to take twice as long. Sleep is futile: the minute I close my eyes I start thinking of her. At last the plane touches down. *Why does it take so long to taxi to the gate? And why does some elderly soul, who was assisted onto the plane by wheelchair, now choose to deplane unaided and get herself stuck in the middle of the aisle? And why is there such a long line-up to get through customs? And why does it take forever for the baggage to arrive, and why-o-why is my suitcase among the last to be unloaded?*

Finally! I exit the terminal and there is Janette, waiting for me in her car. As soon as she sees me, she gets out of the car while I quickly make my way to where she is standing. *Beautiful.* The sun is shining, and Janette's presence is casting a shadow against a brick wall. Imagine for a moment how she would feel if, instead of gathering her into my arms, I turned and tried to hug the shadow on the wall! Why would I want the shadow when I can have the real thing? Why would I give my attention to an *effect* when I can take hold of the *substance*?

That is exactly what the writer to the Hebrews is dealing with when he refers to *copies* or *shadows* of those things that are real or ultimate.[1] Like Paul in his letters to the Galatians and the Colossians, he wants us to recognize that when the real has arrived—once God has fulfilled what was promised—it's time to leave the shadows behind. Regulations about food and drink and special days on the calendar—these are all "things which are a mere shadow of what is to come; but the *substance* belongs to Christ."[2] That sounds simple enough, but the actual transition from shadow to substance can prove surprisingly difficult.

The people of Israel had waited centuries for the promised Messiah, but when He actually appeared in their midst, most preferred the shadow of their pre-Messianic traditions and preconceived ideas. Matthew relates that when the wise men reported the arrival of the king of the Jews, Herod was disturbed, and all Jerusalem with him.[3]

Even the Early Church struggled with the implications of the new covenant. Reporting to the church in Jerusalem after his third missionary journey to the Gentiles, Paul received a warm response when he related what God had done among the Gentiles, but was quickly reminded about the Jewish believers and how *they* viewed the new Christian life: "You see, brother," the Jerusalem elders said to Paul, "how many thousands of Jews have believed, *and all of them are zealous for the law.*"[4]

In this chapter, we look at some of the changes that took place when ultimate Reality in the form of Jesus Christ invaded a world of shadows. We will consider some key questions: What exactly were the shadows that God was eliminating, and what expressions of substance was He bringing in? As we do that, I would ask us to consider another question: If we continue to hold on to shadows instead of embracing God's new order, are we in essence eating of the tree of the knowledge of good and evil?

Old Covenant, New Covenant

Some Christians have been taught that Old Covenant means the Old Testament, and New Covenant the New Testament. Actually, these words are used in the Bible to describe God's *order* in terms of His promises, laws, and means of grace. The theology of certain groups leads them to view the old and new order as completely different, while others believe there is an essential unity in God's order, and that the various covenants—with Adam, Noah, Abraham, Israel, David, Christ and the Church—should be viewed as expressions of one harmonious covenant of God with man.

As usual, we try to package God's truth in one neat bundle so that our minds can handle it better. But God doesn't necessarily accommodate our theological packages. Scripture presents the Old and New Covenants in terms of continuity as well as contrast. There is one God who is unchanging: He did not have a "conversion experience" between covenants nor between the Old and New Testaments; He was not judgmental in the Old and then merciful in the New.[5] On the other hand, Scripture does speak in terms of a "new" and "better" covenant ushered in by Christ, a covenant that is "superior" to an old one that was rendered "obsolete."[6]

Again, *covenant* here refers to God's order at a particular time. The New Testament writers certainly did not consider the Old Testament to be obsolete; neither would today's Christians regard as obsolete the moral law encompassed by the Ten Commandments. Jesus not only affirmed God's eternal law, He also explained more fully its application (for example, in the Sermon on the Mount).

However, the Old Covenant as such had built-in limitations—as we see illustrated by the "gifts and sacrifices being offered," things that the writer to the Hebrews declared could not clear the conscience of the worshiper. Instead:

> They are only a matter of food and drink and various ceremonial washings—external regulations applying *until the time of the new order*.[7]

Jesus completely fulfilled the law and all of its righteous demands. The New Covenant sealed in Christ's blood is the fulfillment of the covenant originally made with Abraham, and is a covenant of grace. But this new order brought with it massive change for God's people in the first century—both in their way of thinking and their way of life. Many of these changes are recorded in the Book of Acts where, for example, Peter receives a supernatural vision concerning God's acceptance of the Gentiles; then, at a later date, the Jerusalem Council tries to decide if new Gentile believers should comply with laws like circumcision.

It was a shift of seismic proportions. You could summarize it all by saying, "Out went the shadow; in came the substance."

External Law vs. Internal Law

When God wrote His laws for Israel on tablets of stone, it was easy for people to regard the law as very much external to their being. The law, as it seemed to them, was holy but it was "out there." Their duty as unholy people therefore was to try to conform to what was (literally) written in stone and hidden away in the tabernacle.

But human effort was never intended as the means of keeping the law or producing perfect people. In fact, as the apostle Paul tells the Galatians, those who try to achieve salvation by keeping the law are under a curse!

> All who rely on observing the law are under a curse, for it is written: "Cursed is everyone who does not continue to do everything written in the Book of the Law." Clearly no one is justified before God by the law, because, "The righteous will live by faith."[8]

Paul's language is particularly passionate in the first three verses of the same chapter where he suggests the Galatians must be out of their minds to think they could achieve godliness by trying harder:

> You foolish Galatians! Who has bewitched you? Before your very eyes Jesus Christ was clearly portrayed as crucified. I would like to learn just one thing from you: Did you receive the Spirit by observing the law, or by believing what you heard? Are you so foolish? After beginning with

the Spirit, are you now trying to attain your goal by human effort?[9]

They did not understand that the ultimate purpose of the law was to reveal our fallen nature and to lead us to Christ. As Paul wrote to the Romans concerning the law: "But in order that sin might be recognized as sin, it produced death in me through what was good, so that through the commandment sin might become utterly sinful."[10] Dr. Martyn Lloyd-Jones adds this observation:

> The word "trespass" suggests a violation of the law, a transgression of law. Notice, then, that God's way of forgiveness is first of all something that exposes the sin. Our tendency is always to cover it up in order that we may be happy. But God first of all exposes it, He unmasks it, He defines it, He pinpoints it. That was the real function of the law. Sin was in existence, as Paul argues in the fifth chapter of the Epistle to the Romans, from the moment Adam fell. But he argues further, "sin is not imputed when there is no law" (5:13). The law was designed to define sin and to bring it home to us by imputation.[11]

In place of the external law under the Old Covenant—the law that was "out there" written on stone tablets—came God's law *written on the heart*. This had been foretold many centuries earlier by the prophet Jeremiah, in words that stand like a beacon of hope amidst the despair of man's darkened state:

> "This is the covenant I will make
> with the house of Israel
> after that time," declares the Lord.
> "I will put my law in their minds
> and write it on their hearts.
> I will be their God,
> and they will be my people."[12]

The writer to the Hebrews quotes these Scriptures, clearly identifying the New Covenant with the new order established by the sacrifice of Jesus. While the ceremonial laws were fulfilled in Christ, the moral laws are the same—but with one significant change: *location*. What was external has now become internal by the Spirit.

For those who reject Christ's redeeming sacrifice and free grace, the law written on stone still stands in judgment. But for those who receive God's grace, the command "you shall not..." becomes, in Christ, a promise that says, "For sin will have no dominion over you, since you are not under law but under grace."[13] Remember: Christ lives in me and He loves righteousness.

ANIMAL SACRIFICES VS. THE LAMB OF GOD

Out went the sacrificing of animals to cover sins. As the writer to Hebrews tells us, "it is impossible for the blood of bulls and goats to take away sins."[14] But then why was the system of sacrifices instituted in the first place? The Pharisees, for all their spiritual blindness, were correct when they said, "Who can forgive sins but God alone?"[15] Even they seemed to know that sacrificing an animal was essentially an act of obedience and faith toward God who alone had the power to forgive.

But the Pharisees failed to grasp the basic, underlying message of the sacrificial system, namely, that no man could atone for his sins and achieve righteous standing before God by his own efforts. That could happen only through the death of Another. More importantly, they didn't realize that the sacrificial animal and its blood were the shadows of the Reality standing before them in the Person of Jesus of Nazareth: that the shadows were being replaced by substance.

We find this transformation described in chapters 9 and 10 of Hebrews:

> The law is only a shadow of the good things that are coming—not the realities themselves. For this reason it can never, by the same sacrifices repeated endlessly year after year, make perfect those who draw near to worship. If it could, would they not have stopped being offered? For the worshipers would have been cleansed once for all, and would no longer have felt guilty for their sins. But those sacrifices are an annual reminder of sins...[16]

> ...but he [Christ] entered the Most Holy Place once for all by his own blood, having obtained eternal redemption. The blood of goats and bulls and the ashes of a heifer sprinkled on those who are ceremonially unclean sanctify them so

that they are outwardly clean. How much more, then, will the blood of Christ, who through the eternal Spirit offered himself unblemished to God, cleanse our consciences from acts that lead to death, so that we may serve the living God![17]

The shadows of the sacrificial system were superseded in a very public way when John the Baptist cried out, "Behold, the Lamb of God who takes away the sin of the world!"[18] These words came from a strange-looking desert-dweller wearing clothes made of camel's hair, speaking to a small crowd of people in an insignificant corner of the Roman Empire. He himself may not have fully understood the significance of those momentous words, but he simply and obediently pointed us to the Reality, the Substance: Jesus Christ, "the Lamb that was slain from the creation of the world."[19]

CIRCUMCISION OF THE FLESH VS. CIRCUMCISION OF THE HEART

From the time of Abraham, circumcision had been understood as a sign of God's covenant with His people. Most probably did not comprehend the spiritual meaning of this ritual, regarding it as nothing more than a physical act of obedience that distinguished Jews from other peoples. Eventually, in the early days of the New Testament Church, we find the traditional view of circumcision being challenged, then defended, and finally being settled (at least on an official level) by a high-level church council at Jerusalem.

Paul wrote to the Roman Christians: "A man is not a Jew if he is only one outwardly, nor is circumcision merely outward and physical."[20] So if circumcision of the flesh is actually a shadow, symbolic of a spiritual reality, what is the substance that takes its place? To the Colossians, Paul wrote:

In him [Christ] you were also circumcised, in the putting off of the sinful nature, not with a circumcision done by the hands of men but with the circumcision done by Christ..."[21]

When Jesus died on the cross, our sinful nature died with Him. That is why Scripture says to "count yourselves dead to sin but alive to God in Christ Jesus,"[22] and "with regard to your former way of life, to put off your old self..."[23]

But this was more than an issue of theological metaphors. Some teachers in the Early Church were insisting that the Gentiles couldn't be saved unless they were physically circumcised. Paul takes on these "defenders of the shadows" in no uncertain terms:

> Watch out for those dogs, those men who do evil, those mutilators of the flesh. For it is we who are the circumcision, we who worship by the Spirit of God, who glory in Christ Jesus, and who put no confidence in the flesh— though I myself have reasons for such confidence.

> If anyone else thinks he has reasons to put confidence in the flesh, I have more: circumcised on the eighth day, of the people of Israel, of the tribe of Benjamin, a Hebrew of Hebrews; in regard to the law, a Pharisee; as for zeal, persecuting the church; as for legalistic righteousness, faultless.

> But whatever was to my profit I now consider loss for the sake of Christ. What is more, I consider everything a loss compared to the surpassing greatness of knowing Christ Jesus my Lord, for whose sake I have lost all things. I consider them rubbish, that I may gain Christ and be found in him, not having a righteousness of my own that comes from the law, but that which is through faith in Christ—the righteousness that comes from God and is by faith.[24]

When Paul uses terms like *dogs* and *mutilators of the flesh*, he could hardly be more insulting to his fellow Jews—although he probably went one step further when he wrote to another church, "As for those agitators, I wish they would go the whole way and emasculate themselves!"[25]

This is very strong language. Was Paul overreacting, or was he expressing the anger of God against those who were trying to keep His people in the shadows? We find a significant parallel in the life of Jesus, who used His strongest words not against cruel Romans or flagrant sinners or even those who tortured Him, but against the religious teachers of the law who were keeping others from the truth. He called them *hypocrites, sons of hell, blind guides, blind fools, whitewashed tombs, snakes, a brood of vipers.*[26] (We would do well to take note of what makes God angry: legalism and hypocrisy are very high on the list.)

A final point: Under the Old Covenant, there were class distinctions between Jew and Gentile, male and female, slave and free, circumcised and uncircumcised. These were done away with under the new covenant, as Paul explains to the Galatians:

> There is neither Jew nor Greek, slave nor free, male nor female, for you are all one in Christ Jesus. If you belong to Christ, then you are Abraham's seed, and heirs according to the promise.

> Neither circumcision nor uncircumcision means anything; what counts is a new creation.[27]

While our *function* in the church will differ according to our God-ordained calling and gender,[28] we all stand on the same ground as sinners saved by grace; we are one in Christ. As Paul told the Christians in Rome, "a man is a Jew if he is one inwardly; and circumcision is *circumcision of the heart*, by the Spirit, not by the written code."[29]

TEMPLES MADE WITH HANDS VS. GOD'S DWELLING IN HIS PEOPLE

It was at the dedication of the original temple in Jerusalem—an incredibly beautiful building made of the most costly materials on earth—that mention was first made of its limitations. As King Solomon prayed, he asked rhetorically:

> "But will God really dwell on earth? The heavens, even the highest heaven, cannot contain you. How much less this temple I have built!"[30]

A thousand years later, Paul picks up the same point in his debate with the Epicurean and Stoic philosophers in Athens:

> "The God who made the world and everything in it is the Lord of heaven and earth and does not live in temples built by hands."[31]

Yet God Himself had ordered the construction of Solomon's temple, and initiated the rebuilding of the temple under Zerubbabel, Ezra and Nehemiah. How do we explain this paradox? It can be understood only in the context of God's long-term strategy for revealing His eternal plan: first using types and shadows, and then, "in the fullness of time," ushering in the substance.

When the Samaritan woman encountered Jesus at the well, she argued, "Our fathers worshiped on this mountain, but you Jews claim that the place where we must worship is in Jerusalem." To which Jesus responded, "Believe me, woman, a time is coming when you will worship the Father neither on this mountain nor in Jerusalem."[32] In other words, when it came to worshiping God under terms of the New Covenant, buildings and geographical locations would be non-issues.

Howard A. Snyder, in his excellent book *The Problem of Wineskins*, had this to say about church buildings:

> The conclusion that the church, theologically, does not need buildings is reinforced by the distinction we have seen between tabernacle and temple. We have noted God's apparent preference for the tabernacle over the temple as the sign of His habitation with His people, for the tabernacle emphasizes God as dynamic not static, as mobile, as a God of surprises. And it thus shows God's people—the church—as mobile and flexible, as pilgrims. But the image of the temple is strikingly incompatible with the idea of a pilgrim people. There is a certain incongruity to the portable Ark of the Covenant resting securely within Solomon's temple. A temple cannot be moved: it can only be destroyed. It is static. And so in the Bible, God does not command the church to build temples. The tabernacle is the truer sign of His presence, and even it has been fulfilled and has passed away.

> So if church buildings have any justification, it can only be practical—simply a place to meet and carry on essential functions as necessary. Beyond this, buildings become a return to the shadow of the Old Testament and a betrayal of the reality of the New.[33]

Is there then no place for great cathedrals with their awe-inspiring architecture and majestic pipe organs? Isn't it true that many people report feeling a sense of reverence and spiritual inspiration in these settings? That may be true, but since I do not subscribe to the view that "the end justifies the means," I cannot advocate the cathedral as a New Covenant model just because some people are blessed through it. St. Paul's Cathedral in London is an architectural treasure and a tribute to its designer, Sir Christopher Wren. Seen as a work of art, it can certainly glorify the One who inspires all great artwork, but as a prototype of a Christian meeting place, it seems closer to the temples of old than a structure fostering New Covenant worship.

Under the New Covenant, we acknowledge that, as the apostle Paul put it, "God's temple is sacred, *and you are that temple*."[34] It's true that God's people don't always seem to be as sacred and awe-inspiring as cathedrals, but we are in fact God's temple: the substance that the physical temples portrayed in shadow. Furthermore, we need neither a religious building nor a crowd to function as a temple; it is sufficient that two or three come together in His name, and He promises to be there.

I must tell a brief story about a building that was not quite "cathedral" status. The little Baptist building where I first pastored had previously served as a bacon factory. When the small group of Baptists took over the building, they decided to make it more appropriate for public worship by upgrading the front structure with a brick façade. They set in place one or two suitable foundation stones, one of which was engraved with the words, *To the glory of God. This stone was laid by A. Bird*. Someone, somewhere must have had a sense of humor!

To summarize this section, I would like to quote a brief but profound statement by John Havlik:

> The church is never a place, but always a people; never a fold, but always a flock; never a sacred building, but always a believing assembly. The church is you who pray, not where you pray. A structure of brick and marble can no more be a church than your clothes of serge or satin can be you. There is in this world nothing sacred but man, no sanctuary of man but the soul.[35]

Worshiping in Special Buildings vs. Worshiping in Spirit

When asked where he worships, a friend of mine will typically name the local Wal-Mart or Safeway store. For myself, I find I can worship God in my study, in the shower, on a plane, while driving my car, out walking or while shopping—as well as in church facilities and school gymnasiums when I gather with other believers for corporate worship.

How is this possible? It's because we live in two worlds: a place called Earth, and a "place" referred to by the apostle Paul as *heavenly realms*:

> And God raised us up with Christ and seated us with him
> in the heavenly realms in Christ Jesus...[36]

Furthermore, Scripture tells us that these heavenly realms include the real place of worship where Christ Himself is the high priest:

> The point of what we are saying is this: We do have such a
> high priest, who sat down at the right hand of the throne of
> the Majesty in heaven, and who serves in the sanctuary, the
> *true tabernacle* set up by the Lord, not by man.[37]

That is why the Early Church did not spend a lot of time, energy and money building designated places of worship. They certainly used the temple in Jerusalem and various local synagogues for evangelistic outreach purposes, but their places of worship and fellowship included homes, marketplaces, riverbanks, beaches, prisons and catacombs.

The annual Passover meal became a frequently held covenant meal in remembrance of Christ's offering for sin, and was an actual meal with real meat, bread and wine. Out went the religious artifacts and holy furniture, just as God promised long ago through the prophet Jeremiah:

> "In those days, when your numbers have increased greatly
> in the land," declares the Lord, "men will no longer say,
> 'The ark of the covenant of the Lord.' It will never enter
> their minds or be remembered; it will not be missed, nor
> will another one be made."[38]

No more altars, no more sacrifice. Calvary was the once-and-for-all sacrifice, never to be repeated. Religious festivals, Sabbath regulations, rules regarding food and drink—all were superseded when Christ satisfied the demands of the Old Covenant and fulfilled its every type and shadow. Paul confirmed this fact to the church at Colosse:

> Therefore do not let anyone judge you by what you eat or drink, or with regard to a religious festival, a New Moon celebration or a Sabbath day. These are a shadow of the things that were to come; the reality, however, is found in Christ.[39]

Rituals, ceremonies and pageantry may impress people, but, according to Jesus, there is only one kind of worship that impresses God—worship that is "in spirit" and that is real:

> Yet a time is coming and has now come when the true worshipers will worship the Father in spirit and truth, for they are the kind of worshipers the Father seeks. God is Spirit, and his worshipers must worship in spirit and in truth.[40]

LIMITED PRIESTHOOD VS. A FULLY FUNCTIONING BODY

Some time ago, Janette and I happened to be watching a televised church service that was very liturgical in style and manner. I recall how, at one point, three priests dressed in cassocks and surplice, each with hands folded in a reverential posture of prayer, walked in line from the side of the chancel to the front of the altar, then turned and faced the congregation. I didn't doubt for a moment that they were intensely sincere in what they were doing, but I turned to Janette and said, "What on earth does that have to do with Jesus?"

I don't wish to be uncharitable, but is there anyone, anywhere, who believes that Jesus walked around that way—even during synagogue meetings? The point is: if He didn't, why do we? There is no indication that his demeanor was unctuous or religious at all; he was viewed by many as just a carpenter from Nazareth. Jesus wasn't carried about on a throne, nor did He wear special religious garb. According to the prophecy of Isaiah, He must have been very plain-looking— "no beauty or majesty to attract us to him, nothing in his appearance that we should desire him."[41] He wore no miter on His head and there was no golden halo surrounding His hair. On the other hand, he evidently had the kind of warm and natural manner that children found disarming.

At this point, it may be tempting for those of us in "non-conformist" circles to feel a little self-righteous because we avoid many of these outward "trappings." But perhaps we need to consider how our own clergy-laity distinctions may serve to create a gap between one group of Christians and another—titles like *Bishop* or *Senior Pastor*, distinctive clothing such as clerical collars, and perks like designated clergy parking spaces. (While visiting Vernon Christian Fellowship recently, I was delighted to see that the only designated parking spaces were assigned to the physically disabled members of the congregation.)

The late Willie Burton, who helped plant nearly 1,500 churches in what was then the Belgian Congo, was a great influence on my life. Two things he couldn't abide were clerical collars and the use of *Reverend* as a form of address. In one episode I shall never forget, I had made the mistake of wearing a clerical collar for a wedding at which I was to speak. Mr. Burton was staying at our home in England at the time, and was in his bedroom painting a watercolor picture for us. When I went to tell him where he could find the lunch that Janette had prepared for him, I noticed immediately that he was taken aback by my appearance. "It's no good," he said, "I can't hear a word you're saying with that wretched thing around your throat. Go on; go away." I slunk away like a scolded dog with his tail between his legs.

On another occasion, Mr. Burton was invited to speak at a Pentecostal missionary meeting in southern England. As he alighted from the car, his attention was seized by the church notice board that advertised the visit of the *Rev. W. F. Burton*. He visibly staggered at the sight. Even though he was 82 at the time, he somehow managed to clamber over a metal fence and, drawing a couple of felt pens from his top pocket, crossed out the word Rev. with the red pen and replaced it with *Mr.* using the black pen. He then proceeded to walk into the building with a look on his face that said, *Well, that's my good deed done for the day.*

We may enjoy these anecdotes of an unconventional leader, still filled with conviction and vigor at age 82, but if we write off his views as merely eccentric, we will have missed it. From a biblical standpoint, it is our clergy-laity distinction that is eccentric—in fact, it's Old Covenant. In speaking of the Church, the apostle John declared that Jesus Christ "has made us to be a kingdom and priests to serve his God and Father,"[42] while the apostle Peter called us a "royal priesthood."[43] In the New Covenant, we are all priests!

That is not to say the Early Church did not recognize certain people for their gifting or pastoral responsibility. But when you look at the ministry lists in Romans chapter 12 and 1 Corinthians chapter 12, the designations refer to *function*, not some elevated position. And everyone is included: elders are to shepherd the flock, teachers are to teach, servers are to serve, encouragers are to encourage, and those whose gifting is showing mercy are to do so cheerfully. It sounds simple—even obvious—but that pattern still is far from common among "Bible-believing" churches.

What I am proposing is simply this: With the advent of the New Covenant, out went a special, limited priesthood that dressed in priestly attire, and in came the priesthood of every believer. *Out* went one-man-ministry and in came "body ministry"—each member of Christ's Body functioning properly, with special honor being given to the parts deemed weaker or less honorable.[44]

To those entrenched in the one-man-ministry model, Paul would say (in the words of the Living Bible), "What a strange thing a body would be if it had only one part!"[45] The New English Bible translates it this way: "If the whole were one single organ, there would not be a body at all."[46] It doesn't take 21st century training in anatomy to grasp the concept that a body is made up of many parts, and that it can function effectively only when each part is working as intended.

This is the essence of the analogy used by Paul in his letters to the Roman and Corinthian believers. God's intention was (and is) for each part to function properly, operating according to God's specific allotment of grace. And that is where the various *equipping* ministry gifts come in. Their function is to draw out the grace that God deposited in each member, so that the whole Body can grow, develop and function as it should. Paul tells us that these equipping gifts were apportioned by Christ:

> It was he who gave some to be apostles, some to be prophets, some to be evangelists, and some to be pastors

and teachers, to prepare[47] God's people for works of service, so that the body of Christ may be built up...[48]

Here is how Howard Snyder, author of *The Problem of Wineskins* and *The Community of the King*, comments on this passage:

> These then are the four or five basic leadership or enabling ministries in the New Testament—apostles, prophets, evangelists, pastors and teachers. They are God's gift to the Church "to prepare God's people for works of service."
>
> It would be well if each present-day denomination and each local church would take this list and lay it alongside a list of the leaders prescribed by the church's official organizational structure and, before God, make a comparison...
>
> What is the relationship between these basic leadership or equipping gifts and the ministry gifts of the Christian community in general? Our two scriptures make it plain: these leadership gifts are to equip the saints for their work of ministry, and these works of ministry involve (representatively, not exclusively) the exercise of such gifts as healing, prophecy, miracles, tongues, helping, administering and interpretation of tongues (Eph. 4:11; 1 Cor. 12). The goal is the edification of the Church, and thereby the glorification of God and the accomplishing of his cosmic plan.
>
> The pattern of leadership and ministry outlined above allows for no rigid distinction between clergy and laity. The New Testament simply does not speak in terms of two classes of Christians—"minister" and "laymen"—as we do today. According to the Bible, the people (*laos*, "laity") of God comprise all Christians, and all Christians through the exercise of spiritual gifts have some "work of ministry." So if we wish to be biblical, we will have to say that all Christians are laymen (God's people) and all are ministers. The clergy-laity dichotomy is unbiblical and therefore invalid. It grew up as an accident of church history...a throwback to the Old Testament priesthood.
>
> It is one of the principal obstacles to the Church effectively being God's agent of the Kingdom today because it creates

the false idea that only "holy men," namely, ordained min-isters, are really qualified and responsible for leadership and significant ministry.[49]

There are, of course, differing views on the "tenure" of the five equipping ministry gifts of Ephesians 4, with some Christians assuming that they operated only during the time of the original 12 apostles. Still others believe that the nine gifts noted in 1 Corinthians 12 (often referred to by their Greek name *charismata*) lasted only until the canon of Scripture was complete.

Both sets of gifts are linked with the Body of Christ being built up. The mandate given to the apostle, prophet, evangelist, pastor and teacher is ultimately a singular one: to equip each part of the Body of Christ so that the Body will grow to maturity and do what it is intended to do. Equipping also means ensuring that parts of the Body that may be paralyzed (inactive) or malfunctioning (perform-ing in a sphere devoid of God's enabling grace) are helped to regain their proper scope of operation.

My question is this: Is it likely that the apostle Paul, led by the Holy Spirit to write this letter to the Ephesians around A.D. 60, would be instructing the church about the validity and necessity of the five equipping gifts if they were about to become obsolete in a few years as the remaining members of the Twelve died? The fact is: limiting these gifts to the lifespan of the Twelve is not suggested anywhere in the Bible. Instead, the Scripture indicates that this process whereby we are prepared for works of service by the apostle, prophet, evan-gelist, pastor and teacher—and thus build up the Body of Christ—continues *until* we arrive at a certain point, namely:

> ...until we all reach unity in the faith and in the knowledge of the Son of God and become mature, attaining to the whole measure of the fullness of Christ.[50]

Unless your reading of church history is very different from mine, I would suggest we have not yet reached that glorious state of complete unity and maturity—meaning that we still need the min-istry gifts Christ gave to the Church. In fact, knowing the condition of the Church of Jesus Christ in many different countries, I would have to say we couldn't afford the loss of *any* of these gifts. (Of course, one of the main points of contention centers around the apostolic gift, with some claiming that the number of apostles was limited to the Twelve. There are actually 22 apostles named in the pages of the New Testament, and many more inferred.[51])

Others disparage the nine charismata by claiming that they are superseded by love—"the most excellent way." But that is not Paul's argument in 1 Corinthians 13. That famous chapter on love is sandwiched between chapter 12—where Paul is arguing that the believers need to recognize, appreciate and make room for all the nine gifts—and chapter 14, where he is expressing concern about how the gifts are being used.

I am reminded of a well-known advertising slogan used by florists: *Say it with flowers.* The most excellent way, Paul is saying in these chapters, is not choosing between the gifts of the Spirit and love; it's *love with a gift.* Thus he encourages the Corinthians: "Follow the way of love *and* eagerly desire spiritual gifts..."[52] The words *eagerly desire* are translated from a Greek word meaning to *be zealous towards,* which tells us that a casual "take-it-or-leave-it" attitude is not a biblical approach to these gifts.

In chapter 12, Paul says, "to each one the manifestation of the Spirit is given for the common good."[53] This tells us two things: first, every member of the Body is included in the distribution of these gifts; second, the gifts are meant for "the common good," that is, for the sake of others:

> To one there is given through the Spirit the message of wisdom, to another the message of knowledge by means of the same Spirit, to another faith by the same Spirit, to another gifts of healing by that one Spirit, to another miraculous powers, to another prophecy, to another distinguishing between spirits, to another speaking in different kinds of tongues, and to still another the interpretation of tongues. All these are the work of one and the same Spirit, and he gives them to each one, just as he determines.[54]

One thought that is repeated four times in these verses is the fact that the *same Spirit* is behind all these gifts. Why the repetition? Probably because the manifestation of these gifts is so diverse that people are tempted to think the source must be different. (Unfortunately, new denominations have arisen out of much smaller differences than these.) It also is clear from this chapter that a particular gifting is not a matter of a member's preference, personal ambition or specialized training, but rather the result of God's sovereign choice:

> But in fact God has arranged the parts in the body, every one of them, just as he wanted them to be.[55]

Another important means of grace for our maturing in Christ is outlined immediately following the passage on the five equipping gifts:

> Then we will no longer be infants, tossed back and forth by the waves, and blown here and there by every wind of teaching and by the cunning and craftiness of men in their deceitful scheming. Instead, speaking the truth in love, we will in all things grow up into him who is the Head, that is, Christ.[56]

The phrase *speaking the truth in love* is sometimes used as a biblical basis for reproof or confrontation, as in: "Brother, I have a concern about the way you are treating your dog. The Bible says to speak the truth in love, so I'm just saying this out of love for you."

There may well be a good and proper reason to confront someone about an issue of unrighteousness, but the true context of this passage is maturity in the face of "winds of doctrine" and the schemes of men. Thus "speaking the truth in love" could be understood as *speaking a truth from God's word in love.*

God's plan was that every member of the Body would grow to the point where they could and would teach His word to others. The writer to the Hebrews complained, "In fact, though by this time you ought to be teachers, you need someone to teach you the elementary truths of God's word all over again. You need milk, not solid food![57] Here is how the apostle Paul encouraged the Church to function:

> What then shall we say, brothers? When you come together, everyone has a hymn, or a word of instruction, a revelation, a tongue or an interpretation. All of these things must be done for the strengthening of the church.[58]

STEPPING FROM THE SHADOWS

To what lengths are we willing to go in abandoning the shadows in favor of the substance? What will motivate us to exchange the old, inflexible, leaking "wineskins"[59] of our old church structures for the "new wineskins" of the New Covenant? When will we discard our man-made "Plan B" schemes in order to recover God's original "Plan A" design?

I well remember hearing a report of Howard Snyder's presentation at the 1974 International Congress on World Evangelization in Lausanne, Switzerland. His paper, "The Church as God's Agent of Evangelism," had an innocuous-sounding title, but the content was anything but standard fare. Snyder may not have expected every proposal to be taken at face value, but his stated goal of church transformation was deadly serious, and it set the conference abuzz. Here are some excerpts:

> For a radical gospel (the biblical kind) we need a radical church (the biblical kind). For the ever-new wine, we must continually have new wineskins.
>
> In short, we need a cataclysm.
>
> Something could be done. The institutionalism could be stripped away.
>
> What would a denomination do that really wanted to become a church with a New Testament dynamic? Let us suppose...
>
> First, all church buildings are sold. The money is given (literally) to the poor. All congregations of more than two hundred are divided into two. Storefronts, garages or small halls are rented as needed. Most publicity, including Sunday school promotion, is dropped. Small group Bible studies, meeting in private homes, take the place of mid-week prayer services.
>
> Pastors take secular employment and cease to be paid by the church; they become, in effect, trained "laymen" instead of paid professionals. "Laymen" take the lead in all affairs of the church. There is no attempt to attract unbelievers to church services—which are primarily for believers and, perhaps, held at some time other than Sunday morning.[60]

Now that *would* be cataclysmic! While I do not consider Snyder's recommendations as "prescriptive" for every local church, I do believe we need to take whatever radical steps the Lord may ask us to take. Let me relate some structural changes that took place in the early years of my own ministry in England—changes that some certainly would have considered cataclysmic (perhaps even catastrophic). Assisted by six deacons, I pastored a Baptist church for nearly ten years. Until my induction, the church always had been led by a pastor who was a one-man-ministry, but controlled democratically by the congregation who could hire and fire him at will.

By God's grace, major changes took place during my time there: the members of the church gathered mid-week in small groups; the five equipping gifts—apostles, prophets, evangelists, pastors and teachers, were recognized and received; and the congregation participated fully in exercising the gifts of the Holy Spirit. We also changed our approach to church decision-making, with the congregation voting (ironically) to dispense with voting as a means of control, and instituting a governing elders' council along with congregational consultations that we called "Family Forums."[61]

While no structure will guarantee the attainment of God's purposes, we believed then—and still do now—that the Church cannot improve on the basic pattern given to us in Scripture. God can still work through other structures (as indeed He has many times), but the further we stray from His pattern, the more limitations we introduce and the more problems we encounter.

In 1976 we were sent to Canada by our congregation in England, but we are still part of that church family today. They affectionately receive me as a spiritual father, and I am blessed to receive their financial support.

Going back even further in my history, I was raised in the Plymouth Brethren and had the blessing of living in a godly, Christ-centered home. I have much appreciation for the solid, scriptural grounding I received in my youth, and the influence of my father's evangelistic outreach using Scripture texts. But these Scriptures, in the end, cut across my earlier traditions and preconceived ideas. For instance, I could not understand from God's Word why many churches allowed no place for the public ministry of women (other than in women's meetings) nor the gifts of the Holy Spirit.

Neither did many churches recognize Christ's equipping gifts as outlined in Ephesians chapter 4. But over the years, my conviction concerning the necessity of these gifts has only deepened. I believe they are essential if we are to attain the biblical goals of unity in the faith and full maturity in Christ.

Embracing the substance

We have considered seven themes connected with life in the New Covenant:

1. Internal law: God writing His laws on our hearts and minds.

2. The Lamb of God: the once-and-for-all sacrifice of Christ.

3. Circumcision of the heart: putting off our sinful nature by the Spirit.

4. God dwelling in His people: we are now God's temple.

5. Worshiping in the Spirit: rituals and ceremonies giving way to life in the Spirit.

6. A fully functioning Body: every member of the Body of Christ equipped for service.

7. Stepping from the shadows: moving toward substance through steps of faith and obedience.

I submit to you that these are the constituent elements of the New Covenant, the *substance* spoken of by the apostle Paul and the writer to the Hebrews. If the Church were described as God's garden (to borrow an analogy from Isaiah), then surely the "tree of life" in the midst of the garden is Christ, who is the heart and life of the New Covenant.

The life of this *Christ*-centered New Covenant comes to us through God's inerrant Word, His Holy Spirit, the ministry of apostles, prophets, evangelists, pastors and teachers, the gifts of the Holy Spirit, the work of elders and deacons, and the motivational gifts of Romans 12. It flows freely when each member is using the gift that God specifically has chosen for him or her. And it results in the building up of the Body of Christ and the advancement of the King-dom of God on the earth.

In speaking of the headship of Christ over His Body, the Church, Paul declares:

> From him the whole body, joined and held together by every supporting ligament, grows and builds itself up in love, as each part does its work.[62]

In the New Covenant, the motivation, the energy, the wisdom, the power—everything that we need to do the will of God—flows ultimately from Christ our Head. And we have the awesome privi-lege of being workers together with Him.

ENDNOTES

1. Hebrews 8:5, 9:23, 10:1.
2. Colossians 2:17 (NASB) (emphasis added).
3. Matthew 2:1-3.
4. Acts 21:20 (emphasis added).
5. A reading of books like Jeremiah, Psalms and Revelation should quickly dispel the popular notion that Jehovah was primarily a God of regulations and retribution while the Son was meek and merciful. Jesus was, and is, the "exact representation" of God's being (Hebrews 1:3), full of grace and truth. Man's view of God may have changed over time, but God Himself is immutable.
6. Hebrews 7:22, 8:6,8,13.
7. Hebrews 9:10 (emphasis added).
8. Galatians 3:10-11.
9. Galatians 3:1-3.
10. Romans 7:13.
11. Martyn Lloyd-Jones, *The Exposition of Ephesians, Vol. 1* (Grand Rapids, Michigan: Baker Books, 1998), 167.
12. Jeremiah 31:33.
13. Romans 6:14 (RSV).
14. Hebrews 10:4.
15. Luke 5:21.
16. Hebrews 10:1-3.
17. Hebrews 9:12-14.
18. John 1:29 (NASB).

19. Revelation 13:8.

20. Romans 2:28.

21. Colossians 2:11.

22. Romans 6:11.

23. Ephesians 4:22.

24. Philippians 3:2-9.

25. Galatians 5:12.

26. Matthew chapter 23.

27. Galatians 3:28-29, 6:15.

28. Functional differences relating to gender are essentially issues of headship based on our being created in the image of God. The members of the Trinity are equal in essence and worth, but are not the same in their function and authority.

29. Romans 2:29 (emphasis added).

30. 1 Kings 8:27.

31. Acts 17:24.

32. John 4:20-21.

33. Howard S. Snyder, *The Problem of Wineskins* (Downer's Grove, Illinois: InterVarsity Press, 1975), 67.

34. 1 Corinthians 3:17 (emphasis added).

35. John Havlik, *People-Centered Evangelism* (Nashville: Broadman Press, 1971), 47.

36. Ephesians 2:6.

37. Hebrews 8:1-2 (emphasis added).

38. Jeremiah 3:16.

39. Colossians 2:16-17.

40. John 4:23-24.

41. Isaiah 53:2.

42. Revelation 1:6.

43. 1 Peter 2:9.

44. 1 Corinthians 12:22-25.

45. 1 Corinthians 12:19 (TLB).

46. 1 Corinthians 12:19 (NEB).

47. Or equip (NASB).

48. Ephesians 4:11-12.

49. Howard A. Snyder, *The Community of the King* (Downers Grove, Illinois: InterVarsity Press, 1977), 94-95.

50. Ephesians 4:13.

51. This subject is discussed more fully in my book *Apostles Today: Christ's Love-Gift to the Church* (Tonbridge, England: Sovereign World, 1996).

52. 1 Corinthians 14:1 (emphasis added).

53. 1 Corinthians 12:7.

54. 1 Corinthians 12:8-11.

55. 1 Corinthians 12:18.

56. Ephesians 4:14-15.

57. Hebrews 5:12.

58. 1 Corinthians 14:26.

59. Wineskins are a metaphor used by Jesus in Matthew 9:17 referring to structures and methodologies that are flexible enough to allow for change (as a new wineskin for new wine).

60. Excerpts taken from paper by Howard A. Snyder presented at the 1974 International Congress on World Evangelization.

61. Democracy may be an excellent model for the government of nations, but the Bible provides a different pattern for church governance, one that is designed to avoid the pitfalls of both populism and autocracy.

62. Ephesians 4:16.

TWELVE

THE GOOD, THE BAD, AND THE UGLY

*Go on, rack, torture, grind us to powder: our numbers
increase in proportion as ye mow us down. The blood
of Christians is their harvest seed.*

—Tertullian, A.D. 200[1]

INTRODUCTION

There is an old western movie called *The Good, the Bad and the
Ugly* in which three main characters vie for dominance: a bad guy
who is a classic villain, an ugly fellow with a particularly nasty
demeanor, and a good guy (Clint Eastwood, naturally) who is *somewhat* good *some* of the time. These may be little more than amusing
caricatures, but I must admit to thinking of such types when I read
certain parts of church history. The people of God are indeed a "mot-
ley crew," a fact that makes me appreciate all the more the amazing
grace and patience of our God.

Of course, we cannot automatically assume that all church leaders in history were genuine people of God. Jesus said, "Not everyone
who says to me, 'Lord, Lord,' will enter the kingdom of heaven, but
only he who does the will of my Father who is in heaven."[2] On the
other hand, we should be careful about writing off everyone who
doesn't measure up to current theological standards.

God's plans and purposes are eternal and the Scriptures are
unchanging, but our understanding of these is "in process." It grows
over time as we allow God to deal with the dullness of our natural
minds, and as God's truth gradually penetrates the barriers of our
preconceived ideas, traditions and cultural mindsets. But even with
the benefit of two millennia of church history, our understanding is

incomplete. In fact, the apostle Paul indicates that full knowledge of the truth won't be ours until we're with the Lord in eternity: "Now I know in part; then I shall know fully..."[3]

That calls for a certain degree of forbearance and humility on our part: forbearance because God's people—whether in the Old Testament, New Testament, or church history since then—have always functioned with impaired understanding; and humility because we too must have spiritual blind spots.[4] Should the Lord wait a few more centuries before returning, I could imagine some future writer dutifully warning his contemporaries about the mistakes of church leaders in the 21st century A.D.—and some of *us* might end up under the microscope!

Having said that, I believe it will be both inspiring and instructive for us to review some highlights and "lowlights" of church history from the first century to the present. The New Testament itself includes a few historical summaries: notably, Stephen's speech to the Sanhedrin in Acts 7, and the "faith honor roll" in Hebrews 11. None of these are comprehensive chronicles of Old Testament history, but simply lists of various people and events that tell a story or illustrate a theme.

Similarly, what follows in the next three chapters is not presented as a complete or even balanced compilation of church history. Rather, my intention is to provide an historical overview from the perspective of God's unfolding purposes and ultimate intention. In the light of our present understanding, I will also seek to point out (honestly yet, I trust, graciously) the shortcomings and blind spots of historical church leaders. I do so, however, with a growing sense of appreciation for what our spiritual forebears have contributed.

But appreciating the value and contribution of church leaders should not rule out challenging them when they stray from essential truth. We find in the Book of Galatians that Paul submitted his teaching to the scrutiny of the church leaders at Jerusalem, in particular, James, Peter and John. However, in the very same chapter, Paul mentions that he publicly opposed Peter to his face because he was being hypocritical in his behavior toward the Gentiles.[5]

The Bible is surprisingly candid in its description of the faults of spiritual leaders, including the great heroes of faith. Paul says that the failures of God's people through the ages were recorded in Scripture "as a warning for us."[6] My hope is that the history covered in these chapters will also serve that purpose, so that we avoid repeating the errors of the past.

One final introductory thought: We see occasional examples in biblical history where God accommodates Himself to man's cultural/ natural thinking patterns. An example of this occurred during Samuel's time when God gave Israel a king. Even though the record shows that this was not God's primary choice for how His people were to be governed, He chose to work within the framework of Israel's "king" mentality—to the extent that a subsequent monarch, King David, became a prototype for the future Messiah-King, our Lord Jesus Christ.

We don't know, however, how often—and to what extent—God accommodates Himself to man's ideas, and how exactly this may be reflected in the historical record. With the benefit of hindsight, we may now be able to identify certain methods or patterns as being "man's good ideas" rather than God's perfect way, but that doesn't necessarily mean God has removed Himself from the situation. Having said that, we should never presume upon God's mercy by continuing in a pattern that we know is contrary to His will. Our goal always should be to conform our will and ways to His, rather than expecting *Him* to accommodate *us*.

Therefore, whenever God gives the opportunity to build or "rebuild" in His Church, I want to build only according to His design. For all of us in the twenty-first-century Church, my desire is that we learn from the successes and failures of those who preceded us: to be warned by their mistakes and inspired by their faith: that we may build with "gold, silver and precious stones"[7]—spiritual materials that will withstand the test of time and eternity.

THE FIRST FOUR CENTURIES

The rapid growth of Christianity in the first 400 years of its inception represents one of history's great marvels. As historian Philip Schaff points out, this was not due to famous leaders, organizations or programs:

It is remarkable that after the days of the apostles, no names of great missionaries are mentioned until after the arrival of Patrick in Ireland somewhere around 432, followed by Columba to Scotland in 560, Augustine of Canterbury to England in 597, St. Boniface to Germany, St. Ansgar to Scandinavia, St. Cyril and Methodius amongst the Slavs. There were no missionary societies, no missionary institutions, and no organized efforts in the ante-Nicene age. Yet in less than 300 years from the death of the apostle John, the whole population of the Roman Empire, which then represented the civilized world, was nominally Christianized.[8]

Schaff goes on to describe the dynamic that propelled the expansion of the early Church:

Christianity, once established, was its own best missionary. It grew naturally from within. It attracted people by its very presence. It was a light shining in the darkness. And while there were no professional missionaries devoting their whole life to this specific work, every congregation was a missionary society, and every Christian believer a missionary, inflamed by the love of Christ to convert his fellow men.

The seed grew up while men slept, and brought forth fruit, first the blade, then the ear, after that the full corn in the ear. Every Christian told his neighbor, the laborer his fellow laborer, the slave his fellow slave, the servant his master and mistress.[9]

Justyn Martyr, converted after meeting an old man walking at the seashore who directed him to the Scriptures, wrote these words around A.D. 150:

There is no people—Greek or barbarian or of any other race, by whatever appellation or manners they may be distinguished, however ignorant of arts or agriculture, whether they dwell in tents or wander about in covered wagons—among whom prayers and thanksgivings are not offered in the name of the crucified Jesus to the Father and Creator of all things.[10]

Half a century later, Tertullian, speaking to the heathen, defiantly declared: "We are but of yesterday, and yet we already fill your cities, islands, camps, your palace, senate and forum; we have left to you only your temples."[11]

It is estimated that by the beginning of the fourth century, despite intense persecution, the number of believers had risen to approximately 10 million. Roman emperors from Nero to Diocletian to Galerius were obsessed with the constant growth of the Christian "sect" and stopped at nothing to bring about its demise. But the more they tried to destroy the Church, the more it expanded.

In Rome itself, the very heart and nerve center of the empire, there remains to this day a silent yet eloquent testimony of the triumph of Christ in His people. The catacombs, comprising over 900 miles of underground rooms and corridors beneath the city, served as both sanctuary and gravesite for a multitude of Christians during the years of persecution. Among the nearly seven million graves discovered in the catacombs were many Christian martyrs. They were possessed of a hope that was steadfast and sure. Nothing separated them from the love of God in Christ Jesus; they proved to be "more than conquerors."

The martyrs included many of the great leaders of the early Church: Clement of Rome, Ignatius of Antioch, Polycarp of Smyrna, Justin Martyr of Rome, Tertullian and Cyprian of Carthage, and Origen of Alexandria. When I consider the courage of these men of God in the face of sadistic torture and martyrdom, and when I stop to think about the tens of thousands of ordinary believers who bore the same fate with calmness and good cheer—even singing songs of triumphant hope while being led to the stake or to the coliseum—I can only respond, "I am not worthy to wash their feet or tie up their shoe laces." Many times, while reading accounts of their suffering, I have been unable to hold back the tears. The writer to the Hebrews said of the Old Testament martyrs, "the world was not worthy of them."[12] I would have to say the same of these.

SATAN'S STRATEGIES AGAINST THE EARLY CHURCH

There were countless examples of courage, dedication and good works among the leaders of the Early Church. But that doesn't mean everything they said and did was from the Lord. Even disciples like

Peter were quite capable of going off on a tangent and drawing a strong reprimand like this one from Jesus: "Get behind me, Satan! You are a stumbling block to me; you do not have in mind the things of God, but the things of men."[13]

As we look back over the first 400 years of Christianity, it is clear that satan, the enemy of Christ and the indefatigable foe of the Church, did not succeed in curtailing the advance of Christ's Kingdom by means of persecution. However, from the very beginning of the New Testament Church, he began to undermine the Church's effectiveness by other means: drawing the disciples into sin, sowing seeds of discord among the believers, and introducing heretical teaching. The latter often proved the most dangerous.

Added to this was man's propensity to allow new wineskins to harden into old wineskins by developing structures designed to preserve *not* the new wine of the Spirit, but the old structures themselves. An unknown author describes this regression—a process repeated throughout the centuries—with a sense of profound tragedy:

> The history of Christianity from the latter days of the apostles is a history of prisons. Not literal, material prisons (though there have been not a few of these), but prisons which are the result of man's inveterate habit of taking hold and bringing into bondage. How many times has the Spirit broken loose and moved in a new and free way, only to have that way brought under the control of man and crystallized into another form, creed, organization, denomination, sect, order or community?

> God gives a vision, and every God-given vision has unlimited possibilities and potentialities. But, all too soon, the vision is laid hold of by men who never had it by the Spirit, and the grapes of Eshcol turn to raisins in their hands. Altogether the result has been that the free movement of the Spirit has been cramped, or even killed, by the prison of the framework into which it has been forced.[14]

When we read such a description, we can respond in several ways: discouragement concerning our dismal track record in handling vision and truth; denial that things are really that bad; or renewed commitment to shun the lure of man-made structures and methods in favor of God's "wineskins" (which are subject to change as and when required by the new wine of the Spirit). May He grant us hearts to respond in faith and obedience to His will.

We now consider some of satan's specific strategies against the Church.

1. Doctrinal Heresies—"Jesus Plus...":

Even though the apostles had been careful to lay a solid foundation of truth, it didn't take long for certain elements in the Church to begin eating of the tree of the knowledge of good and evil and, as a result, being drawn into heresy. In fact, much of the content in the letters of the New Testament—from Romans to Revelation—is focused on correcting doctrinal errors and destructive heresies. It must have been an exasperating and, at times, heart-breaking experience for the apostles, dealing with one error after another and seeing some of their good friends go astray.

The problem in the Galatian church was extreme Judaism, while Philippi embraced both Judaism's strict adherence to the law as well as a form of sensuous, gluttonous antinomianism (where "anything goes"). At Colosse, it was an ascetic form of Gnosticism that included ritualistic elements from Judaism—circumcision, abstention from certain meats and drinks, keeping of Sabbaths and New Moons— while at the same time mixing certain aspects of heathenism such as mystical, secret knowledge, theosophy and the worship of angels. Paul responds to this by saying to the Colossian believers:

> Do not let anyone who delights in false humility and the worship of angels disqualify you for the prize. Such a person goes into great detail about what he has seen, and his unspiritual mind puffs him up with idle notions. He has lost connection with the Head, from whom the whole body, supported and held together by its ligaments and sinews, grows as God causes it to grow.

> Since you died with Christ to the basic principles of this world, why, as though you still belonged to it, do you submit to its rules: "Do not handle! Do not taste! Do not touch!"? These are all destined to perish with use, because

they are based on human commands and teachings. Such regulations indeed have an appearance of wisdom, with their self-imposed worship, their false humility and their harsh treatment of the body, but they lack any value in restraining sensual indulgence.[15]

By the time John wrote his first epistle around A.D. 90, the heresy of Gnosticism was spreading like wildfire. As one of the most dangerous heresies of the first three centuries, it combined elements of Greek philosophy, Eastern religions and Christianity. Gnostics denied Christ's true humanity because they believed that *spirit* was absolutely good while *matter* was entirely evil. This belief often led to asceticism, which involved harsh treatment of the body. Ironically, it also led to licentiousness. Some Gnostics reasoned that since the body was matter and therefore evil, what was done with it was of no moral consequence.

In all of these heresies—and in all heresies ever since that time—there is a common thread: that the Cross was not enough; that *Christ was not enough*. Yes, they preached Jesus, but it was Jesus *plus* circumcision, Jesus *plus* the law, Jesus *plus* Sabbaths, Jesus *plus* man's philosophy, Jesus *plus* tradition, Jesus *plus* secret knowledge. (Does this theme sound familiar? Do we still make the mistake of adding our little bit to the essence of the gospel?) These beliefs were like a virus in the Body of Christ, a contagion that was to spread throughout Christendom, and one that would require many rigorous "treatments" to re-establish healthy orthodoxy and practice.[16]

2. Revering the Saints:

It all started so innocently. The church at Smyrna began to commemorate annually the martyrdom of their bishop, Polycarp. It seemed fitting that the celebration took place at his grave, which, in time, became part of a new trend. Just as temples and altars were built previously to honor heroes, church buildings and chapels now came to be built over the graves of the martyrs, and were consecrated in their names. Sacred gifts of silver and gold were hung there—just as in the temples of pagan gods. According to Chrysostom, the martyrs' graves were more splendidly adorned and more frequently visited than the palaces of kings. Their relics were believed to possess miraculous virtue and were preserved with scrupulous care.

In addition, statues and carvings depicting Mary, the apostles and martyrs began to be produced. Although the Greek church rejected these carvings and statues, they welcomed the use of icons,[17] reasoning that they helped to educate the illiterate in biblical truths concerning Christ, Mary and other New Testament personalities.

By the beginning of the fourth century, some of the church fathers began praying to the saints. Ephraim Syrus addresses the departed saints with these words: "Remember me, ye heirs of God, ye brethren of Christ, pray to the Savior for me, that I through Christ may be delivered from him who assaults me from day to day."

Even Chrysostom became an enthusiastic advocate of invoking the help of the saints. On one occasion he exhorted his hearers to implore the saints to be their protectors: "For they have great boldness, not merely during their life, but also after their death. For now they bear the stigmata of Christ [the marks of martyrdom], and when they show these, they can persuade the King to anything."[18]

3. Veneration of Mary:

In the second century, a new heresy arose when Mary, the mother of Jesus, began to be seen as the spiritual counterpart to Eve. According to this view, just as sin came into the world through Adam and Eve, so redemption came through Jesus and Mary; as Eve was the natural mother of all living, Mary was the spiritual mother of all living. This concept was even espoused by church leaders like Justyn Martyr, Irenaeus and Tertullian.

After the middle of the fourth century, the church's veneration of Mary became even more extreme as she was transformed from *Mother of our Lord* into *Mother of God*; from *Highly favored one* into a *Dispenser of favors*; from *Blessed among women* into an *Intercessor above all women*; from *Redeemed daughter of Adam* into a *Sinless, holy co-redeemer.*

By the beginning of the fifth century, the worship of saints appeared in full bloom, with Mary placed at the head as the most blessed *Queen of the heavenly host.* From that time on, numerous buildings—including the church building at Ephesus—were dedicated to the *Holy Mother of God, the perpetual Virgin.* Mary was declared to have had a "sinless conception, sinless birth, resurrection and ascension to heaven" and to be "a participator of all the power of heaven and earth." Leaders like Proclus of Constantinople and Cyril of Alexandria couldn't find enough superlatives to describe Mary:

> She was the crown of virginity, the indestructible temple of God, the dwelling place of the Holy Trinity, the paradise of the second Adam, the bridge from God to man, the loom of incarnation, the scepter of orthodoxy; through her the Trinity is glorified and adored, the devil and demons are put to flight, the nations converted, and the fallen creature raised to heaven.[19]

It is true that there was strong reaction to much of this, but in one way or another most of the Early Church Fathers subscribed to these extra-biblical doctrines—despite the clear teaching of the apostle Paul that "there is one God and one mediator between God and men, the man Christ Jesus…"[20] As for the pagans who were "Christianized," the veneration of Mary and the saints was reminiscent of their worship of multiple gods; for many of these converts, the distinction between veneration and worship was not altogether clear.

4.   Marriage of Church and State:

Constantine the Great, who ruled the Roman Empire from A.D. 306 to A.D. 337, is broadly viewed as a positive influence on the Early Church and is credited with the wide acceptance of Christianity among the masses. But what seemed like a great victory turned out to be a very mixed blessing.

The Empire at that time was very polytheistic, worshiping many gods. It was a veritable "multi-cultural and multi-faith" society, and Constantine himself reflected this mixture. While claiming he had become a Christian, Constantine did not abandon his pagan roots during his lifetime. He would consult mediums for advice from time to time, and retained the title and dignity of a *Pontifex Maximus* or high priest of the heathen hierarchy.

His coins bore the name of Christ on one side, but on the other, a figure of the sun god and the inscription *Sol Deus Invictus*. In fact, Constantine never formally renounced paganism until he was on his deathbed. Just hours before his death, he suddenly exclaimed, "Now let us cast away all duplicity," and requested baptism. With that he took off his imperial purple robe and put on the white baptismal robe.

In retrospect, the worst aspect of Constantine's legacy may have been the marriage of church and state, resulting in the use of coercive force (including the power of the sword) to achieve spiritual goals. The problem of state religion has dogged the Church through the ages since then. Even today there are several European nations who tax their citizens in order to support the state church. And in the U.K., where the official head of the Church of England is by law the head of state, we face the distinct possibility of the highest church office being held by a self-confessed adulterer when Prince Charles becomes King. (That is not intended as an unkind or critical comment, but simply as a factual statement illustrating the problem of mixing church and state.)

THE DARK AGES

After Constantine, the church throughout Europe sank slowly into the murky waters of what became known as the Dark Ages. Instead of being "the light of the world," the Church degenerated into darkness, debauchery, politics, murder and unspeakable distortions of the faith. The Crusades, the Inquisition and other events provide ample evidence for this sorry description.

In spite of these horrors, there were many outstanding examples of men and women who, by and large, stood true to the faith. Among these was St. Bede of Durham, an eighth-century monk whose writings are considered the finest historical work of the early Middle Ages. Bede also translated John's Gospel into Anglo Saxon, but while writing, became very ill. Close to death and with no strength left to write, a young man was provided to finish the translation at his dictation.

At 3 A.M. of his last day, only one chapter remained to be completed. On being informed of this fact, he instructed the youth, "Take your pen and make ready, and write fast." Even though his strength was draining away, he continued dictating until 9 A.M. He then asked for the priests of the monastery to come and gather around him and, from his wooden chest, drew out such items as pepper, napkins and incense, and distributed his meager possessions to his fellow monks while praying a blessing over each one.

Later that day his young scribe spoke up, "Dear master, there is yet one sentence not written," to which Bede answered, "Write quickly." Not long after, the lad said, "It is ended." He replied, "It is well, you have said the truth. It is ended. Receive my head into your hands, for it is a great satisfaction to me to sit facing my holy place where I was wont to pray, that I may also sitting call upon my Father." And thus on the pavement of his little cell, he sang, "Glory be to the Father, and to the Son, and to the Holy Ghost." When he had named the Holy Ghost, he breathed his last and so departed to the heavenly kingdom.

More than three centuries later, in A.D. 1090, Bernard of Clairvaux was born.[21] He was known as the founder and abbot of the convent of Clairvaux, but also as a man of great holiness. It was said of him that "in his countenance there shone forth a pureness not of earth but of heaven, and his eyes had the clearness of an angel's and the mildness of a dove's eyes."

While Bernard denied the doctrine of the immaculate conception of Mary, and constantly referred to Scripture as his authority, he nevertheless remained very supportive of the Pope, especially in his preaching in support of the Crusades.[22] He was also known throughout Europe for healing many who were sick and ministering to hundreds for deliverance from demons.

Centuries later, both Calvin and Luther were to hold Bernard in high regard. Luther praised him for not having depended on his monk's vow but upon the free grace of Christ for salvation, commenting on one occasion, "Bernard loved Jesus as much as anyone can." This was very evident in some of the songs Bernard wrote, such as: *Jesus Thou joy of Loving Hearts, O Sacred Head Now Wounded,* and one of my favorites:

> Jesus the very thought of Thee
> With sweetness fills my breast,
> But sweeter far Thy face to see
> And in Thy presence rest.
>
> No voice can sing, nor heart can frame,
> Nor can the memory find
> A sweeter sound than Thy bless'd Name,
> O Savior of mankind.

O Hope of every contrite heart,
O Joy of all the meek
To those who fall how kind Thou art!
How good to those who seek!

But what to those who find? Ah this
No tongue nor pen can show;
The love of Jesus, what it is,
None but His loved ones know.

Jesus, our only joy be Thou,
As Thou our prize wilt be;
Jesus, be Thou our glory now
And through eternity.

Another great French believer of that period was Peter Waldo of Lyon, a wealthy merchant who began to preach his newfound faith and employ others to translate parts of Scripture into the local French dialect. This angered both the local bishop and the Pope who were further infuriated when they discovered he was sending out disciples, two by two, to preach the gospel all over Europe. These Waldensian preachers (as they were called) encouraged the memorization of Scripture (up to the whole New Testament!), rejected the priest and laity divide, and administered communion themselves.

This led to severe persecution from Rome, including imprisonment, confiscation of goods, the destruction of homes, and even death by burning. Not all the beliefs and practices of the Waldensians were commendable, but one cannot dismiss their immense courage or the new paths they opened up—sealed with their own blood—that led on toward the Reformation. As in the days of Elijah when there were still 7,000 who had not bowed the knee to Baal, these believers chose rather to die than renounce their faith. The faithful witness of the Waldensians and others of this period would serve to set the stage for the next move of God. The tide had begun to turn, and was about to come in like a flood.

ENDNOTES

1. Philip Schaff, *The History of the Christian Church*, Vol. 2 (Peabody, Massachusetts: Hendrickson Publishing, 1996), 76.

2. Matthew 7:21.

3. 1 Corinthians 13:12.

4. As Bob Mumford once put it, "If I saw where my blind spots were, I would change!"

5. Galatians 2:1-14.

6. 1 Corinthians 10:11.

7. 1 Corinthians 3:12.

8. Philip Schaff, op. cit., 19-20. In the interest of brevity, this excellent history, originally published in 1858, is cited in a somewhat abridged form.

9. Ibid., 20-21.

10. Ibid., 22.

11. Ibid.

12. Hebrews 11:38.

13. Matthew 16:23.

14. Author unknown. Excerpt from G. Milton Smith, *God Acting in Human History* (Auckland, N.Z.: Faith Bible Course, 1981), 18.

15. Colossians 2:18-23.

16. Some of these "treatments" came in the form of creeds that were established (often through major church councils) such as the Apostles', Nicene and Athanasian Creeds.

17. Icons typically were images painted on small wooden panels.

18. Philip Schaff, *The History of the Christian Church, Vol. 3* (Peabody, Massachusetts: Hendrickson Publishing, 1996), 439 (abridged).

19. Ibid., 421.

20. 1 Timothy 2:5.

21. Most of these details are drawn from Philip Schaff, *The History of the Christian Church, Vol. 5*.

22. According to one source, Bernard had even promised forgiveness of sins and entry after death into Paradise for those who fought in the Crusades. However, this represented an aberration from his normal preaching (not to mention Scripture) for which he later expressed regret.

THIRTEEN

BACK TO BASICS

All authority in heaven and on earth has been given to me. Therefore go and make disciples of all nations, baptizing them in the name of the Father and of the Son and of the Holy Spirit, and teaching them to obey everything I have commanded you. —Jesus Christ[1]

We now come to a very exciting time in church history: an era in which reformers and pioneer evangelists challenged a corrupt status quo. Although it was a period of upheaval, conflict and persecution, it brought about much-needed cleansing in the Church and a return to key foundational doctrines. The reformers we will meet in this chapter were not without their own faults and blind spots, but they demonstrated extraordinary leadership and unflinching courage as they challenged the errors of the established church.

WYCLIFFE:

One of the giants among the early reformers was John Wycliffe. Born in 1324 and educated at Oxford University, Wycliffe first expressed his theological differences with the church hierarchy as a university scholar. He strongly repudiated the doctrine of transubstantiation (the belief that the bread and wine of Communion are transformed into the real body and blood of Christ), and claimed that the Church, as the people of God, did not need priests as mediators between themselves and God.

About 1380, Wycliffe began training and sending out traveling evangelists, many of them Oxford graduates, who became known as *Lollards*. They were a sensation. They spread out from Oxford, preaching and setting up small groups in the surrounding villages and towns and eventually all across England. This innovation soon aroused the ire of the church hierarchy, as we see in this description of the Lollards by Bishop Courtenay: "...itinerant, unauthorized preachers who teach erroneous, yea heretical, assertions publicly, not only in churches but also in public squares and other profane places, and who do this under the guise of great holiness, but without having obtained any Episcopal or papal authorization."[2] (Of course, this ignores the fact that Jesus and His disciples often ministered in public places, and did so without the approval of religious authorities.)

Meanwhile, Wycliffe devoted himself to translating the Bible from the Latin *Vulgate* into English. As a result, the ordinary people of England were able to read the Scriptures in their own language, rather than being restricted to hearing God's Word through a priest's interpretation in a Sunday service. Wycliffe was eventually banished to Lutterworth, where he spent the rest of his days, and from where he wrote several treatises. One of the most important of these, the *Trialogus*, basically stated that where the Bible and the Church do not agree, we must obey the Bible, and where conscience and human authority are opposed, we must follow our conscience.

On December 29, 1384, after suffering the second of two strokes, Wycliffe passed into the presence of his Lord and Savior. Those who loved him referred to him as the "Evangelical Doctor" (and years later as the "Morning Star of the Reformation"), but the church establishment viewed him otherwise. Announcing his death, Walsingham, chronicler of St. Albans, had this to say:

> On the feast of the passion of St. Thomas of Canterbury, John de Wyclif, that instrument of the devil, that enemy of the Church, that author of confusion to the common people, that image of hypocrites, that idol of heretics, that author of schism, that sower of hatred, that coiner of lies, being struck with the horrible judgment of God, was smitten with palsy and continued to live till St. Sylvester's Day, on which he breathed out his malicious spirit into the abodes of darkness.[3]

I suspect that if Wycliffe could have heard that particular eulogy, he would have considered the source and taken personal satisfaction in being thus vilified. It showed he had made a difference. In fact, the impact of this courageous man was staggering: the Bible was unchained from the pulpit and released into the hands of all who had a hunger for God's Word; the preaching of the gospel was heard once again in the marketplace; the Pope's secular authority over the state was challenged; the "priesthood of all believers" was reintroduced; and the doctrine of the sole sufficiency of Christ's mediatorial ministry was re-established.

LUTHER:

Born in 1483 in Eisleben in Saxony, Martin Luther grew up with an abiding sense of unworthiness.[4] One day, on his way to Erfurt University, he was overtaken by a violent thunderstorm and fell to the ground. "Help, beloved St. Anna!" he cried out, "[and] I will become a monk."[5] Luther survived and, true to his word, entered an Augustinian monastery.

The monks were given to worshipful veneration of the Virgin Mary, a practice that Luther was quick to embrace. He became a model monk who, because of his rigorous self-discipline in prayer, fasting, night watches and self-mortification, was held up as one to be emulated. He was later to say, "If ever a monk got to heaven by monkery, I would have gotten there."[6] But no matter how hard he tried, he still could not find rest for his soul. His burden of guilt grew ever greater.

A turning point came when an elderly teacher of novices at the monastery (or *convent*, as it was then called) reminded Luther of an article in the Apostles' Creed relating to forgiveness of sin, and pointed out Paul's teaching in Scripture on justification by grace through faith. Another godly man who helped Luther (and became a spiritual father to him) was Johann von Staupitz, a Doctor of Divinity and Vicar-General of the Augustinian convents in Germany. He taught that the law "makes known the disease, but cannot heal," and that the central issue in life is to have Christ in our hearts. Furthermore, he believed that the knowledge of the Christian faith and the love of God are gifts of pure grace, beyond our ability, works and merits. Staupitz helped Luther begin a journey that would bring fundamental change: from a preoccupation with his own sinful state to a focus on the merits of Christ, from the law to the Cross, from works to faith, from the tree of the knowledge of good and evil to the tree of life.

Luther became a professor of Biblical Studies at the University of Wittenberg, and it was there while lecturing on Romans and Galatians that he became joyfully convinced of the truth that *the just shall live by faith.* Describing his reaction to the realization that righteousness was a gift, Luther stated, "A gateway to heaven had opened...I was reborn." But included in this revelation was also a "gateway" to conflict. Truth indeed sets us free—as Jesus promised—but it also may bring trouble for those who embrace it.

On October 31, 1517, at the hour of noon, Luther nailed 95 theses to the wooden doors of the castle-church at Wittenberg, taking issue with an envoy of the Pope who was selling indulgences to raise money for building St. Peter's basilica in Rome. The church had invented indulgences as a means of pardoning sin, but these had "progressed" from sacrificial acts expressing repentance to contributions toward a worthy cause. The latter became an increasingly popular fundraising tool, and it was this "abuse" of indulgences to which Luther objected. Years later in A.D. 1545 when he published his collected works, Luther referred to the 95 theses as follows:

> I allow them to stand, that by them it may appear how weak I was, and in what a fluctuating state of mind, when I began this business. I was then a monk and a mad papist, and so submersed in the dogmas of the Pope that I would have readily murdered any person who denied obedience to the Pope.[7]

Luther's spiritual journey led him to conclude from Scripture that forgiveness could not be bought through indulgences, nor could salvation be earned through good works or inherited through Christian parents. It was inevitable that Rome would take drastic measures against him. First, he was excommunicated, then, shortly afterwards, ordered to appear before Emperor Charles V at the *diet* (governing assembly) at Worms, Germany. Stating that his conscience was captive to the Word of God, Luther made his famous declaration, "Here I stand. I can do no other."

While Luther was active in public life, he remained a scholar, producing many theological works, a hymnbook and liturgy, and a translation of the entire Bible into German—which not only gave the people the Bible in their own tongue, but also established the standard form of the German language. He was fearless in his conviction of the supremacy of Scripture over extra-biblical teachings and traditions of men. He also advocated the priesthood of all believers, and restored congregational singing to the common people. (It has been said that Luther even took some old drinking songs and wrote new words to them—an example being the well-known hymn *A Mighty Fortress is Our God*.)

Luther spoke out strongly against clerical celibacy, declaring, "God has created man for marriage, and those who oppose it must either be ashamed of their manhood, or pretend to be wiser than God!" He married a former nun named Katherine von Bora (who had a reputation for being very bossy, but who nonetheless bore him six much-loved children).

Space does not permit more than a glimpse of the lives of the great reformers, but I do want to acknowledge the contribution of courageous men like Luther who, by God's grace, enabled the Church to crawl out from the religious mire of the Dark Ages and recover the simple truths and lifestyles of the Early Church. They were not perfect—either in character or doctrine—but were willing to pay the ultimate price for truth, and the Church was transformed as a result.

THE ANABAPTISTS:

Next to emerge in sixteenth-century Europe were the Anabaptists. This group rejected the validity of infant baptism because they believed that the Bible taught repentance from sin and faith in Christ as prerequisites to baptism. They required anyone converting from Catholicism to be re-baptized, hence the term *Anabaptist*. For this truth they paid with their lives. A saying of that time was, "He who dips, shall be dipped," meaning, "He who is re-baptized shall be drowned." And that is in fact what happened. Many men and women were bound and thrown into rivers and lakes, while others were burned at the stake, hanged or beheaded.

Anabaptists opposed government involvement in religion (as, for example, in state churches). They were not interested in simply reforming the Church, but wanted to restore it to the pattern they saw in the pages of the New Testament. There they observed a church that was not rich or politically involved, but instead one where members were all brothers and sisters in Christ—and even shared things in common. While some Anabaptists held to radical, socialist beliefs concerning property and were caught up in a fanatical anticipation of Christ's return (in which, according to one leader, Strasbourg was to be the New Jerusalem[8]), in general they represented a sincere, Bible-based movement whose descendants were to include the Mennonites, Hutterites and Amish.

The Anabaptists also believed they should celebrate the Lord's Supper—or, as they called it, "breaking of bread"—as a simple meal of bread and wine that commemorated the Lord's death. They neither agreed with the Catholic doctrine of *transubstantiation* (that the bread and wine were transformed into the actual body and blood of Christ) nor accepted Luther's *consubstantiation* (that the real "presence" of Christ was with the bread and wine). Not only were the Anabaptists opposed by the Catholic Church, they were also strongly denounced by Luther, Zwingli, Calvin, and later by John Wesley.[9]

CALVIN:

John Calvin was born in 1509 in France. He experienced a sudden spiritual conversion in late 1532 and, within a few months, declared himself to be a Protestant. He became a forceful advocate of the doctrine of grace, and strongly asserted, "Only one haven of salvation is left open for our souls, and that is the mercy of God in Christ. We are saved by grace—not by our merits, not by our works."[10]

However, Calvin's emphasis on salvation by grace did not deter him from advocating good works. Believing that Christianity was intended to reform all of society, Calvin lectured and wrote on various political, social and international issues and strongly encouraged Christian education. His letters and other writings fill nearly 57 volumes, and include his famous *Institutes of the Christian Religion*. In more recent years, a theological summary of key Calvinist doctrines was developed using the mnemonic TULIP:[11]

T - for the total depravity of man.

U - for unconditional election.

L - for limited atonement or, more precisely, definite atonement.

I - for irresistible grace.

P - for the perseverance of the saints.

During his time in Geneva, Calvin became the first Protestant leader in Europe to gain partial independence for the church from the state—although he himself sometimes used the power of government to compel conformity. His followers in France were later called *Huguenots*, while those he influenced in England came to be known as *Puritans*.

THE PURITANS AND NONCONFORMISTS:

The struggle for truth and religious liberty continued in the 17th century as the Puritans and Nonconformists (including the Dissenters, the Covenanters and the Quakers) frequently became targets of persecution. In one way or another, these groups of believers believed passionately in their cause and were willing to die for it. The following is just one incident illustrating the strength of their commitment.

It's the story of two women who were martyred for their faith: 70-year-old Margaret MacLachlan and 18-year-old Margaret Wilson.[12] Their crime? Attending field meetings and cottage meetings of the Scottish Covenanters and refusing to swear that the church was a department of the state. Grierson of Lagg, a vicious opponent of the Covenanters, sentenced them to death by drowning. They were taken from their dark, filthy prison cell to the Blednoch Burn, which is inundated by water whenever the tide rushes in. It was here that they would soon pass into the presence of their beloved Savior.

In the early 1980s, Janette and I celebrated our 25th wedding anniversary by spending six weeks in Scotland (where she was born). During our time there we visited several historic places, including those where martyrs had been executed or buried. So it was that we stood on the bank of Blednoch Burn, picturing the scene where the elder Margaret had been fastened to a stake further down the beach to await the incoming tide that would eventually rise to cover her head. The younger Margaret had been tied to a stake higher up so that she could witness the death of her fellow sufferer.

At any time they could avoid death simply by saying "God save the King" and acknowledging him as head of the church. This they resolutely refused. As the waves rose higher around Margaret MacLachlan, the younger Margaret began to sing psalms. It wasn't long before the elder lady began to struggle with the waves at her head, whereupon Grierson began to taunt Margaret Wilson: "So what do you think of her now?" "Think? Margaret replied, "I see Christ wrestling there. Think ye that we are sufferers? No; it is Christ in us, for He sends none a warfare at their own charges." Margaret continued to pray and to sing Psalm 25 until it was her turn. She also quoted from Romans chapter 8:

> ...whom he justified, them he also glorified...we are more than conquerors through him that loved us. For I am persuaded, that neither death, nor life, nor angels, nor principalities, nor powers, nor things present, nor things to come, nor height, nor depth, nor any other creature, shall be able to separate us from the love of God, which is in Christ Jesus our Lord.[13]

She finally collapsed unconscious into the water, whereupon Grierson dragged her out and gave her one last chance to recant and pray for the king. Her family and friends who were gathered there began to plead with her, "O Margaret, say it!" But Margaret would respond only by praying for the king's repentance, salvation and forgiveness. "Damn bitch," raged Grierson. "We do not want such prayers. Tender her the oaths." Margaret now became distressed. "No! No! No sinful oaths for me. I am one of Christ's children. Let me go." Then he threw her back into the water where she quickly expired.

Janette and I walked silently away from the beach and visited the churchyard cemetery where the remains of these martyrs are buried. I shall never forget, standing by their joint grave, the overwhelming sense of gratitude I felt for those two heroines of the faith. The tears were not easy to keep back.

Prior to 1980, our church family in Vancouver was known as St. Margaret's Community Church,[14] named—according to some sources—in honor of Margaret Wilson. But I had no doubt whatsoever that the last thing Margaret would have wanted was for a church to be named after her; she would have regarded it as *anathema*.[15] After this visit, I was especially grateful that we had changed the name of our church to "West Coast Christian Fellowship." It was the least we could do to honor Margaret's faith!

Another Scottish Covenanter, 20-year-old Marion Harvie, wrote on the eve of her martyrdom:

> Now farewell, lovely and sweet Scriptures, which were aye my comfort in the midst of all my difficulties! Farewell, faith! Farewell, hope! Farewell, wanderers, who have been comfortable to my soul, in the hearing of them commend Christ's love! Farewell, brethren! Farewell, sisters! Farewell, Christian acquaintances! Farewell, sun, moon and stars! And now, welcome my lovely, heartsome Christ Jesus, into whose hands I commit my spirit throughout all eternity.[16]

The Nonconformists represented a range of beliefs and practices, but shared several notable characteristics: simplicity of worship, the primacy of preaching, the publication of quality doctrinal books from authors like John Owen and Thomas Brooks,[17] structuring of church government to align more closely with Scripture, and the freedom to gather and break bread together in homes or other "non-consecrated" buildings.

These groups emphasized piety and personal devotion to Christ, and some encouraged the manifestation of the Holy Spirit in public worship. Early Quakers, for example, would begin to shake involuntarily during worship (hence the name by which they came to be called: *Quakers*), attributing this to the anointing of the Holy Spirit. They also included dancing in some of their worship services, with the men in one circle and the women in another.

THE MORAVIANS, CONGREGATIONALISTS AND METHODISTS:

The name of Jonathan Edwards, a Congregational pastor and evangelist, is linked inseparably with the Great Awakening of the 18th century. Born in Connecticut in 1703, Edwards was a brilliant scholar from his youth—achieving fluency in Greek, Hebrew and Latin by age 13! Like English evangelist George Whitefield, his doctrinal views reflected Calvin's reformed theology.

The 18th century brought a dramatic increase in Christ-centered preaching and the subsequent inner transformation of many souls. The spiritual tide was turning—and starting to come in with a rush. Unusual visitations of God began to occur whereby whole towns and cities seemed to come under a heavenly siege. Edwards once observed: "Those who were wont to be the vainest and loosest, and those who had been most disposed to think and speak slightly of vital and experimental religion, were now generally subject to great awakenings."[18]

Meanwhile, on the other side of the Atlantic, God was working in the hearts of men like George Whitefield, John and Charles Wesley, as well as Count Zinzendorf, who led the Moravian Church in Germany. The Moravians were known for their dedication in prayer (evidenced by their continuous, 24-hour-a-day prayer meeting that lasted 100 years!), their *Koinonia* love feasts, and their divine "obsession" to see the gospel proclaimed to every group of people in every corner of the earth. While other Protestant churches averaged one missionary out of 2,500 members during the last two centuries, the Moravians averaged one in 92. The seal on all their official documents was: *Our Lamb has conquered; let us follow Him.*

The first Moravian missionaries, Leonard Dober and David Nitschmann, went out from Germany to the West Indies in 1732 after hearing the pleas of a black slave who had been converted. Filled with concern for the salvation of his people, the slave pleaded with Count Zinzendorf to send missionaries to preach the gospel to the black natives of the West Indies. (Existing churches were for whites only.) After much soul searching and an emotional farewell (at which they sang 100 hymns), Dober and Nitschmann sailed from Copenhagen in a Dutch ship bound for the West Indies, ready to be sold into slavery in order to be able to preach the gospel to the slaves.

Many people tried to dissuade them from going, saying that they were mad. Others called from the dock as the boat was leaving, "Why are you doing this?" Their reply was simple, but it speaks volumes about their motivation and vision: "That the Lamb who was slain might receive the reward of His suffering." After they arrived, some local inhabitants took pity on them and provided them with accommodation. In time they led a number of slaves to Christ, and were subsequently joined by other Moravian missionaries. Sadly, of the first 29 who came, 22 died within the first few months; they called it the "dying season."

One of my dear and loyal friends for over 30 years, the late Ron Trudinger, was a descendant of the Moravians. Ron told of how his grandmother, Clara Schammer, unable to be a missionary herself, prayed for a large number of children so that she could send as many as possible to the mission field. God answered, giving Clara and August Trudinger 13 children, 12 of whom survived, with 8 becoming missionaries to China, Tibet, Africa and Australia. At Ron's memorial service in late 2002, we heard testimonies of how he had ministered the love of Christ to the Australian Aborigines—at a time when they were being exploited and even killed by whites. He first created a written form of their language, Pitjantjatjara, and then translated the Gospel of Mark. Three months before Ron died, he was thrilled to receive one of the first copies of the entire Bible in that language.

GEORGE WHITEFIELD AND JOHN WESLEY:

Connections among the reformers often crossed cultural and national barriers, as we see in the following instance involving John Wesley and spiritual influences between English and German reform groups:

> It is interesting to note that the circle of influence was completed when Wesley was helped to personal faith in Christ by the Moravians. Wycliffe's teachings had influenced Hus, the founder of the Bohemian Brethren, out of which the Moravian church, which was to have such an influence on the spiritual life of the Englishman John Wesley, emerged.[19]

The 18th century saw a steady increase in both the quality and quantity of preaching. Whitefield preached over 18,000 sermons in 34 years of ministry, while Wesley preached about 42,000—many of these after completing arduous journeys. Wesley traveled over 200,000 miles by horseback all over England, Scotland and Ireland during his days of field preaching. At first he found open air preaching distasteful but, after observing the vast numbers attending Whitefield's meetings and turning to Christ, he soon changed his mind and was similarly blessed with a great spiritual harvest. The following is an excerpt from George Whitefield's diary:

Sunday, March 25th. Preached at Hanham to a larger congregation than ever...upwards of 23,000. I was afterwards
told that those who stood farthest off hear me very plainly.
O may God speak to them by His Spirit, at the time that He
enables me to lift my voice like a trumpet. The open firma-
ment above me, the prospect of the adjacent fields, with the
sight of thousands and thousands, some in coaches, some
on horseback, and some in trees, and at times all affected
and drenched in tears together. My preaching in the fields
may displease some timorous, bigoted men, but I am thoroughly persuaded it pleases God, and why should I fear
anything else![20]

Wesley believed that the gifts of the Holy Spirit were given not
just for first century believers. In a lengthy public letter to Dr. Cony-
ers Middleton, he stated his belief that all the spiritual gifts were
fully operative in the third century but that the degeneracy of the
Church had led to the lapse in their use. Moreover, were the Church
reformed and truly spiritual, one could expect the re-introduction of
all the gifts—the "ordinary" and the "extraordinary" (or miraculous)
as he distinguished them.[21]

Both Whitefield and Wesley saw some remarkable signs and
wonders. On one occasion, Wesley was experiencing severe pain in
his teeth. When a friend related that he had been healed supernatu-
rally of similar pain after praying, Wesley responded in simple,
childlike faith by following his example and was likewise healed.
Other examples are recorded in Wesley's journal: a woman, bedrid-
den for several months, made an immediate recovery after he prayed
for her, as did another woman who was close to death.

And it wasn't only for *people* that he prayed. On a least three
occasions when his horses were injured, Wesley sought supernatural
healing for his animals, noting in his journal, "It being impossible to
procure any human help, I knew of no remedy but prayer. Immediately the lameness was gone." Wesley's own records show that he
also was deeply concerned for those under the oppression of evil
spirits, and prayed over them for deliverance:

"At St. Thomas's (Workhouse) was a young woman, raving
mad, screaming and tormenting herself continually. I had a

strong desire to speak with her…The tears ran down her cheeks all the time I was telling her, 'Jesus of Nazareth is able and willing to deliver you.' O where is faith upon earth? Why are these poor wretches left under the open bondage of Satan? Jesus, Master! Give thou medicines to heal this sickness and deliver those who are now vexed with unclean spirits."[22]

On another occasion, Wesley wrote about the general absence of spiritual gifts during long periods of church history:

"The grand reason why the miraculous gifts were soon withdrawn was not only that faith and holiness were well nigh lost, but that dry, formal, orthodox men began even then to ridicule whatever gifts they had not themselves and to decry them all as either madness or imposture."[23]

It was also during this time that the social conscience of the renewal movement was aroused. Whitefield was the first of this period to pioneer schools for the poor and illiterate, while Wesley established the first free medical dispensary in England and worked to abolish the gin trade, slavery and war. Some historians credit the preaching and social reforms of Wesley and Whitefield with helping England avoid the anarchy experienced just across the English Channel—the savage uprising now known as the French Revolution.

Although John Wesley remained within the Anglican Church, he increasingly felt marginalized.[24] In order to help his many followers grow in faith and function effectively, he formed what were called societies, small groups of 10 to 20 people who met regularly for prayer, Bible study and outreach. These meetings were also blessed by the new hymns that his brother Charles wrote—some 6,000 songs including the beloved carol *Hark! The Herald Angels Sing*.

As we can see, Wesley recognized the value of a new wineskin for the new wine. But even the best leadership and the best structure can take a movement only so far. Despite his razor sharp mind, his clear ideas on what needed to be done, his communication skills and ability to sway multitudes into following, Wesley, in the end, could not impart some of his core values to the next generation. When he passed on to his reward, Wesley's methods remained and were zealously preserved, but his vision and values—the "fire" that drove him to take such radical action in the first place—faded away like the morning mist.

PIONEER MISSIONARIES:

In the latter part of the 18th century and throughout the 19th, many missionary pioneers set sail for foreign ports on a voyage of adventure, danger, and hardship. Some were courageous, some fool-hardy, but many clearly were motivated by a God-given longing to evangelize the world. For some particularly brave souls, the journey was understood to be a one-way trip, so they packed their belongings into a wooden coffin instead of a steamer trunk.

Men such as William Carey, David Livingstone and Hudson Taylor were used by God to affect not only individuals and groups, but also nations. Carey set sail for India in 1793 with the intent of spending the remainder of his life in the service of his Master. For him there were no furloughs, and letters from home could take up to two years to arrive. He never did return to England. In the face of severe trials and very limited resources, the accomplishments of Carey and the other pioneer missionaries of his time were awe-inspiring. Only Heaven will reveal the true measure of their sacrifice.

GEORGE MULLER:

The 19th century also saw a great upsurge in ministry to the poor—both in terms of bringing them the gospel and caring for their physical needs. One who modeled God's heart for the poor in this way was George Muller, who pioneered orphanages that operated strictly by faith.

Muller had no religious background as a child, and at age 16 was jailed as a thief. When he was 20, his life dramatically changed after attending a home meeting of Christians who gathered for prayer, worship and teaching in the Word. Muller became deeply impressed by the work of August Franke, who had established a large orphanage in Germany solely through dependence on God's provision. When Muller opened his first Orphan House in Bristol, England, he gave three reasons for embarking on such a venture:

> Firstly, that God might be glorified, should He be pleased
> to furnish me with the means, in its being seen that it is not
> a vain thing to trust in Him; and that thus the faith of His

children may be strengthened. Secondly, the spiritual welfare of fatherless and motherless children. Thirdly, their temporal welfare.[25]

Muller continued to oversee this ever-increasing work until his death at 93. He never deviated from the practice of refusing to make his needs known to others, trusting God at all times and in every circumstance to provide for both his needs and those of the orphans. He lived a frugal life and died a poor man, leaving a personal estate of about $850. However, it was later discovered that he himself had given $407,450 to the orphanage during his lifetime.[26]

CHARLES FINNEY:

Charles Finney was an American lawyer who was converted by a remarkable experience of God in 1821 and who became one of the most effective evangelists in history. For a time he served as minister of the Second Free Presbyterian Church in New York City, where it is said he experienced almost continuous revival. He later became president of Oberlin College in Ohio.

Finney's ministry took him to many states, and wherever he went, revivals broke out. In some towns where he preached, liquor stores had to close down after the entire population was converted. During his lifetime, which coincided with a period known as the Second Evangelical Awakening, it is estimated that over 1,000,000 people were converted to Christ.

THE SALVATION ARMY:

On August 20, 1865, the *Wesleyan Times* gave this brief report of an evangelistic crusade led by a certain William Booth:

The Reverend William Booth has been engaged for the past seven weeks holding a series of special meetings in the East End of London near the London Hospital and in the Mile End Road. Hundreds of working men and numbers of persons who never enter a place of worship have listened night after night to appeals of this devoted servant of God, and many conversions have taken place. In no part of the Metropolis is there a greater need for an evangelistic effort.

Even though the name *Salvation Army* was not yet in use, this was, in retrospect, the birthing of a powerful, new army of godly zealots who would eventually spread throughout the world. But the future success of William and Catherine Booth could not have been anticipated from their humble beginnings, as suggested by this early account:

> With a few musicians and loyal followers, Booth marched to open-air meetings or to revivals in the Quaker Burial Ground tent. Never mind that along the way they might be bombarded with stones, tomatoes, eggs, dead rats and cats, or other missiles by drunkards or hecklers. He held his Bible high, inviting people to follow, and proclaimed the gospel of love.[27]

While the Salvation Army has gained a great deal of respect since those days (escaping the barrage of dead rats and tomatoes it once attracted), it has continued to focus on reaching those who are most needy in society. Today there may not be the same emphasis on the need for Holy Ghost fire, but the Army still is a major player when it comes to caring for the poor in the name of Christ. Their reputation for charity with integrity is unparalleled in most of the major cities of the western world.

A REFORMATION LEGACY:

As we began this chapter, we noted that the reformers and pioneer evangelists of church history were not without their flaws and blind spots—an observation that biographical records will readily confirm. Nevertheless, the fact is that God used these men and women to change the face of Christianity: to overthrow corrupt, man-made structures; to re-establish biblical truth and patterns of church life; and, most importantly, to help renew the relational life of Christ in His Body—the new wine within a new wineskin. It was a revolution that moved us forward in the purposes of God by bringing us "back to basics."

Yet, not all these movements succeeded in maintaining their initial momentum. Would the Church regress once more? What would the 20th century hold in store? The answers in the next chapter may surprise you.

ENDNOTES

1. Matthew 28:18-20.

2. Philip Schaff, *The History of the Christian Church, Vol. 6* (Peabody, Massachusetts: Hendrickson Publishers, 1996), 320.

3. Ibid., 324.

4. One cannot help but think that if Luther's "low self-esteem" had been addressed by one of the well-meaning therapists of our time, the Reformation might have taken a very different course!

5. Philip Schaff, *The History of the Christian Church, Vol. 7* (Peabody, Massachusetts: Hendrickson Publishers, 1996), 112.

6. Ibid., 116.

7. Ibid., 157.

8. Earle E. Cairns, *Christianity Through the Ages* (Grand Rapids, Michigan: Zondervan, 1981), 307.

9. For further insights into the tensions that existed among the reformers, and between them and the Catholic Church, I highly commend *The Reformers and their Stepchildren* by Leonard Verduin (published by Eerdmans).

10. Philip Schaff, *The History of the Christian Church, Vol. 8* (Peabody, Massachusetts: Hendrickson Publishers, 1996), 311.

11. TULIP is not, however, a summary of Calvin's overall beliefs, as noted by J. I. Packer in his excellent book *A Quest for Godliness* (published by Crossway, 1990). Dr. Packer goes on to outline Calvin's challenge of Arminian doctrine.

12. Details of this story are taken from *Fair Sunshine* by Jock Purves (Edinburgh: Banner of Truth Trust, 1968), 77-84.

13. Romans 8:30, 37-39 (King James Version).

14. The original name was St. Margaret's Free Church of England, and later, St. Margaret's Reformed Episcopal Church.

15. Some of the best known reformers—notably Calvin and Luther—objected to having a church or movement named after them, but their successors ignored their wishes.

16. Jock Purves, *Fair Sunshine*, op. cit.

17. Thomas Brooks is also a favorite author of mine.

18. Jonathan Edwards, *The History of Christianity* (Oxford: A Lion Handbook, 1990), 441.

19. Earle E. Cairns, op. cit., 382.

20. Arnold Dallimore, *George Whitefield* (Edinburgh: Banner of Truth Trust, 1970), 267, 269.

21. Details on Wesley's life are drawn from *The Radical Wesley Reconsidered* (Bangor, U.K.: Bangor Christian Trust Publications, 1984).

22. Ibid., 51.

23. Ibid., 53.

24. It was following Wesley's death that his followers established a Methodist Church separate from the Anglican Church.

25. E. H. Broadbent, *The Pilgrim Church* (London: Marshall Pickering, 1931), 367.

26. Basil Miller, *George Muller* (Minneapolis, Minnesota: Dimension Books, 1941), 127. Note that dollar amounts were converted from British currency, and that the value in today's terms would be approximately ten or fifteen times those amounts.

27. Helen K. Hosier, *William and Catherine Booth* (Uhrichsville, Ohio: Barbour Publishing), 96.

FOURTEEN

A Century of Growth

It has been reserved for the twentieth century to experience an unexampled acceleration in the course of events. As an avalanche begins its slow movement, which, from being almost imperceptible, gains speed until it comes down with overwhelming power, so the slow development of earlier years has become the rushing torrent of our time. —E. H. Broadbenti

And he will be called
Wonderful Counselor, Mighty God,
Everlasting Father, Prince of Peace.
Of the increase of his government and peace
there will be no end.[2] —Isaiah, ca. 700 B.C.

With all the bad news we hear on a daily basis, it would be easy to think that Isaiah's prophecy of Christ's *unending, increasing* government was somewhat optimistic, and that evil, at least for now, may have gained the upper hand. It probably was in order to challenge such discouraging thoughts that Christian missions researcher Patrick Johnstone wrote a book entitled *The Church is Bigger Than You Think.*[3] From this—and other recent sources—we learn that there are, on average, 178,356 people around the world being added to the Church *every day.*

One hundred and seventy-eight thousand, three hundred and fifty-six. Did *your* newspaper report that astonishing statistic in today's headlines? Or did it concentrate on who was murdered, molested and robbed—plus the latest story on worldwide terrorism? The tragic events around us *are* serious and should not be minimized, but just because the world focuses on the latest developments in the kingdom of darkness doesn't mean we must follow suit. If we take seriously the words of Jesus that there is rejoicing in Heaven over one sinner who repents, we have to conclude that there is now a continual "celestial party" underway—and we can rightfully celebrate the fact.

In this chapter we will focus on the good news of the growth of the Kingdom of God in the 20th century, highlighting a few statistics and stories from different parts of the world. While there are no extensive critiques of the various leaders and movements, I certainly do not endorse all that has appeared under the banner of Christianity. The failings of the Church in the past 100 years—selfishness, divisiveness, racism and apostasy—could fill books.[4] But rather than dwell on the negatives, I want to direct our attention to the advancement of God's Kingdom through evangelism, the spread of His written Word, and the ongoing restoration of His ways. To that end, I will summarize some of the most influential movements of the past century, giving special attention to the areas of the greatest growth, and offering some personal perspectives.

Among the major ministries and events affecting the Church on a global basis were: the outstanding ministry of Billy Graham[5]; the arrival of the Wycliffe Bible Translators pioneered by Cameron Townsend; the 2nd Vatican Council under Pope John XXIII; the example of Mother Teresa of Calcutta (including her strong pro-life witness); the World Congress on Evangelism—Berlin 1966, Lausanne 1974, Manila 1989; and the Amsterdam conferences for Itinerant Evangelists in 1983 and 1986. But the most predominant influence of all came from the Pentecostal, Charismatic and Restoration movements.

PENTECOSTALS

The century began with an extraordinary visitation of God in a warehouse and horse stable at 312 Azusa Street in Los Angeles. (It would seem that God enjoys using stables for big events!) For several years there had been a growing sense of spiritual anticipation, with many churches in Los Angeles seeking God in prayer and engaging in door-to-door evangelism. Then, in 1906, God chose to use

William J. Seymour, a humble African American from Louisiana, the son of ex-slaves, to give leadership to the new Azusa Street Mission.[6] Seymour was wary of programs and orders of service, preferring to wait on the Holy Spirit and then proceed with the way he believed the Spirit was directing.

In the days that followed, many people were filled with the Holy Spirit and spoke in other tongues. Thousands of Christians from all over the world visited 312 Azusa Street and took back with them a burning desire to see a similar visitation in their own countries. (With reference to "burning," on one occasion the fire brigade was called to the warehouse by anxious neighbors who reported seeing flames shooting out of the top of the building. But this was no natural fire, it was God's holy presence—as was the fire that Daniel, Ezekiel, Isaiah and the apostle John witnessed.) By the end of three years, the revival at Azusa Street had given rise to the planting of many new churches.

Besides the new churches that came to be known as Pentecostal, there were several major preaching and healing ministries that touched the nation, notably Oral Roberts and Katherine Kuhlman. These ministries were no strangers to controversy, in part because they challenged the status quo of traditional church life, in part because of occasional words and actions that were unwise, and in part because they represented a threat to the kingdom of darkness. Space does not permit an adequate description of these pioneer Pentecostal ministries, but books like Jamie Buckingham's *Daughter of Destiny*—the life story of Kathryn Kuhlman—provide a rich yet painfully honest portrait of how the frailties of human character intersect with the power of the Holy Spirit.

Meanwhile, in England and other parts of Europe at the beginning of the century, amazing healings and various signs and wonders were accompanying the gospel preaching of Smith Wigglesworth. Here is how Wigglesworth described one such healing in Sweden:

> At Stockholm, long lines of people waited to get in. The hall held eighteen hundred people. At nearly every meeting crowds were unable to enter the building, but they

waited on, often hours and hours, for the chance, if any left the building, to step in the place.

Here a man with two crutches, his whole body shaking with palsy, is lifted onto the platform. (Behind him five or six hundred more are waiting for help.) This man is anointed and hands laid upon him in the Name of Jesus. He is still shaking. Then he drops one crutch, and after a short time the other one. His body is still shaking, but he takes the first step out in faith. Will it be? He lifts one foot and then the other, walks around the platform. The onlookers rejoice with him. Now he walks around the auditorium. Hallelujah![7]

In the same meeting, a woman stood up on a chair, much to her husband's embarrassment, waving her arms and shouting, "I am healed, I am healed!" She had been healed of mouth cancer. In speaking of Wigglesworth's audacious faith, James Salter observed:

We accompanied him on his great crusades with trepidation, for we never knew what he was going to do next. We were always afraid he would go "too far." But he never did. He always said, "You can't go too far with God; in fact, you can't go far enough."[8]

Around that time, a close friend of Wigglesworth, Thomas Myerscough, began to assemble a group of young men in order to train them for the mission field and evangelism. Among them were George Jeffreys and W. F. P. (Willie) Burton, two men whose ministry would be powerful and far-reaching. Willie Burton received Myerscough as a spiritual father, describing their relationship as similar to that of Paul and Timothy. I had the inestimable privilege of spending a considerable amount of time with Mr. Burton, particularly on occasions when he stayed in our home.

Myerscough planted a hunger for the mission field in these young men, while Wigglesworth, who sometimes took young Burton with him on evangelistic endeavors, imparted a strong faith and conviction in their hearts that preaching the gospel "with signs following" was normal evangelism. Accordingly, when Willie Burton and James Salter went to Africa in 1915, to the region known then as the

Belgian Congo, they saw extraordinary miracles, some of which are recorded in Burton's little book *Signs Following*. (As noted in an earlier chapter, Willie helped to plant almost 1,500 churches during his ministry there.)

George Jeffreys, meanwhile, began to hold major evangelistic crusades throughout the United Kingdom, crusades that drew huge crowds to salvation in Christ and where praying for the sick was an integral part of the ministry. A friend told me of one meeting at which he was present where a man with only one eye came forward to be healed. Suddenly the man cried out in pain because of a burning sensation in the empty socket.

Jeffreys assured him that all was well: "God is healing you." And, sure enough, a new eye grew in the socket while everyone else stood back and watched in amazement. The healed man's wife was beside herself with joy and wonderment. "Is it the same color as the other one?" she asked nervously. "Don't be foolish, woman," Jeffreys replied condescendingly, "Do you think God's color-blind?"[9]

Evangelistic zeal, the full expression of the gifts of the Holy Spirit, and healing as an essential part of the gospel—these were key elements of early British Pentecostal belief and practice. Men like Wigglesworth and Myerscough had seen that in the Scriptures, from Genesis through Revelation, God is portrayed consistently as the God of wonders. They could not understand the teaching of some Christian leaders that signs and wonders had ceased when the canon of Scripture was completed.

This view is also bewildering to many of our brothers and sisters from non-western countries. A certain prominent, evangelical Bible scholar was teaching at a seminar on the subject of healing, maintaining that there is no more need for miracles and the gifts of the Spirit because we now have the Scriptures, and declaring that in all his many years of ministry he had never witnessed anything supernatural. An East Indian friend of mine was listening to this in utter disbelief. Finally, he could not contain himself any longer. He raised his hand and managed to catch the speaker's attention: "Please, brother," he appealed, "where have you been?"

It is true that our eternal salvation is of far greater value than any physical healing we receive, but that does not make healing unimportant. If God, in His infinite wisdom, chooses to demonstrate His power and His love in this way, we cannot afford to treat it as an issue of doctrinal "preference." Our task is to represent our Father as accurately as possible to the world around us, in terms of His power, His truth, His wisdom and His heart of love toward people. That was the pattern of our Lord Jesus and the example of the apostles.

Jesus told His disciples, "Believe me when I say that I am in the Father and the Father is in me; or at least believe on the evidence of the miracles themselves. I tell you the truth, anyone who has faith in me will do what I have been doing."[10] Paul wrote the Corinthians, "My message and my preaching were not with wise and persuasive words, but with a demonstration of the Spirit's power..."[11] To the Romans, he said:

> I will not venture to speak of anything except what Christ has accomplished through me in leading the Gentiles to obey God by what I have said and done—by the power of signs and miracles, through the power of the Spirit. So from Jerusalem all the way around to Illyricum, I have fully proclaimed the gospel of Christ.[12]

For Jesus and Paul, there was no artificial divide between preaching the gospel and demonstrating its supernatural power. Yes, spiritual gifts can be misused by those seeking power or financial gain, and they can be falsified by charlatans. That was true in the pages of the New Testament[13] and it still is true today. In this life there always will be counterfeit copies of the real thing (because of the work of the enemy), but that does not change the fact that the real exists, and remains part of God's strategic plan.

Charismatics and the Restoration Movement

Early in the 20th century, a branch of Pentecostalism developed that emphasized not only the gifts of the Holy Spirit, but also the equipping gifts outlined in Ephesians chapter 4: apostle, prophet, evangelist, pastor and teacher. Calling themselves the *Apostolic Church*, they were convinced that these gifts were just as valid today as when they were first distributed by the ascended Christ. As time went by, there was such a proliferation of those claiming to be apostles and prophets that the effect was a cheapening of the very gifts they were eager to see restored. Little is heard from this movement today.

With the emergence of Watchman Nee of China, DeVern Fromke of the United States, and several leaders from England—Arthur Wallis, Cecil Cousen, Austin Sparkes and David Lillie, a whole new emphasis on the simplicity of New Testament doctrine began to take root. This time, the new development was not springing forth from the Pentecostals, but from people who would later be known as Charismatics and Restorationists. They came from the Open Brethren, Anglicans, Methodists, Baptists and, eventually, Roman Catholics.

Most of the leaders of this new movement[14] subscribed to the restoration of the fivefold ministries of Ephesians 4 and the gifts of the Spirit, but they also stressed the priesthood of all believers. Based on the example given in 1 Corinthians 14:26-33, they believed that any believer led by the Spirit of God could function in a church meeting through a teaching, a song, a prophecy, a tongue or an interpretation of a tongue. They also held that the Church is indeed the visible, functioning Body of Christ, and that, according to Romans 12 and 1 Corinthians 12, it is essential for each part to function properly according to the measure of grace given by Christ.

In many cases, this new direction was accompanied by a theological departure from a *dispensational, pre-tribulation-rapture* eschatology. The latter was a teaching that claimed Christ would secretly—and at any time—rapture the Church before it could sink into total apostasy and evil could gain complete victory on earth. The words of an old song epitomized this view:

> Hold the fort for I am coming,
> Jesus signals still;
> Wave the answer back to heaven,
> By Thy grace we will.

This view was replaced with a victorious eschatology that said, in essence: although the world was getting darker as evil flourished, the growing darkness would coincide with (and ultimately be surpassed by) the increasing light of Christ in the Church. Also, according to Scripture, Jesus was coming back for a Church that would, in the glorious moment of His return, appear "radiant...without stain or wrinkle or any other blemish."[15] Furthermore, before Christ's return, the gospel of the Kingdom would be preached to every tribe, tongue, people and nation on the entire earth; and there would be a great outpouring of the Holy Spirit[16] resulting in millions being swept into the Kingdom of God.

So, which view of end-time history is correct? Is the Church in decline, desperately hanging on by its fingertips? Or is the "knowledge of the Lord" filling the whole earth "as waters cover the sea,"[17] with the Church significantly advancing in its proclamation of the gospel? Where do we stand today in terms of the restoration of God's original plan? The reports, facts and figures that follow do not provide a *complete* answer to those questions (for one thing, numbers do not tell us the condition of the heart), but they do tell a story—one that I personally find greatly encouraging.

AROUND THE WORLD

According to the new edition of the *World Christian Encyclopedia*, about 2 billion (or 31percent) of the world's population is now Christian, making it the world's largest religion.[18] The second largest is Islam at 1.2 billion. Other sources[19] tell us that biblical Christians (those with a biblical, personal faith in Jesus Christ as Lord and Savior) are growing at an annual rate of 6.9 percent, while the earth's population growth is just under 2 percent. As noted earlier, the average number of new Christians each day is 178,356. The net increase in the number of churches is estimated at 44,000 each year.

And Christianity is no longer a "white man's religion." While 81 percent of Christians were white in 1900, that proportion was only 45 percent by the year 2000. (Of course, Christianity originally started with Jewish disciples and added white-faced Gentiles only later.) The numbers we will see as we take a brief tour around the world will help to explain the colorful change in the family of God during the 20th century.

In 1900 there were fewer than 300,000 born-again Christians in the whole of Latin America. By 1980 there were 20,000,000 such believers. Within 12 years this number had doubled, and estimates for the turn of century were close to 100,000,000. On average, 400 people are coming to Christ every hour in this region, four times the population growth rate.[20] Meanwhile, in sub-Saharan Africa, just 3 percent were evangelical Christian in 1900. By 1990, that number had grown to over 50 percent.

Kenya:

John Brown (J. B.) Masinde, a much-loved friend of mine, pastors Umoja Deliverance Church, which meets not far from Nairobi Airport in Kenya. When I first met J. B., he had to conduct two services to accommodate a membership that totaled just under 2,500. (I counted them.) The place was so crowded that members were listening through windows and standing in doorways, which necessitated going to three services. But again the building filled to overflowing.

They then made the decision to double the size of their facility to seat 2,400 and have only two services. But within one week of the new extension being built, they had to return to three services. I visited their building not long after, and was assured that all three services continue to be crowded out. That means they have now grown to over 7,000 members. In addition, they have pioneered a Christian school and have planted eight new churches. I met the pastor of one of those new churches who told me it was already being attended by over 2,000.

Burundi:

Despite years of civil unrest, God is working in a powerful way in Burundi. At the final meeting of a recent evangelistic crusade, over 500 people declared their decision to follow Christ. I have had the privilege of meeting a number of Christian leaders in this country, and would like to relate a story that took place at the African Revival Ministries Hospital in the capital city, Bujumbura. One morning, Mama Pascal, a cleaner in the hospital maternity unit, arrived for work to find that a lady was in labor, but having difficulties delivering the baby. Since Mama Pascal had witnessed many healings in church services, she decided it was time to "launch out into the deep" spiritually.

She began by asking the Lord to move in the situation and for the baby to be born normally. Then she told the nurse to be ready to receive the baby. Eventually the baby was born, but he was dead. They washed him and examined him again, but he clearly was dead. Mama Pascal was not satisfied, and directed her complaint to God:

"Lord, I didn't ask you for a dead baby! The maternity unit is a place for the living, not for the dead, so I'm asking you to revive this baby."

She continued thus for 80 minutes and was seen pacing up and down outside the ward, crying out to God. Then the miraculous happened. The baby began to breathe and move—and, at the time of this writing, was a healthy three-month-old! They called him Lazarus. Both his parents gave their lives to Christ as a result of this amazing act of God.

Guatemala:

This Central-American country caught the attention of the Christian world when General Rios Mont, who served as a deacon in one of the Verbo churches in Guatemala City, came to be President. There are eight Verbo congregations in the capital, the largest numbering over 3,000 members. When I was speaking in some of those churches in the late '90s, I was told that Verbo had been given a permit to start a Christian university, something that would have been unthinkable a few years earlier. The spiritual climate had changed so much that evangelical believers were now estimated to number more than 51 percent of the population.

In 1999, under the oversight of Verbo Ministries, a group of Canadian and British young people from Gateway Christian Community in Winnipeg and West Coast Christian Fellowship in Vancouver visited Guatemala for a four-week mission. During the first two weeks they designed and built classrooms for *Casa del Alsarero*, an outstanding ministry reaching out to the "garbage dump kids" of Guatemala City, and helped in the construction of an orphanage. For the final two weeks, they traveled to rural areas, visiting schools, preaching in the open air and holding evangelistic meetings. Altogether, 450 adults and children received Christ into their lives as Lord and Savior.

Argentina:

I always will remember a particular November morning in 1995 when I heard about the revival in Argentina. I was sitting in my office (at that time located in Scotland at the King's Bible College), looking out at pheasants and rabbits foraging for food, when the sound of the phone ringing interrupted my thoughts. It was Steve

Thomas from Oxford Community Churches, and I could tell by the tone of his voice that he was excited. He told me about Abby, a young lady from their church who was spending a year in Argentina and who had sent an amazing letter about the church she was attending in Buenos Aires. Here are some excerpts:

> First, I want to talk about the young people in the church. There are about 1,000 of them, mostly converts, some from the streets or difficult backgrounds, aged between 13 and 25 years…There are no half-hearted Christians; all of them have given themselves 100% over to God…This is the basic idea: to renounce everything from the world and live a life totally ruled by God with the help and guidance of the Holy Spirit.

> It is not acceptable to compromise with God. We cannot keep one foot in the world and also share fully in God's blessing…They are all wonderful, exciting, vibrant human beings—but energetic for God, not material pleasures. All the effort that could be spent arguing and rebelling is channeled into God. I've never before seen such a group of simply happy—no, joyous—young people.

By the time Steve finished reading the letter, I was almost in tears. "Steve," I said, "we have to go there. Whatever they have got, I want it!" So it was that a few months later, Steve Thomas and I led a group of eleven men to visit Claudio Freidzon and the 6,000-member King of Kings Church in Buenos Aires. Everything Abby had testified of the church was true. Every member was discipled in the foundations of the faith and godly character, and they in turn would disciple others. Discipleship was not an extra; it was the heart of the church.

During our visit, we also spent time with Claudio's close friend, Carlos Annacondia, one of the pioneers in the Argentine revival. We learned that two things coincided to change the spiritual climate there: One was Argentina's 1982 defeat in the Maldives/Falklands war, which broke many Argentines' strength and pride in themselves and created a spiritual vacuum. The second was President Alfonsin's decision in 1983 to grant complete freedom for preaching the gospel. Christians seized this opportunity. Under Annacondia's ministry since 1983, it is reckoned that about 3 million people have acknowledged Christ as Lord and Savior.

Among the highlights of our time in Argentina was a visit to Olmos Prison, a penitentiary that housed 3,500 of the worst offenders of the criminal fraternity. All the prisoners were serving long sentences for murder, armed robbery, rape and other violent offences. For a long time, darkness reigned in this prison of horror. Inmate gangs would terrorize other inmates, murder fellow prisoners and carry out homosexual gang rapes. The inmates called the prison "Swiss cheese" because of all the holes between cells that allowed easy access for terror and murder.

Juan, a local Pentecostal pastor, had made attempts to share the claims of Christ in the prison but was always rebuffed by the authorities. He concluded that the only way he could get inside was to become a prison guard. While undergoing training, he inquired of the senior instructor whether it was permissible to speak about Christ to the prisoners. "What religion are you?" asked the instructor. "Evangelical," replied Juan. "Well, get this straight," said the instructor, "there will be no such religious discussion in this prison. Do you understand?" "Yes," responded Juan, "but I will have to talk to God about this." With this, the instructor went red in the face and proudly announced, "I am god in this prison."

Today, that instructor is still there, but he is now one of five pastors who lead *Church of Christ the Only Hope*—the largest prison church in the world, with 1,500 members.

This is also a church with a continuous (24-hour-a-day) prayer meeting attended by at least 200 Christian prisoners. Every night between midnight and 6 A.M., 144 men in teams of six divide into pairs, with each pair taking two-hour time slots. These comprise two hours of Bible reading, two hours of intercessory prayer, and two hours of walking around every believer's bunk, laying hands on it and praying for his life and for the lives of all his family members. Each church member is expected to participate in this all-night prayer vigil once a week.

We were especially delighted that the prison authorities allowed us to attend the afternoon church service. Long before we reached the meeting hall, we were struck by a "wall" of praise. No microphones, just a small drum kit, an acoustic guitar, 1,000 pairs of hands and 1,000 male voices praising God with all the strength they could muster. Never before, anywhere, had we heard such praise and such volume!

According to Scripture, "...the foolishness of God is wiser than man's wisdom, and the weakness of God is stronger than man's strength."[21] If ever there was a demonstration of that truth, this is it. Men who were the worst that society could find, made righteous and pure by the blood of Jesus. Men, too depraved to be in their home community, now able to stand with dignity before God. Men who were full of hate and violence, transformed into men of love and concern. Men with nothing to offer the world, now fervently praying for others, fueling revival in Argentina and other countries around the globe. Men who had lost all sense of purpose, now finding their unique, God-given mission and calling. Men, physically restricted and living in squalor, set free in their spirits and filled with the joy of the Lord. Is there a better example of the power of the Gospel? Of the extravagant grace of God?

CHINA:

In 1950 there were an estimated 1 million Christians in China. By 1980 the figure had jumped to 40 million. By 1990 it was 60 million, and by 1992 it had grown by another 15 million to 75 million believers. (Even the Beijing Statistical Bureau has acknowledged the figure of 75 million.) In Szechuan province of mainland China, church growth has been so dramatic that communist officials have referred to it as the "Jesus Nest."

SOUTH KOREA:

In 1900, Korea was considered to be impenetrable. There was not a single known evangelical church. By 1986, 20 percent of the population was Christian, and by 1992 the figure was 40 percent. In just six years, the church had doubled from 6.1 million to 12.5 million. There are now 7,000 churches in the city of Seoul, including nine of the largest in the world![22]

Nepal:

As recently as the mid-1950s, there were no known believers in this Hindu kingdom. In 1971, Janette and I visited Nepal where Vic and Jenny Gledhill were working with Operation Mobilisation and operating an International Book Shop in the heart of Kathmandu. While there, I gave a series of Bible teachings to a small conference being held in Vic and Jenny's home. Any Nepalese who became a Christian at that time was subject to a penalty of two years' imprisonment, while the penalty for being baptized was eight years. The number of Christians in the whole country in 1971 was fewer than 200.

I next visited Nepal in 1977, together with Alan Vincent and a group of young men from Vancouver, Canada. We were to speak at a leadership conference in Kathmandu, but the pressure on the church was so intense it became necessary to relocate the conference to a town just across the border in India. I vividly recall several rural pastors from the Himalayan Mountains of Nepal who had walked barefoot through mountainous regions for two weeks in order to hear God's Word—and then returned home in similar fashion. I had never before seen such spiritual hunger.

By 1993, the number of Nepalese Christians had risen to 150,000. At the end of 1999, there were about 500,000. Truly the gospel of Jesus Christ is the power of God unto salvation.

The Spread of God's Word

Coupled with the spread of the gospel of Christ has been the remarkable increase in the distribution of God's written Word. In March of 1804, the British and Foreign Bible Society was formed. Its stated purpose: *To encourage the wider circulation of the Scriptures without note or comment.* Similar societies soon spread throughout the world.

Within 100 years, they had circulated 203,931,768 Bibles, New Testaments and portions of the Scripture. By 1963, the annual distribution totaled 54.1 million, and by 1992, the Bible societies had sent out 618,185,347 Bibles and portions of Scripture.[23] In 1900 there were 517 languages into which at least one book of Scripture had been translated. By 1975, the count was at 1,577 languages or dialects, and by 1990 it had reached 2,000. The complete Bible is now available in 329 languages.

In 1934 Cameron Townsend founded the Wycliffe Bible Translators, which has since grown to become one of the largest missionary societies in the world, with over 4,500 people sent to the four corners of the earth. Thus far they have worked in over 1,200 languages. In some cases, providing a Bible for non-literate tribes means Wycliffe workers first have to create a written language and then teach the people how to read it. I consider these translators among the bravest and most self-sacrificing believers of the western church in the 20th century.

For the first time in the history of the Church, the completion of the Great Commission potentially lies within reach of a generation currently alive on the earth. Patrick Johnstone told a group of denominational leaders in 1994: "If the present trends continue in terms of reaching out to unreached people groups, the final unreached people group on this planet should be addressed with the gospel no later than 2005."

Jesus said, "And this gospel of the kingdom will be preached in the whole world as a testimony to all nations, and then the end will come."[24] If indeed we are near that point, this has got to be the most exciting time in history: when all creation is "standing on tip-toe" to see the outcome of God's eternal plan. Paul put it in these words: "The creation waits in eager expectation for the sons of God to be revealed."[25] And Daniel, hundreds of years earlier, prophesied:

> Then the sovereignty, power and greatness of the kingdoms under the whole heaven will be handed over to the saints, the people of the Most High. His kingdom will be an everlasting kingdom, and all rulers will worship and obey him.[26]

Daniel adds, enigmatically, "This is the end of the matter." It is certainly within the realm of possibility that we may witness "the end of the matter" as far as history is concerned. One day there *will* be such a generation. Why not us? One thing is certain: When God says that "the earth will be full of the knowledge of the Lord as the waters cover the sea," then that is exactly what we can expect, no matter what the enemy may do. And contrary to the prognostications of certain prophets of doom, I am convinced that our eternal, omnipotent God will see to it that his eternal Word is fulfilled: that there will be *no end to the increase* of the government of our Lord Jesus Christ.

Endnotes

1. E. H. Broadbent, *The Pilgrim Church* (London: Marshall Pickering, 1931), 392.

2. Isaiah 9:6-7.

3. Patrick Johnstone, *The Church is Bigger Than You Think* (Fearn, Scotland: Christian Focus Publications, 1998).

4. A good example would be Francis Schaeffer's insightful book *The Great Evangelical Disaster*.

5. For a comprehensive and inspiring summary of Billy Graham's evangelistic ministry, I would commend his autobiography entitled *Just As I Am* (HarperCollins, 1997).

6. There were earlier signs of spiritual revival (including speaking in tongues) at Bible colleges operated by Charles Parham in Kansas in 1901 Texas in 1905. Seymour had been a student at the Texas school.

7. Smith Wigglesworth, *Ever Increasing Faith* (Springfield, Missouri: Gospel Publishing House), 35, 37.

8. Albert Hibbert, *Smith Wigglesworth: The Secret of His Power* (Tulsa, Oklahoma: Harrison House, 1982), 106.

9. Perhaps the apostle Peter would have had more patience with her, having experienced the phenomenon of an unthinking response at the Transfiguration ("If you wish, I will put up three shelters—one for you, one for Moses and one for Elijah").

10. John 14:11-12.

11. 1 Corinthians 2:4.

12. Romans 15:18-19.

13. Examples of wrong motives in ministry include: Matthew 7:21-23, Acts 8:9-23, and Philippians 1:15-18.

14. For purposes of brevity, I am referring to the Charismatic and Restorationist movements as one group.

15. Ephesians 5:27.

16. This has been referred to as the "Latter Rain," applying various prophetic words about the autumn rains (KJV latter rains) to the "rain" of the Holy Spirit.

17. Isaiah 11:9.

18. David B. Barrett, *World Christian Encyclopedia, 2nd ed.* (New York: Oxford University Press, 2001). It should be noted that statistics for the world totals do not distinguish between nominal adherents to a religion and practicing believers.

19. For example: Patrick Johnstone, *The Church is Bigger Than You Think*, op. cit.

20. Most of these statistics have been compiled by Patrick Johnstone of the U.S. Center for World Missions.

21. 1 Corinthians 1:25.

22. Statistics obtained from the *1992 Yearbook of the Korean Church*. With the rapid expansion of Christianity, these numbers have no doubt been exceeded.

23. It was interesting that *Time* magazine's choice for the Person of the Millennium was Johannes Gutenberg, inventor of the first printing press capable of mass production. I'm sure the Bible societies would heartily agree with that choice!

24. Matthew 24:14.

25. Romans 8:19.

26. Daniel 7:27.

FIFTEEN

To Him Be Glory in the Church

⌒

His intent was that now, through the church, the manifold wisdom of God should be made known to the rulers and authorities in the heavenly realms, according to his eternal purpose which he accomplished in Christ Jesus our Lord. —Ephesians 3:10-11

⌒

With all our reminders of the faults and shortcomings of the Church, it is vital to be reminded of God's vision for His people—a vision that, if it weren't God's, we would probably dismiss as hopelessly optimistic. As someone wisely pointed out, God has no "Plan B" in case the Church doesn't work out. He is committed to using us: meaning that we, along with our brothers and sisters in the Lord through the ages, are "it."

To help stimulate our faith and renew our understanding of God's eternal plan for Himself and His family, I want to quote at length from a description of God's design and purpose for the Church written by G. Milton Smith:

> Conceived in the heart of God, redeemed by the precious blood of Christ, sanctified and empowered by the Spirit of God, the church is the masterpiece of divine wisdom. The individual members were personally selected by the Father, and predestined to live a life of holiness and nearness to God. Each has been granted the special position of a son in the family of God, having been sealed by the Holy Spirit.
>
> Selected from both groups of the human family—Jew and Gentile—members have lost their identity in Adam and are

now members of one new Man—a new creation in Christ. So great are the blessings bestowed on those who are in the church that every blessing that the wisdom of God can conceive is theirs—they are indeed the actual members of the mystical body of Christ, His fulness or complement! So great, too, is the purpose of God for the church that it has become the object lesson which God uses to display the manifest wisdom of God to the highest angelic orders in heaven.

Just as Christ, the Head of the church, died and was buried and is now seated in royal authority at God's right hand, so, too, the members have not only died to sin, but have also been raised from the dead and have been enthroned with Christ in the heavenly realms. The supreme purpose of the exceeding riches of divine grace being bestowed upon the church is that Christ Himself should become the ultimate Head of the entire universe, thus reconciling all the various parts to Himself. The love of Christ in seeking lost sinners who were under the dominion of satanic powers, surpasses all knowledge. The message that brought the good news of their salvation is described as the unsearchable riches of Christ.

The church is destined to become the church glorious, with neither spot nor defect, resplendent with beauty and youthfulness. One day she will indeed attain to the position of maturity, the measure of the stature of the fulness of Christ Himself! Yes indeed, one day the church, the bride of Christ, which is also the glorious inheritance of God, shall be empowered with the immeasurable greatness of His power—such power that set Christ at the pinnacle of divine glory.

Moreover, the church shall personally experience the breadth, length, depth and height of the unknowable love of Christ, being filled with all the fulness of God Himself. He who planned all this is fully able to do far more abundantly than all we ask or think, for He is determined to lavish on us the immeasurable riches of His grace. To Him be glory in the church and in Christ Jesus to all generations, for ever and ever. Amen.[1]

MAKING IT PERSONAL

As we conclude our consideration of God's original design for mankind, for the Church, and for us as individuals, I would like to turn to some honest reflection and personal application. Sometimes we reach a certain point where we know it's not more information that we need, but an opportunity to respond. At such times, without giving way to morbid introspection, I try to be brutally honest with myself. Why? Because according to Scripture, "Everything is uncovered and laid bare before the eyes of him to whom we must give account."[2] That includes my heart.

William Still said it well when he pointed out:

It is the simplest things that are most difficult to understand and accept, and one of those which seems in my experience to have been most difficult for people to understand and accept has been the fact that the Lord demands of His servants, each and every one of them, to listen to Him only and obey His will implicitly, irrespective of what it costs.[3]

For me, it all comes down to a few critical questions. What am I going to do with all this teaching? Will I continue with the status quo? Will I capitulate to prevailing systems of thought to be remembered by future generations as one who knew the truth but drew back into his "comfort zone"?

Will those I led view me as a trustworthy shepherd, or as someone who turned out to be a hireling—who, in the end, put his own safety and reputation ahead of the well-being of the sheep that God entrusted to his care? God forbid that my spiritual sons and daughters would have to say, "He talked a lot about the problem of wineskins and the futility of clinging to shadows, but when God introduced him to the substance, he chose popularity and shrank back into the shadows, thereby becoming a 'shadow' of what he might have been in Christ."

When I think about such things, my heart cries, No! May it never be. And I come back, again and again, to the words of the apostle

Paul, "...I press on to take hold of that for which Christ Jesus took hold of me."[4]

I have always liked that phrase "take hold of" (sometimes translated "apprehend") because it expresses a very deliberate, purposeful action—similar to an arrest by a police officer. When I was at Hendon Police Training College many years ago preparing to be a London "bobby," we were taught that when arresting a suspect, we were to "use only as much force as was necessary to effect the cause."

One night I went to arrest a man trying to break into a Post Office, but instead of coming quietly, he punched me in the stomach and ran off. When I caught up with him, he became extremely violent, requiring the application of my truncheon[5] to the top of his head—an action he didn't appreciate but one that proved successful in "effecting the cause." I realize God doesn't literally hit us over the head when we resist His call, but I appreciate the strength of Paul's words here. We could translate it: "I press on to arrest that for which I have been *arrested*."

Jesus has apprehended us through the extremity of Calvary with the intent that we would discover the plan He has for our lives and apprehend it, using "as much force as is necessary to effect the cause." That does not mean we use our own strength and wisdom to do God's will, but that we take the radical steps necessary for God to have His way. The good news is, it doesn't take superstars to make a real difference in the Kingdom of God. In fact, Paul (in one of my favorite Scripture passages) goes to great lengths to point out that God loves using ordinary people to do His work:

> Brothers, think of what you were when you were called. Not many of you were wise by human standards; not many were influential; not many were of noble birth. But God chose the foolish things of the world to shame the wise; God chose the weak things of the world to shame the strong. He chose the lowly things of this world and the despised things—and the things that are not—to nullify the things that are, so that no one may boast before him.[6]

To underline the truth that this is all of God, not man, Paul mentions in his letter to Timothy that God "has saved us and called us to a holy life—not because of anything we have done but because of his own purpose and grace."[7] What then is our response? I would like to quote a familiar Scripture passage from a less familiar source, the J. B. Phillips translation:

> With eyes wide open to the mercies of God, I beg you, my brothers, as an act of intelligent worship, to give him your bodies, as a living sacrifice, consecrated to him and acceptable by him. Don't let the world around you squeeze you into its own mould, but let God re-mould your minds from within, so that you may prove in practice that the plan of God for you is good, meets all his demands and moves towards the goal of true maturity.[8]

PRAYER

Join me as I close with a personal response to God:[9]

Almighty God, Creator of Heaven and earth, I know I am not on this earth by mistake. Thank You that You knew me before I was born, that You planned me from all eternity and have a wonderful design and purpose for my life.

My heavenly Father, I believe that You created me in order that I would live to the praise of Your glory, and that You are most glorified in me when I am most satisfied in You.[10] Please forgive me for the many times I have chosen selfish pursuits at the cost of intimacy with You. And forgive me for the many wasted opportunities to bring Your love and Your life-giving Word to those in need.

Lord, I don't want to be counted among those who have "seen the Promised Land," but through fear and unbelief have forfeited the right to enter in. Keep me from devaluing my heritage, thus wasting my inheritance; or selling my birthright in You for a "pot of stew." I don't want my life's work to be burned up because it turned out to be wood, hay and straw. And I don't want to be ashamed at Your coming because I buried the gift You graciously entrusted to my stewardship.

Search me, O God, and know my heart; try me and know my anxious thoughts; and see if there be any hurtful way in me, and lead me in the everlasting way.[11]

Lord, deliver me from acting independently and trusting in my own strength, wisdom and good ideas. Help me instead to eat from the tree of life—the wisdom and grace that You provide. By whatever means You see fit, keep me in the place where I am useful to Your purposes, and cause me to be a son who always pleases You, loving righteousness and hating wickedness.

Lord Jesus, I want to be counted among those who offer themselves willingly in the day of Your power. I want to know You and the power of Your resurrection and the fellowship of Your sufferings, and be made like You in Your death. Thank You that Your rod of correction is actually the assurance of Your love and care for me.

Help me to "arrest that for which I have been arrested"— Your holy calling and purpose in my life. I desire to live by what You say, and to delight to do Your will. Help me, by Your Holy Spirit's enabling, to finish the course and to be found faithful and alert at Your return. Amen!

May the words of my mouth and the meditation of my heart be pleasing in Your sight, O Lord, my Rock and my Redeemer.[12]

ENDNOTES

1. G. Milton Smith, *God Acting in History* (Auckland, N.Z.: Faith Bible Course, 1981), 141.

2. Hebrews 4:13.

3. John Blanchard, *Sifted Silver* (Durham, England: Evangelical Press), 212.

4. Philippians 3:12.

5. A truncheon is a baton or nightstick. Very few police officers in England carry firearms.

6. 1 Corinthians 1:26-29.

7. 2 Timothy 1:9.

8. Romans 12:1-2, J. B. Phillips, *The New Testament in Modern English* (London: Geoffrey Bles, 1960).

9. I have chosen to include many phrases from Scripture in this prayer; only the longer ones are noted in the references.

10. Phrase quoted from John Piper, *The Pleasures of God* (Portland, Oregon: Multnomah Press, 1991), 9.

11. Psalm 139:23-24 (NASB).

12. Psalm 19:14.

CONTACT ADDRESSES

North American Office:

Salt and Light Ministries
5-3459 River Road West
Delta, B.C. Canada
V4K 4Y6

Tel: 604.946.6186
Fax: 604.946.6996
e-mail: bcoombs@saltlight.org

European Office:

Salt and Light Ministries
The King's Centre
Osney Mead
Oxford OX2 0ES
England

Tel: 01865 297440
Fax: 01865 297441
e-mail: european@saltlight.org

Additional copies of this book and other
book titles from DESTINY IMAGE are
available at your local bookstore.

For a complete list of our titles,
visit us at www.destinyimage.com
Send a request for a catalog to:

Destiny Image₍ᵣ₎ Publishers, Inc.
P.O. Box 310
Shippensburg, PA 17257-0310

*"Speaking to the Purposes of God for This
Generation and for the Generations to Come"*